Fazisi
The Joint Venture

Fazisi
The Joint Venture

Skip Novak

SIDGWICK & JACKSON
LONDON

First published in Great Britain in 1990 by
Sidgwick & Jackson Limited

Copyright © 1990 by Skip Novak
Map © 1990 by Chris Wood

ISBN 0 283 06053 0

Typeset by Hewer Text Composition Services, Edinburgh
Printed by Mackays of Chatham plc, Chatham, Kent
for Sidgwick & Jackson Limited
1 Tavistock Chambers, Bloomsbury Way
London WC1A 2SG

For the crew of *Fazisi*,
travellers through time – our present and their future

'To be truly challenging a voyage, like life, must rest on a firm foundation of financial unrest. Otherwise you are doomed to a routine traverse.'

Sterling Hayden

Contents

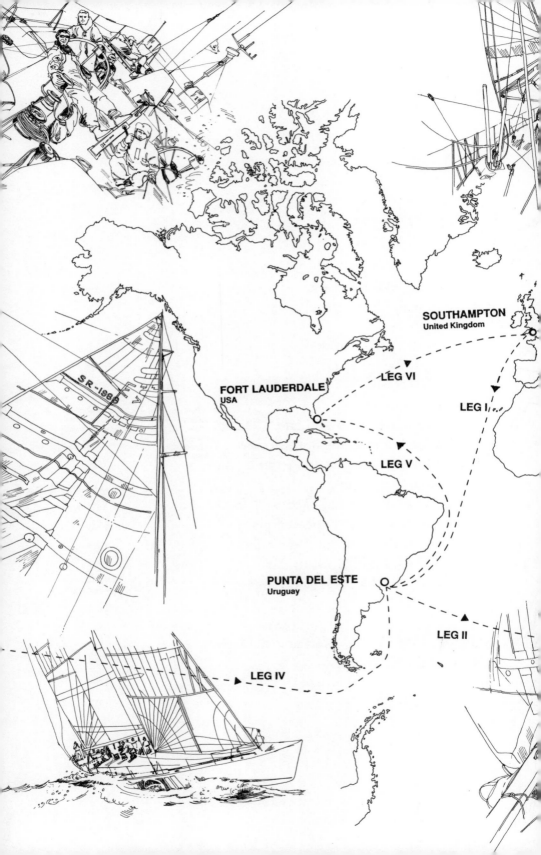

SOUTHAMPTON
United Kingdom

FORT LAUDERDALE
USA

LEG VI

LEG I

LEG V

LEG II

PUNTA DEL ESTE
Uruguay

LEG IV

SR-1988

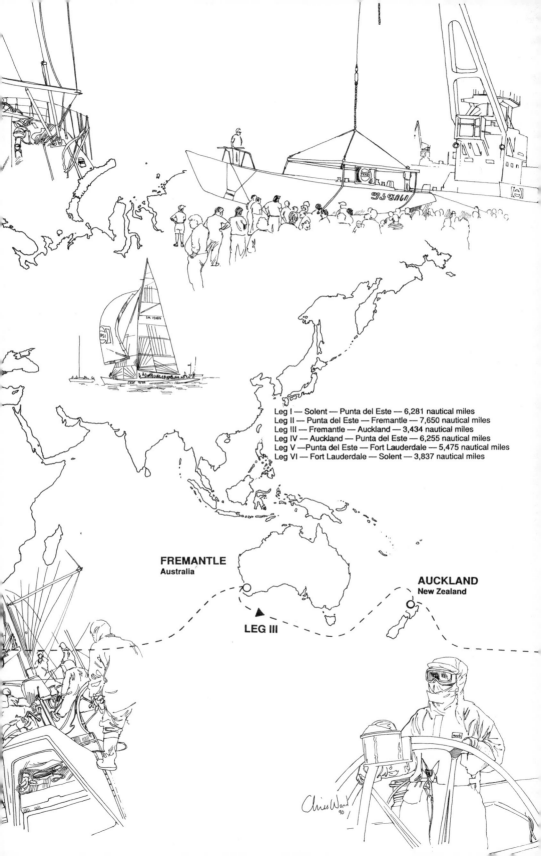

Leg I — Solent — Punta del Este — 6,281 nautical miles
Leg II — Punta del Este — Fremantle — 7,650 nautical miles
Leg III — Fremantle — Auckland — 3,434 nautical miles
Leg IV — Auckland — Punta del Este — 6,255 nautical miles
Leg V — Punta del Este — Fort Lauderdale — 5,475 nautical miles
Leg VI — Fort Lauderdale — Solent — 3,837 nautical miles

FREMANTLE
Australia

AUCKLAND
New Zealand

LEG III

Foreword

Skip was first introduced to me in April 1989 by Vladislav Murnikov, director of our Golden Fleece syndicate which had been established to create the first ever Soviet entry in the Whitbread Round the World Race. Our aims were simple: to build the first Soviet maxi yacht; to participate in that legendary race around the world; and to give Soviet yachtsmen the opportunity to compete in an event they had previously only dreamed about.

At the same time, we wanted to demonstrate to other nations that the Soviets are not 'devils with horns' as Rear Admiral Charles Williams, chairman of the race committee, had once remarked. Also, we wanted to show the potential of our company to build high-tech yachts and establish new business.

Skip did not sail the last leg of the Whitbread to England with *Fazisi* which, of course, was sad. But on the other hand, it was good that the experience he brought to the crew enabled them to attempt it on their own.

One of the sayings of Dchammapada is: 'Tell the truth. Offer no hate. And, if someone asks of you, give. To come close to these ideals is to come close to the gods.'

Of course both Skip and those of us on the Soviet side were far removed from such ideals. Sometimes we argued, sometimes we wouldn't give way, but I do believe we were always honest with each other.

Skip's book is full of truth and optimism about the events we all shared, events that were sometimes dramatic, sad and hard but often full of delight. He describes the satisfaction following those days of striving when the boat was being constructed at the Poti Shipyard, the amazing flight out of Russia to Heathrow, the completion of the boat at Hamble, the critical last-minute keel change just before the start and the overwhelming happiness of finishing 6th at the end of the first leg.

Here you will find our problems with language barriers, the tragedy in Punta del Este where we lost our first skipper Alexei Gryshenko, whose titanic work gave life to *Fazisi*. And you will find the raw excitement and anxiety of the Roaring Forties, the good times ashore, our financial problems and just about everything in fact that life consists of.

So, reader, let's go! Downwind and with plenty of water under the keel!

Viktor Tichov
President, Golden Fleece Syndicate

Introduction

At 33,000 miles the 1989/90 Whitbread Round the World Race was the longest yacht race ever, the equivalent of fifty-five Fastnets. This, the fifth time the race has been run, was somewhat special. The Whitbread had come of age. There were seventeen eighty-footers in the fleet of twenty-three yachts, no fewer than twelve of them newly built for the race.

The fleet also included an all-woman crew. Clare Francis had been the first woman Whitbread skipper in 1977/78, but Tracy Edwards' handling of the Maiden project, skippering the yacht to victory in the small boat class in two of the toughest legs of the race, was a triumph. And of course, there were the Soviets aboard *Fazisi*, making the USSR's debut in grand-prix yachting with their country's first ever maxi yacht.

Soviet sailors are far from being a novelty in international sailing. In the Olympic arena they have formidable strength in the dinghy and small keelboat classes. Their top sailors, like their athletes, are privileged citizens, employed by the Ministry of Sport. Their Tall Ships are frequent overseas competitors, their crews familiar with many of Europe's cities. But when it was learned there was to be a Soviet entry in not only the Whitbread Race but the America's Cup too, two of the Western world's most heavily capitalized, technologically advanced and endlessly hyped yacht races, then it was quite clear the wind of change was blowing through the USSR.

Yet the *Fazisi* enterprise owed nothing to state-sponsored

sport. It was essentially the dream of one man, an architect named Vladislav Murnikov, who, against all odds, found a sponsor in the USSR. The Fazis company of Moscow was one of the earliest Joint Venture companies in the Soviet Union, and the first in the republic of Georgia, to be set up when the then General Secretary Gorbachev's *perestroika* reforms were adopted by the Party Congress in 1986.

All this happened while the Berlin Wall was still resolutely standing, democracy in Eastern Europe was but a cherished dream and the Soviet Union as monolithic as at any time since Lenin. For the sailors aboard *Fazisi*, the country they left behind for the West in July 1989 may have looked the same on their return 12 months later but it could not have changed more drastically. Queues and chronic shortages may still be a part of everyday Soviet life, but expectations and ambitions had been catapulted to new levels.

Longstanding curiosity about the Soviet Union and the anticipation of something significant in the *Fazisi* story took me to the USSR in June 1989. The unknown soldier's tomb just outside the Kremlin's bastion walls; Lenin's blockhouse mausoleum familiar from TV news reports of the May Day parades; and the bells striking midnight from the Disneyesque St Stephen's church in Red Square made for wonderful memories. But other images stuck just as firmly: peeling paint; crumbling concrete; air thick with fumes from out-of-tune Ladas running on low-grade fuel; shops with empty shelves; and, above all, the dull eyes of a population in whom hope had largely been extinguished a long time ago.

The *Fazisi* crew were different. Even the perpetually preoccupied Alexei Gryshenko had the aura of a man embarking on a grand adventure. Unlike most Whitbread crews who could count an America's Cup, a previous Whitbread or world-class regatta on their sailing CVs, the *Fazisi* crew were ordinary men from an extraordinary country. Their eyes popped when they saw the Hamble River overflowing with yachts. In Hamble village, their first precious few spare hours were spent not in the pubs but in the Tesco supermarket watching shoppers walking up to overburdened shelves and putting all manner of goods in their baskets.

Into this scene stepped Skip Novak, a singular American with a penchant for the unusual. With three Whitbreads behind him he had a reputation for firefighting, getting a grip on campaigns that were going astray. This was never more evident than in 1985, when *Drum*'s keel fell off during the Fastnet Race. Novak's eclectic range of skills came instantly into play, and somehow the boat was ready four weeks later to start the Whitbread Race. *Drum* then began to fall apart in a gale on the approach to Cape Town at the end of Leg 1, yet Skip not only nursed the boat home but kept his crew's morale and commitment intact. Though he is clearly a self-contained person, whose intolerance of the unnecessary can be mistaken for aloofness, there is absolutely no doubt that he has the respect of those who sail under him; and his friendships, once made, are firm and lasting.

It was during the *Drum* saga that I first came across Novak. It was in Falmouth in fact, where I was loitering on a quay while the still upturned *Drum* was moored off in the harbour, hoping to catch Skip to get the crumb of news or information on which a journalist's business exists. He stepped ashore late in the day, still clad in his dripping orange and black drysuit having been diving in and out of *Drum*'s hull preparing her for righting. Even thus encumbered, he managed to stride right past, saying 'Not now' to my questions. His daggers look would have done justice to someone emerging from court and trying to run the gauntlet of TV crews and reporters. He was clearly a man with a lot on his mind and even more on his shoulders. I was unnecessary. He was intolerant. Off he went.

In the five years since then, I've seen him relaxed, enjoyed his slightly off-beat humour, admired his wide-ranging interests and appreciated that unlike many other Whitbread race pros his life revolves around much, much more than simply the next project, the next air ticket and the next crew uniform. A one-dimensional professional sportsman, who can talk only about the game, he is clearly not.

Novak maintains his equilibrium by seeing far beyond the esoteric world of Whitbread racing; where as some sailors spend their whole lives trimming afloat and drinking ashore. He is the complete outdoors man – rock climber;

mountaineer; photographer; diver; paraglider; rider; and expedition leader.

I remember walking into the Pier 66 resort hotel in Fort Lauderdale during the 1990 Leg V stopover with Novak when he noticed an architect's attempt to make a blank end wall 'interesing' by leaving some bricks standing proud as 'features'. 'Good training wall,' muttered Skip, his mind always tuned into life beyond the race.

By then he had embarked on this book. We knew *Fazisi*'s presence in the race with significant. We had already signed Skip up as columnist for the *Daily Telegraph* and knew his weekly pieces were well received by readers not just in Britain but elsewhere in the world. Such was the interest that his second column was cut from the newspaper and faxed to the 50-foot World Championship Regatta in Japan, not by me, nor the *Telegraph*, but by a friend who knew that the sailors out there wanted to read how Skip and the Soviets were shaping up.

It was less of a decision and more of a simple, logical step for us to ask Novak to tackle a book. We knew he could write formidable prose. We knew the *Fazisi* story was exceptional. For my part, I thought I knew most of what had gone on in and around the Soviet Union's entrée into the yachting big time. But as each chapter passed my desk, I realized how little in fact I did know.

It is a remarkable story.

Tim Jeffery
June 1990

1

The Enemy has Landed

The group looked rag-tag and dog-tired sitting on the bench outside Sheremtievo Airport in the heat and humidity of a Moscow July. Like refugees waiting for an improbable clearance into asylum, they were nervous, fidgety and worried.

These were not Soviet tourists on a *glasnost* holiday, nor students off on an exchange programme abroad. This was a sailboat crew due to take part in the Whitbread Round the World Race, leaving the UK in September. They were scheduled to fly into London's Heathrow airport that afternoon, 10 July 1989, but there had been so many hold-ups and delays since the flight had begun in the Soviet Republic of Georgia almost three days ago that they seemed to have abandoned hope of ever making it.

This was understandable because what they were doing was so outlandish by Soviet standards I got the impression that if the plan failed here and now, and they were told to pack up and go home, they would have just thrown their hands up in the air and proclaimed to the American travelling with them, 'Well, there's nothing we can do; it's just the Soviet system'.

We were not travelling in business or even tourist class. This was a cargo flight. Out on the boiling tarmac sat the Antonov 124, the largest transport plane in the world. And in its belly, chained to the load deck, were cradled the hopes and dreams of these eighteen Soviet sailors, something they had built with their own hands, the 82-foot aluminium hull of an ocean-racing greyhound – the USSR's first-ever entry into the rarefied world of professional, sponsored yacht-racing.

The administrative hitch today had been the lack of UK visas for the loading crew of the Antonov, so instead of flying directly from Kiev yesterday, we had to divert to Moscow this morning to sort it out – yet another hurdle in the bureaucratic obstacle course only the Soviet Union could have devised.

After eight hours of waiting, finally the moment came. A jackbooted airport official led us out across the runway, in single file, towards our aircraft that dwarfed everything else at the terminal. No one said much. The turbines were already run-up and idling and the air was thick with unburned jet fuel and our own nervous sweat. We climbed up into the cargo bay, sidled around the unfinished bare hull that had been christened *Fazisi* in Soviet Georgia only ten days before, and made our way up a rickety metal ladder into the spartan upper deck for passengers and aircrew.

Thirty cheap, plastic bucket seats lined each side of the cabin. Mattresses were strewn about the floor, a free-standing cafeteria table stood aft to serve as a mess, and we later discovered a cubicle off to one side with a chemical toilet that wasn't working. There was little else. In each of the two emergency doors was a window about the size of a soup bowl, now our only link with the Soviet Union.

Randomly seated around the cabin were my companions whom I hardly knew and whose names I could barely pronounce: burly Georgian faces, strong, Slavic Russian and Ukrainian faces, a round Moldavian face, an Asian face and the calm, composed face of a Jew.

With all aboard we lost no time in taxiing out onto the runway and soon we were climbing into a blinding afternoon sky, westward bound. The air conditioning came on, and with relief we all unbuckled our seat belts and stretched out on the mattresses, heads cushioned by kit bags, each to his own thoughts.

I had been with this crew for the last two weeks while they had struggled to finish as much of the construction of *Fazisi* as possible, culminating in this emergency measure of airlifting the boat to England for completion – the only way

2

to get her to the start on time. In spite of that, I knew very little about this project, other than what was in the official press releases which, as their hired Western consultant, I had helped to write.

I did know, however, that the crew had toiled like slaves for the last eight months, working under what I would describe as not merely primitive, but illegal working conditions, building a machine to meet the technological West head on. But I didn't realize then the personal hardships they had already weathered in their family lives. All but one married with children, they had hardly seen their families during all the months of boat-building, and now they were off for what might be another year.

I knew that they had been selected from all over the Soviet Union for their sailing and boat-building skills. I didn't know, however, that despite their clever craftsmanship, their sailing skills were very basic; more importantly, conflicts were already brewing amongst the crew. Of course, I spoke no Russian and only a few of them spoke enough English to get by; most at that stage merely grunted in response to my questions, observations and suggestions.

Sailboat racing aside, what was important politically, and fascinating for me, was that this was not a government project, but a privately sponsored effort from a new Soviet Joint Venture company. Joint ventures in the Soviet Union are a recent economic tool to facilitate trade with the West involving barter deals and, hopefully, injections of Western hard currency into the beleaguered Soviet infrastructure. The Fazis Moscow Company were entering the Whitbread Round the World Race for all the reasons that Western companies sponsor participants in sporting events, and it was curious to see the Soviets involved in advertising, publicity, sponsorship and media events – concepts that were alien and unacceptable to the old Soviet régime.

The *Fazisi* project appeared to be the first of its kind – the practical result of *glasnost* and *perestroika* – at least in the sporting world – and I was reminded by the Soviets that it would have been impossible two years ago. Something was going on here that was far more significant than ten tonnes of tortured aluminium in the cargo hold; for the crew, it

3

was more than just a yacht race. I think when I realized this, I made an unconscious decision to follow this odyssey through, whatever the conclusion.

'*Kushet, kushet*, Skip,' one of the three Viktors said as he shook me awake from a deep sleep. A quick meal was being served – Russian bully beef and potatoes. Everyone else was up and the windows were now crowded three or four deep as the crew tried to catch their first glimpse of the English countryside. The atmosphere on board had completely changed, with a lot of light-hearted conversation, laughter and jokes, the best of which were enthusiastically translated for me. The pressure was off – at least for now. A psychological frontier had been passed.

'Well, Eugene, it looks like the *Fazisi* will at least get this far,' I said to the bearded Moldavian who spoke the best English.

'Yeah, at least we will see England, Skip. After that, who knows? Do you really think we can build this boat in five weeks, train the crew and make the Whitbread?'

'I don't know. There will be a lot of problems, you can bet on that, and I'm afraid to say most of the problems will be financial. We still have no cash flow and no money from sponsors. The West is a different place, Eugene, and your paper roubles aren't worth jack-shit, as we say in America.'

'Anyway, even to get this far was a huge dream for this crew one year ago. Now we can only hope.'

Half an hour later the big Antonov touched down at Heathrow, silhouetted against a raging red sunset. We grabbed our bags and piled down the ladder just as the big nose cone was opening to reveal those hopes and dreams to a crowd of camera men and reporters jockeying for position in the fading evening light.

*　　*　　*

This is not a yachting book for yachtsmen only – in fact, a lot of the story is about what happens on shore – but I think any sailor will relate to the trials and tribulations – and the joys – of getting a boat and crew ready for sea.

4

But I hope it will be much more than that. Tales of blocks breaking, ropes parting, sails being trimmed and changed and courses across the oceans negotiated with cunning and skill by the navigators are what a sea story should be all about, and certainly there are enough of these around to fill the library of the most avaricious armchair sailor.

But what I feel is far more interesting is the story of the people who trim the sails and plot the courses and the people behind them, supporting them on shore. Only then does it become an account of why, not how. And what better subjects than the crew of *Fazisi*?

I remember Vladislav Murnikov being displeased with me during the third leg of the race when I had mentioned the Soviet crew's interest in pornography in my column for the *Daily Telegraph*. He claimed I was making out that the Soviet crew was different, when of course I had the opposite intention. But the truth came out when, in exasperation, I finally said to him, 'But Vladislav, you people are different!'

This is the story about the *Fazisi* crew's sometimes awkward, sometimes amusing, but always interesting and dignified attempts to come to grips with an 82-foot, high-tech racing yacht, at times out of control at sea, and at the same time with the strange ways of the West ashore, which almost caused us to founder a few times.

What must always be remembered when we think of *Fazisi* is that for her crew the Whitbread Round the World Race was more than just a race, it was a new life.

2

Trying to be a Patriot

To fully appreciate the story of how I, as an American, came to work for the Soviets, we must go back briefly to over 15 years ago. When I was fresh out of college in 1974, instead of treading a conventional path, I did what was, for me, the logical alternative and began delivering and maintaining high-performance ocean-racing yachts on the endless world circuit. Venues like Bermuda, Cowes, Sydney, Malta and Montego Bay, to name just a few, were the stuff of dreams for any harbour rat from the shores of Lake Michigan. I justified what was viewed as only a temporary way of life to everyone, including myself, with the reasoning that my bachelor's degree in geography should not go to waste. Looking back, this ridiculous excuse was nothing more than an indictment on the poor quality of a liberal arts education from a mediocre American university. In fact, going sailing was the best move I could have ever made.

Before long, the novelty of scrubbing other people's decks and changing their jibs had worn pretty thin. It was clear to me early on that I wanted to run the show, and if my ego had anything to do with this attitude, it was bolstered by the simple observation that, at the age of 23, I could sail better than most of the owner-skippers I had worked for.

There was a problem in achieving this in a world of amateur, or Corinthian, yachting, where wealth implies right, especially in America, where the type and style of sailing was ultra-conservative. From what I read and gossip I heard around the wharf, sailing in Europe was beginning to be sponsored, so during the late Seventies I decided to base myself there and follow what is now a well established game of chance. It all began with the love of sailing, but little did I know then that I would have to navigate through the shoals and tide-rips of PR companies, ad agencies and fund-raising wizards, and my skill in the use of marlinspike, sextant, and my ability to push a boat-brush would be of little practical consequence. Luckily, I followed the advice of a dockside clairvoyant who said, 'If you want to find a sponsor, then better wear a suit and tie.'

Ten years later in the winter of 1987 I was on the Whitbread Campaign Trail, suited-up and ready to go. I had already sailed in three Whitbread Races, the pre-eminent international fully-crewed race around the world. But I had never won it. Each time, our weaknesses had been obvious before the race started. In 1977/78, on the British sloop *King's Legend* we came second (good boat, best crew, no money). In 1981/82 on *Alaska Eagle* we came ninth (bad boat, terrible crew, plenty of money!) and in 1985/86 on rock-star Simon Le Bon's *Drum* we came a tough third (bad boat, best crew, marginal money, no time).

All of these projects had thick or thin veils of sponsorship, but were really funded by wealthy individuals. Without those financial buccaneers I would not have sailed in those three races, but it was obvious that compromises were made for their benefit. I was still hoping for the dream project where all the pieces of the puzzle would fall into place – where a racing project could be put together on the strength of its marketing potential, leaving the sailing to people like myself.

The Whitbread race is sponsored by the UK brewing and leisure firm Whitbread, and organized by the Royal Naval Sailing Association. Big changes were planned after the 1985/86 Whitbread, which suffered from a lack of media attention that was incongruous since the budgets of some of the entries then topped $4 million. It was decided to change the course for next time, to get out of South Africa (for the usual reasons) and get into North America, for what it was hoped would be big money; and also into the potentially valuable market of Australia. The new course doesn't go around the world in the classic way, but instead zigs and zags its way to what the organizers were hoping would be better publicity and marketing venues.

Peer-group pressure certainly played a part in my decision to try again. 'Hell, if you can't get sponsorship, nobody can,' they all said. I was one of only a handful of Americans who had skippered boats on two of three occasions. The next Whitbread was coming to North America, Fort Lauderdale, it was announced in the winter of 1986, so as an American I felt obliged to have another go.

My plan was to start my fund-raising efforts in South Florida where, in three years' time, it was all supposed to happen. I was under no illusion. I did not expect to raise $5-6 million of corporate sponsorship by working out of a beat-up briefcase from the back of a rental car. But I was hoping to find local support; maybe a few hundred grand, some city backing, a free building-site for the yacht's construction, all very public, all promotion-orientated, to stretch the sponsor's investment out over three years, from the building stage to the promotion after the race. This would be the first serious American entry. I was optimistic. I generated a lot of paper.

Using my sailing contacts in Miami I arranged a brief meeting with Mayor Xavier Suarez of Miami, a smooth-talking Cuban success story. I came armed with an architect's drawing of the proposed 'public construction' in Bayside Shopping Pavilion on Biscayne Boulevard on Miami's fore-shore, a place that boasts a flow of 20,000 people per day. The boat would be called *City of Miami*, at least until the major corporate sponsors were found.

'It's a great idea,' said the Mayor, as he leaned back in his big leather chair, 'but you have to understand one thing. Seventy per cent of the people in Greater Miami are Hispanic and another 17% are black; and they don't give a damn about sail boats.' He said he couldn't ask the council for any direct funds as the city budget was strapped that year, but being the politician he was, he promised to try and help push the Bayside thing through. And being the politician that he was, I never heard from the Mayor's office again.

Not to be deterred, I went on the road. I began touting round a slide show of the 1985/86 Whitbread on *Drum* to which I added a little sales pitch at the end. Local Chambers of Commerce, Rotary Clubs and Yacht Clubs were my main targets ('Here, take my card, I got a friend in advertising who would like to talk to you; he's got a 30-footer, not a racing man you understand . . .') with the goal of getting someone, anyone, to join me, someone with some financial muscle, because my personal funds were running out fast. I soon realized what a task I had; the whole idea of stopping in a decadent resort town like Fort Lauderdale was as good as useless for my purposes. Any marketing person or media heavy I told about the situation always asked the same question, 'If publicity is what they're after, why aren't you going to the Big Apple?'

Thinking that the Fort Lauderdale Yacht Club would be a logical venue for some advance publicity, since they had agreed to be the host club for the stopover, I was surprised to be flatly refused a platform by the Rear-Commodore on the grounds that they couldn't be involved in anything the least bit commercial or their private club status would be in jeopardy. I explained that the Whitbread Race was indeed commercial, and as the conversation went on I realized that the Rear-Commodore had very little idea what the Whitbread was, where it went and who did it. Of course Whitbreads, who then marketed Cutty Sark Whisky, Beefeater Gin and a small amount of their own brand of beer, were immediately blamed for lack of publicity in what they always said was a critical marketing area.

It is still not clear how Fort Lauderdale was chosen. John Anson, Whitbread Race Commercial Director, explained to me in Uruguay two years later, when it was realized America would not be the media success they had hoped for, 'We thought the race would be lost in New York City. The weather is terrible at that time of year (April) and we thought it would be unpopular with the crews. I don't think it's a problem of Fort Lauderdale. The lack of interest is more of an American problem. If you want to make any impact there you have to spend millions of dollars and we, as a company, were not prepared to do that. A lot of Americans still think the world is flat and the idea of an around-the-world race is something they really can't comprehend.'

9

With no help from Whitbreads in pre-race promotion, and not even a passing interest from the yacht club hosting the fifth leg, I was about to take my one-man roadshow, now bankrupt, back to Europe to have a rethink.

Enter John Baker, yachtsman, ex-CEO and Whitbread Race aficionado. After a chance suggestion by the New Zealand yacht designer Bruce Farr, I telephoned Baker at his home in Virginia and we discussed my ideas. Not a man to mince his words, nor his ideas, he simply said, 'I'm sailing across the Atlantic next week on my 51-footer. Meet me in Portugal on 5 June and make me an offer.'

After a morning's work in a hotel in Lisbon, Baker and I had outlined a deal: he would finance the design and construction of a maxi designed by Bruce Farr and would also lend me money to make the sponsorship search. I, as the fund-raising and management company, would then charter the boat from John with the sponsorship funds, the charter fee being his remuneration for his investment in the boat. This scheme would run 'until I start to get nervous,' he pointed out. He added he was not a Simon Le Bon, implying that I shouldn't assume he had limitless funds (the rock star and his two partners had failed to find sponsorship for *Drum* in the 1985/86 race, and had had to fund it themselves). His bail-out option was to sell the boat; it was likely there would be a buyer – the start of the race was over two years away.

John Baker was the antithesis to my experiences with rock musicians. Conservative by nature, but forward in outlook, the 68-year-old businessman had pioneered lever-aged buyouts over 15 years ago. In the days before corporate raiding was accepted business practice, he organized a man-agement take-over of American Safety Razor, then owned by Philip Morris, and turned the failing company into a success story. Now retired, except for a full-time job managing his stock portfolio, he admitted he needed something to do, and the Whitbread Race was certainly an attraction – the association with yachts, the vicarious experience of doing the Race – but for John the business side was probably the real kick; looking at an apparently hopeless situation and making a success of it. Though John Baker is one in a million, he is, in a sense, a typical Whitbread figure. If you look at most of the Whitbread boats, from New Zealand to Finland to Switzerland, you will find a John Baker behind the scenes somewhere, pushing the effort along with financial muscle, clever management and more than a few good contacts.

During June and July of 1987, John contracted with Bruce Farr Associates of Annapolis, Maryland, to design the 82-foot maxi, and Eric Goetz Custom Sailboats, of Bristol, Rhode Island, began to build the mould that would soon be covered with a fortune in high-tech Kevlar and carbon fibre composite fabrics. It was to be a 'state of the art' racing yacht projected at a cost of over $2 million. At that time it was unique, as we had opted for a ketch rig, a choice given to all Bruce Farr's Whitbread clients. My shipmate from *Drum*, part-time yacht designer Patrick Banfield from England, was hired by John to oversee and co-ordinate the building and fitting out – the fun part – leaving me free to concentrate on the fund-raising side, which any Salvation Army Colonel will tell you is anything but enjoyable.

We formed a few operating companies, and then the work began in earnest: full colour brochure of Team Novak; Gary Jobson, the best yacht racing commentator in the business and TV personality in his own right, on retainer as our mouthpiece and adviser; video newsletter; computer search of CEOs who sail; saturation bombing of the Fortune 1000 companies with a blind mail-shot to the president followed by a telephone call ('Yes we received your letter and it is being referred to our marketing department'); association with an established schools' geography project; contact with Senator Bill Bradley of New Jersey, a geography buff, for possible help with the schools' project. Any ad man or fund-raiser who sounded the least bit credible, I was on a plane to see him. We left no stone unturned, short of a public subscription campaign. Jobson's exhaustive analysis of fund-raising in America for the America's Cup had shown that not to be cost-effective.

These were the early days when we were still optimistic. Jobson lined up meetings for us with his corporate clients whom he advises on sailing sponsorships, among them brewers Anheuser Busch, Cadillac Cars and the Ciba Geigy

11

drugs and chemical conglomerate. Gary Jobson came up through the ranks of amateur yachting, culminating in his famous role as Ted Turner's tactician aboard *Courageous* in the defence of the 1976 America's Cup. A visionary, he realized early on the value of the television camera in an arena that formerly had hardly considered the possibilities of the media at all. Without question he has put yacht-racing, and sailing in general, on the media map and arguably opened up a whole new growth industry in America. In spite of his self-interested reputation and professional TV personality's smile I found him completely engaging and, at heart, a realist. He made it clear from the start what he thought the position would be. 'Look,' he told me in confidence after we had held another meeting with Baker, 'if you're lucky you'll get a million bucks out of one of these companies, but nobody is going to give you four. The way I see it, Baker is in for $2 million.' Jobson was working on the 'hook, line and sinker' theory, a common tactic in dealing with yacht owners, but John was in for nothing of the sort.

Black Monday, 19 October 1987. The consequences of the famous plunge in the stock market were only too evident when John picked me up at Charlotteville Airport in Virginia for a weekend pow-wow. He got right to the point and I admired his candour. 'How are you doing John?' 'Bad,' was his first reply. 'I'm real nervous and we need to talk about options.'

John had outlined a grim scenario – in his mind stopping the construction of the maxi yacht, now in its second building month in Rhode Island, or changing the boat into a cruiser, much to Patrick's disgust – but we still forged ahead in our efforts, trying desperately to get a meeting with corporate America. Finally, during Thanksgiving week, Jobson managed to fix a hearing at Anheuser Busch.

'Dennis (Conner) was here last week looking for $4 million for the Cup, but we had to turn him down,' said the boyish junior marketing manager for Bud Light. 'He's got a plan for twenty sponsors and an enormous budget and we couldn't see where we would get our return. If we're talking exclusivity for the same amount of money, for your

Whitbread campaign, it makes a lot more sense. It's still a lot of cash, but we'll look into it.' We were reasonably buoyant after hearing that and I finally had something positive to tell Baker, but I had learned a valuable lesson abut big sailing sponsorships in America: where you dare to tread in corporate America, Dennis Conner has already been there.

Dennis Conner Sports Inc., a sports marketing company, was formed on the back of his famous turn-around victory over the Australians in the 1987 America's Cup. Not only was he raising money for the next Cup defence (ostensibly his own), with budgets the Pentagon could be proud of, he was also offering his services to other projects. It took little talking to get a meeting with DC Sports Inc. since our figures were significant. John was chuffed about meeting DC, as he is known in the business, while I was a little less enthusiastic. We flew to San Diego for what could be a turning point.

The receptionist welcomed us in the well appointed annexe to Dennis's carpet store on the San Diego foreshore which was overflowing with enough America's Cup artwork and memorabilia to fill a museum, which is what it was destined for. David McGuigen led the initial discussion to soften us up, co-piloted by Bill Trenkle. Recently headhunted from Mark McCormack's IMG in Chicago, McGuigen was suited, bespectacled, a bit pale and looked like the corporate hit-man from the East that he was. Bill Trenkle was tanned, moustachioed and Californian, and also looked his part, a sail trimmer on a 12 Metre, which he was.

McGuigen asked all the right questions, and I was hopeful of getting some help until DC came in to spare us 20 minutes. Preoccupied with the current 'K' Boat challenge from New Zealand (that would, a year and a half later, find its way deep into the judiciary system of New York) and related financial problems, he looked incredibly unhealthy and could not focus on the conversation, if you call 20 minutes of his anecdotes about his America's Cup experiences a conversation about sponsorship for the Whitbread. His assistants were visibly embarrassed. The Great One ambled out and McGuigen promised to look into companies for us that

13

Dennis had not targeted for the America's Cup – obviously there were none. John summed up our feelings in the taxi back to the airport. 'I would have felt a lot better had I never met the man.'

Other fund-raisers and sports marketeers came and went ('I'm still working on it and should have some news for you next week'), some promising results and making contacts, others disappearing into the fug of New York City never to be heard from again. Although results were always negative, more contacts were never in short supply, and their comments on each other's track records were sometimes amusing, if not distressing.

The day we heard that Anheuser Busch, one of our few hopes, had given us the thumbs down ('Really doesn't fit in with our long term marketing plan') signalled the end of our efforts. The boat was half completed on the shop floor in Rhode Island. One month later, in February 1989, John Baker exercised the dreaded option of putting the boat up for sale. She was eventually taken over – the boat, our media contacts, Patrick Banfield, the lot – by a Swedish syndicate led by my ex-navigator on *Alaska Eagle* and *Drum*, Dr Roger Nilson. She raced as *The Card*. So ended the American dream.

The bald truth was obvious to John that no company or group of companies in America was going to risk the necessary $4-6 million for something so esoteric to the American public as a boat race around the world. Of course I knew this all along too, but a blind optimism carried me along, which is all the more understandable since I was not footing the bills.

I've heard a lot of conversation and theorising about why there is no American entry in the 1989/90 Race and it all boils down to one significant factor. Television coverage is the be-all and end-all of any sponsorship campaign. All the print media, the credibility of the schools' project and the goodwill generated did not mean a toss if we couldn't deliver on prime time and guarantee it by contract. And to get that contract years in advance, when we needed the money to operate, was the conundrum. Even though America is a big place with plenty of capital, that bigness works against what we were trying to achieve. How could we focus the media when the media, and especially prime-time television, will only focus on mainstream sport?

Demoralized and exhausted I got as far away as I could from this debâcle; for the first time in 12 years I was right out of what had become a life's game. Instead I returned to an original plan to go to Antarctica for a sailing and climbing expedition on the 54-foot boat *Pelagic* in which I had third share. I had started this project two years earlier but, because of the Whitbread plans, it had been carrying on for a large part without me. I flew to Punta Arenas in southern Chile in the first days of February to catch the six-week voyage down to the Antarctic Peninsula with an international team of climbers, sailors and film-makers, and, most important of all, good friends. I would spend the next six months between Antarctica, Tierra del Fuego and South Georgia, finishing our trip in Cape Town in July of that year.

While I was basking in the purity of the ice, and breathing clean air, in Europe and around the world other Whitbread projects were gathering steam, all big new stories and most with the character of a national project.

Finland, population four million, was boasting three maxis named and sponsored by Union Bank of Finland, Belmont cigarettes (Philip Morris) and Martela Oy, maker of office furniture. New Zealand, population three million, had two flagships in *Steinlager 2*, a local brew now exported, and *Fisher & Paykel*, a large appliance manufacturer just breaking into the Australian and European markets. Even Ireland had a big national entry, sponsored by NCB, the brokerage house, with help from Irish Distillers and government encouragement from the participation of Irish Life (insurance), the Electricity Supply Board and Aer Lingus (airline). The 'Captain's Club' subscription campaign and stunts like touring the country with the building mould painted in the Irish colours had made everyone aware of the project and tapped them for their contributions.

Howard Kilroy, the executive chairman of the Irish entry's management committee, an unwieldy organization of the kind the Irish are famous for, explained the reasoning to a journalist. 'National & City Brokers is a financial institution that is young and up and coming. They took this brave

15

decision to try and accelerate the visibility of their name in the community, which it certainly has done, particularly in Ireland and even abroad where they have other interests. I felt good about their involvement, because it wasn't just about getting back the money; they are really trying to create a national effort and to create a sense of ownership amongst all the people. It's only been partly successful so far, but conceptually it's right and with only three million people it's something that can work.'

In New Zealand, work it did. Besides the 'establishment' organization of the omnipotent Peter Blake and his big ketch *Steinlager 2*, another Kiwi challenge came from the unlikely source of a maker of washing machines. Gary Paykel, managing director of Fisher & Paykel, in the New Zealand tradition of 'do it yourself', looked favourably on skipper Grant Dalton's proposal for an entry in the Whitbread as a long-term commitment to company recognition. In 1988, the yacht and her crew visited all the country's major centres on her maiden promotional tour. 'The level of interest was just fantastic,' he says. 'And you only had to look at the media coverage we had, with frequent front page stories on the boat. Before the tour we were amazed to discover our company awareness was just 12%. That began to lift to 45% when we launched the boat amidst our first television commercial campaign, and by half way around New Zealand it had peaked at 60% and has stayed there ever since.'

Some of the other names read like an international advertisers index: *Merit* from Switzerland (Philip Morris cigarettes), *Fortuna Extra Lights* from Spain (Philip Morris cigarettes), *The Card* from Sweden (Eurocard, Access, Mastercard credit cards), *Charles Jourdan* from France (shoes), *British Satquote Defender* (stock market communications), *Fazisi* from USSR (joint venture), *Gatorade* from Italy (sports drink), *Equity & Law* from Holland (life assurance), *Creightons Naturally* from Britain (cosmetics), *Rucanor Sport* from Belgium (sports goods), *Royal Jordanian's Maiden* (Jordan's national airline) and *Rothmans* of Britain (cigarettes). And they all had an interesting story to tell.

It wasn't until late February of 1989 that I surfaced back in Europe, having had a refreshing mountaineering holiday in

16

East Africa on the way up from Cape Town. Although I had no intention of getting involved with a Whitbread entry that late in the game (the start was in seven months) I did have a practical problem, in that I was stone broke and needed a job.

The south coast of England is my base. In fact, thirteen years ago, during a chance meeting in a pub in Cowes on the Isle of Wight, the whole Whitbread story started for me when I signed on board *King's Legend* after contemplating the offer for a full five minutes. The deal was made with a handshake over a pint. Now the Whitbread game is certainly more premeditated and professionally run, but you still get more interesting information (if not always accurate) from a listening post like the King and Queen, the sailor's favourite watering hole on Hamble High Street, than you would from the Race Committee.

We all had heard rumours about an entry from the Soviet Union called the *Golden Fleece* long before, but not many people took it seriously then. Now, in spite of the fact that something was definitely brewing, there were still no pictures of the boat that was supposed to be already under construction on the shores of the Black Sea in Soviet Georgia.

Only one story appeared in the yachting press, by Englishman Stuart Alexander. He covered a courtesy tour by Dennis Conner to the syndicates dealing with the rumoured Soviet entry for the America's Cup in November 1988 with a side trip to visit the Golden Fleece Project. A poor-quality publicity photo of a portly Conner wearing what looked like a bearskin coat, surrounded by a few Soviets, appeared in the January issue of *Yachting World*, and the short text read like a piece of propaganda from *Pravda* about how this innovative design would amaze Western experts and lay waste to the Whitbread fleet.

It was apparent that whatever they were really up to was supposed to be hidden behind the Iron Curtain from prying Western eyes, and any information that leaked out was done so deliberately, and of course speculated on and distorted – a classic Soviet disinformation campaign. For example, rumour control had that it was being built of space-age materials and would be lighter and stronger in aluminium than the best examples in plastics; that the Soviet crew, rigorously psychologically tested, were at this very moment being blown up on steroids and being programmed to eat food from tubes developed for the cosmonauts. This and a mass of other stereotyped nonsense circulated the pubs and waterfront, but little was of believable substance, least of all the principal dimensions of 85 feet overall length and a displacement of 16 tonnes – impossible under the current International Offshore Rule which is used to handicap Whitbread Race yachts. Of course, Gorbachev was paying for everything as part of his *glasnost* programme and the boat would be called *Perestroika*.

All of this fascinated me, but I knew I had to work fast. Two names were quickly extracted from the race organizers: Murnikov and Wawer. Murnikov was a Soviet and was the project manager, while Wawer, a West German running a sports marketing company in Hamburg, was putting together the PR campaign when the boat got to England. I sent them both faxes and when I didn't hear from them immediately I sent them more. This went on for three weeks.

My idea was simple and logical. If the Soviets were going to sail a maxi boat, they would need to train their crew. This was something I had done for the Fazer Finland project in the autumn of 1984; I had taken good, small-boat sailors and taught them the rudiments of big-boat handling. I made the assumption that there were not any large sailboats in the Soviet Union. Also, their timing was critical as they would be starting late. What a great opportunity – work for the Russians! Maybe get a trip into the Soviet Union out of it – maybe make a few roubles. What a crack!

Vladislav Murnikov eventually answered my fax with a tentative invitation to come to the Soviet Union for an interview. They said my idea was interesting. I was to stand by for more information. The fax was worded in such a way that I could easily imagine that the next message would be by a dead letter drop.

While awaiting my next instructions I amused myself and others by having a serious paragliding accident on the Isle of Wight, running into a tree and rupturing my urethra. Five days later while I was still in hospital in Southampton, plumbed in and out, I got a phone call. The line was weak and scratchy and a heavy accent said slowly: 'My name is Vladislav Murnikov. We've been trying to reach you. Your visa information is now at the Soviet Embassy in London and you will come to Moscow on 12 April.'

I said I would be there. But, 'Christ! That's in ten days. I've got to get out of this hospital,' I told the nurse. She went to find the doctor. He said I could have one of the catheters out the next day and go home, and the other out in one week, leaving me three days before my flight.

Sporting a catheter bag strapped to my knee and good for about a pint I nonchalantly pulled up to the bar at the King and Queen two days later. My shipmate from *Drum*, neighbour and raconteur Neil Cheston was holding his usual court amused with his clever wit, most of whom were signed up on the Rothmans entry, a massively funded Whitbread campaign due to be launched in one month's time. Without asking, he shouted me a pint of bitter.

'So Skip, I hear you're off to Russia. God I'm envious. What do you think they're up to over there? I hear that all the equipment like the rig, sails, deck hardware and electronics are coming from Western suppliers?'

'So I understand,' I said, feeling the catheter bag taking on weight as my first pint started to trickle through. 'I had a long chat to John Green from Sparcraft today who is obviously rubbing his hands together. He's got the order for the rig and he's also putting the package together for the deck stuff. Nudger is working on the electronics order, mostly American stuff, North Germany has got the sails and Speedwave the keel, rudder and steering system. The way I understand it, everything is coming from the West including the paint. All that they're building is the hull and deck. Another thing I know is that nobody has seen any money yet and they don't want roubles, so all this gear is on permanent hold.'

'But what about the design of this thing? All the experts, well at least from what they can see on that drawing from *Yachting World*, say that the boat will never measure under the IOR rules.'

'Does it matter?' I replied almost too casually, the two pints of bitter now in full flood. A noticeable bulge had appeared

19

under my trousers. 'Look I have no intention of sailing on that thing. Strictly a summer's consultant job. Remember I said after *Drum* that I'd never again do a last-minute project? Besides, they already have a skipper, and I wouldn't go as cook.'

'Well, it will be good to see you on the starting line,' he jokingly persisted.

'Not me matey.' I turned to go out the door, the bag taut and about to blow. 'See you when I get back from Russia.'

3

The Defection

I wanted to impress my prospective new employers by taking an Aeroflot plane to Moscow, but a last-minute delay forced me onto the relative comforts of the late-morning British Airways flight.

I was on a personal voyage of discovery. The trend for *Time* and *Newsweek* reports about all things Soviet was only just beginning and I knew very little about the Soviet Union, other than the grim picture Solzhenitsyn has painted in his novels, which I had read many years before. So I started my research at the beginning, and came armed with Berlitz's *Russian for Travellers* and Tolstoy's epic for ballast.

My Russian delegation recognized me before I recognized them in the crowded arrival lobby of Sheremtievo Airport. For one nervous moment it was like being in Japan or China – all the Russians looked the same! Out of a sea of grey overcoats and hats, however, a bearded and balding Vladislav Murnikov, project manager and designer of the yacht, extended his hand with a shy grin. He introduced himself and the Fazis driver he had in tow, before ushering me out to the confusion of the airport car park. The driver reassembled the windscreen-wiper blades and side-view mirrors – a precaution against theft – before we roared down a wide boulevard on bald tyres into the heart of Moscow, with Vladislav pointing out landmarks along the way.

The two of us had dinner that evening in the dining room of the Belgrade, my hotel off Smolensky Square. The hotel, an official Intourist establishment which doubles as a *de facto* hard currency exchange, charges £80 per night, paid in foreign cash or with credit card only. This buys a cubicle with a thin mattress on a plywood base and the joys of dealing with unhelpful reception staff and surly waiters who can growl a first-time visitor into early submission.

Over several rounds of obligatory vodka we discussed the Russian plans, not in any depth, but in general terms, both jockeying for an angle, and neither giving anything away. As the dancing began, a feature of all restaurants in the Soviet Union, Vladislav announced that I would be picked up at 11 o'clock the following morning, and he then left me free to wander down the nearby pedestrian Arbat Street, where the new wave of radicals, artists and pedlars of all things are allowed to gather. A march down to Red Square, which was more impressive than I had imagined, then a few drinks in the Belgrade's tourist bar to gauge the black-market currency rates, rounded out an interesting first evening.

I was met by the driver the next morning and taken to the Fazis Moscow headquarters on Sadovaja-Triumphalnaja Street which is just off the Centrum. The office was a humble, three-room affair in the back of a mezzanine floor in a typical nondescript 1950's Soviet building. Fazis Moscow is a Soviet joint venture company. Joint ventures, whereby a foreign hard currency partner does business with the USSR, have been around for a long time, but only recently, with *perestroika*, have foreigners been allowed a big enough share in the ownership to give them controlling interest and the incentive to participate. Fazis's partner was a slick West German from Saarbrucken whom I later met at his office in Moscow's Hammer Center where Fazis used the Fax machine, not having an 'outside' line of their own. Ostensibly, the West German had nothing to do with the sailing project. Although Fazis maintains a Moscow office, this was the first joint venture officially registered from the Republic of Georgia.

Most joint venture companies engage in any manufacturing, processing or supply operation that promotes growth in the Soviet Union, largely financing these through barter deals. Because the Soviet rouble is not convertible on the foreign exchanges, the emphasis is to get hard currency into the country so they can buy in more technology to operate. The conundrum lies in the fact that what they can manufacture at present is of so low a quality that it is unmarketable in the West so they usually resort to bartering goods from the West for their own raw materials.

There was certainly an air of poverty at the Fazis office. There were a few bare desks, files of paper stood on a few shelves in what were formerly broom cupboards, there was a typical Russian tea service in one corner, an abacus to do the accounts and little else. The only ray of sunshine came not from the windows, which were still dirty and greasy from a long winter's soot and grime, but from a stylized blue and yellow poster of the *Golden Fleece* – the Whitbread racing boat to be – hung on the wall like an icon.

The theme of the project was the Greek legend of Jason and the Argonauts and their search for the Golden Fleece. After the Argonauts weathered their trials crossing the length of the Black Sea they landed in Colchis (now Soviet Georgia) where Jason surreptitiously rowed up the River Phasis and recovered the Fleece that was hanging from a garden tree guarded by the serpent Prometheus. Metaphorically speaking, he who finds the Fleece finds success. What people sometimes forget is that after Jason had found the Fleece, he had a hard time hanging on to it during his voyage back to the west.

Throughout the first day, as they came and went on errands in and about Moscow, I met the Fazis staff: Alexander Kedishvili, one of the company directors, and Ludmilla and Angela, the two administrators, none of whom spoke more than a few words of English. Only Igor, a tall Siberian-looking character, smartly dressed like a Western junior executive, was fluent – really fluent – which immediately made me suspect he was the statutory KGB plant. In my inexperience of Soviet life I was convinced there had to be one and he certainly did fit the bill.

In addition to the company people, Vladislav Murnikov had his own technical group for the Golden Fleece project. In a cramped anteroom the short and squat Valeri Chumakov, decked out in a blue yachting blazer and tie, sat nervously tapping a pencil on the table like a schoolmaster. He overenthusiastically tried to explain himself as a sailing coach who had managed the Olympic Team in Seoul and also led a Soviet delegation to the Worrell 1,000 catamaran race on the American east coast a few years ago. Nadia Ousjannikova, a dark-haired, pale-complexioned wisp of a woman from the Ministry of Sport, on contract to vet the crew psychologically, struggled to be understood in halting French slightly below even my level, which borders on the non-existent. And lastly, skipper elect Anatoly Verba, the archetypal scowling sea captain, who hailed from the Black Sea port of Odessa, was intently ticking off items like marine toilets, lifejackets and signal flags from what looked like a 10-year-old Thomas Foulkes *Marine Hardware Catalogue*.

Of course, language was immediately a problem. Vladislav had to take the burden of translating the panel's greetings and questions into his passable English. With formalities soon over, the discussion became a polite interrogation. It was evident that they were starved for information, not about building an aluminium hull, which, according to Vladislav, was being executed under strict control and to the highest standard and was, as he explained, 'basically on schedule for an end of May launching,' but for just about everything else – sails, machinery, winches and electronics (Anatoly), clothing, hygiene and crew management (Nadia) and running the campaign overseas (Valeri).

The few drawings of the boat were neat and detailed, and from the way Vladislav talked I was sure he had some practical experience. 'Well, what other boats have you seen in the West?' I asked him.

'But I have never been in the West. All our design and engineering is from our own programme at the Leningrad Shipbuilding Institute. Of course, a lot of ideas come from Western yachting magazines about equipment and so on. And that's where we know about you!' I was dumbfounded. I thought about some of the first-time yacht race entries I have seen from other so-called technological countries – more often than not comical disasters crewed by fools. Did the Soviets have any idea of what they were getting into?

After four days, during which they debriefed me of 12 years' knowledge of Whitbread races, they sent me home exhausted. They had agreed that I would train the crew when the boat was launched, check on and co-ordinate the equipment from all the European suppliers that was, according to Fazis, already being made, and finally, generate publicity on their behalf. The simple consultancy job was already becoming complicated.

When I boarded the return Aeroflot flight to London I realized that I still knew very little about the Golden Fleece Project. The few blurred photographs, already out of date, which they had given me to circulate to the press confirmed that something was indeed being built. Their intention was to launch in six weeks' time, put the boat through sea trials in the Black Sea during June, and take the month of July to sail the 4,000 miles to England and then compete in the 1989 Fastnet Race in early August. ASM, the sports' marketing company from Hamburg, was under contract to find the millions of dollars needed to fund this campaign when the boat arrived, and they were apparently confident of doing so. Through the good graces of Dennis Conner's celebrated promotional visit to the Soviet Union the previous December, they already had a letter from Pepsi International in America promising them $250,000 as a start-up fund. They knew they were late, but seemed relaxed about it. 'We in Russia have been waiting for a long time,' they all used to remind me. Back in Western Europe the story was decidedly different. Indeed, Jason was already sailing extremely close to the rocks.

Three main suppliers of Western-made equipment were involved, and all three were not only holding fire on production, but were still struggling contractually with Fazis Moscow. North Sails in Germany were supposed to build 16 sails at a cost of DM 368,000; The Speedwave Company, also of Germany, was expected to supply a custom-made, computer-machined lead keel, a carbon fibre rudder, the two steering wheels and all the ancillary steering equipment for a price of DM 150,000. And finally the Barient Sparcraft Company of Lymington, England, put together an umbrella contract for £380,000 that included not only the rig and winches, but also the scores of blocks and deck fittings, hatches, a full electronics package, the generator and watermaker, plumbing fittings and even the paint.

25

Over half a million pounds sterling of goods had to be paid for in hard currency. This involved a complicated procedure of negotiating foreign contracts and securing bank guarantees via letters of credit – normal business practice really – but the reality of dealing with the fledgling free-market economy of the Soviet Union was almost non-existent communication, misunderstanding as to the chronology of the paperwork needed, and the complications of a Soviet bank guaranteeing a German bank who would then guarantee an English bank. None of us was clear who Fazis really was or where they were getting this cash, because as far as we knew they were a new company and had no other projects. Obviously, companies like Barient Sparcraft were not interested in taking scrap metal or coal in payment, and they were worried.

'The winches and deck gear are all on order, mate,' explained Sparcraft's director, John Green, whom I visited the day after my return. 'Some of the standard stuff has already arrived from California and is on the shelf downstairs. I've got the alloy sections for the mast, in fact I think the guys are due to move them into the factory this week. But until we get a letter of credit from the Russkies, and it passes our banker, there's no bloody way we can start to cut metal. I've already got my neck stuck out to here financially. If IMI [the parent company in America] finds out what I've done, I'll really be in the shit.'

He shoved over a fistful of correspondence in a manila folder. 'Read some of this. This has been going on for months now and we can never get a straight answer. Sometimes they never even reply to our faxes. Frankly I'm getting pretty nervous. Vladislav knows we need eight weeks to build that rig.'

I have known John Green for almost 20 years since the golden days when we both worked on ocean racing yachts as the paid hands. Formerly abrasive, he has mellowed over the years. While I kept on sailing, he took an office job and is now a mainstay in the recognized marine mafia that stretches over two continents and includes mast builders, sail makers, winch manufacturers, electronics suppliers and, not least of all, a network of some of the best sailors in the world which almost guarantees that their products will be where the money is. John was in charge of the UK mast division of the well known American company.

He had met the Soviets in Moscow that winter during the early stages of this project and they had come to an agreement whereby Barient Sparcraft would act as an agent to supply a large portion of the gear for the boat. John has certainly seen more than a few supposedly wealthy clients go belly-up or renege on a deal, so in spite of his genuine enthusiasm for this curious project I knew exactly where his fears lay.

'If we got the go-ahead today, we could have the rig out of the door by the end of May,' he added, as I was leaving, promising to stay in touch. Both of us already knew, without having to say so, that that was a most unlikely scenario.

The essence of this conversation was repeated to me twice more over the telephone with Speedwave and North Sails in Germany. '*Kein Geld, nichts zu tun.*' ('No money, nothing doing.')

Having made adjustments to the specifications for the gear on order after our meetings in Moscow, there was little else to do with the suppliers. I faxed Fazis Moscow, telling them about the financial situation in Europe and how unlikely it was that they would see any of their equipment earlier than the end of June, even if they produced their letters of credit immediately.

I sent a copy of that fax to ASM, the sports' marketing company which was supposed to be helping with these negotiations. The phone rang almost immediately. 'How could that happen?' said Klaus Wawer. 'All these companies have told me they have already started.'

I began to realize the situation ASM was in. After a few conversations it became clear they knew nothing about sailing boats or yacht races. Forging ahead enthusiastically, albeit in the dark on a few issues of fact, they were trying to negotiate the original letter of intent from Pepsi into a contract, in addition to marketing other ideas. Bringing the boat to Hamburg for only four days in August, they said, for the port's 800th anniversary, could clinch a deal worth DM 300,000.

Having done all I could, I left the accountants, lawyers

and managing directors to try and sort it out, and went to Australia for a three-week holiday disguised as a 'prior commitment'. Wasting time waiting for people to make decisions is endemic in the boating business and I felt no guilt in sitting this one out. I kept in touch via the fax machine on minor developments, collecting a stack of insignificant paper about letters of credit, contracts, delivery dates that were already unrealistic and ludicrous schedules that would never be kept. It was during that time that I planted the seed with the Soviets of the possibility of shipping the boat unfinished to the UK and completing the fit-out stage closer to the start of the Whitbread Race.

When I returned to the UK, not a lot had changed. None of the three suppliers had any guarantees! The Soviets had conceded that maybe the boat would be launched later, around the middle to third week in June, and had requested that the keel, rudder and rig be delivered by then.

'If we had the guarantees we maybe could deliver the keel in four weeks, said Hans Waimer from Speedwave, an eternal optimist on production, especially on the tele-phone. '*Nein*,' I could hear his wife shouting at him in the background, '*Nicht moglich, sechs Wochen!*' ('Not possible, six weeks!')

When I called North Sails, loft president, Albert Schweitzer, was disappointed to tell me that they could not afford to stock the cloth without a firm order and now they would not be able to build all the sails there even if they wanted to.

On 31 May I spent a night in Hamburg for a meeting with Klaus Wawer and one of his partners in ASM, Mike Winterfeldt. They were still struggling with the Pepsi con-tract and their biggest concerns were not only whether the boat would get to the starting line on time, only three months away, but also whether it would be able to fulfil the promised summer's schedule, a schedule they were nervously offering as a promotional tour to Pepsi and others. Off to Moscow on my second visit, I promised them a realistic assessment on my return the following week.

I turned 37 years old on 1 June. When the Fazis office staff noticed this in my resumé that afternoon, they kindly presented me with a hand-painted tea tray conjured up out of the back room. Things were different this time around. I was now staying with Vladislav in his apartment outside Moscow and although this put a damper on my black-market dealing on Arbat Street, the atmosphere surely beat the austerity of the Belgrade.

Vladislav is a Ukrainian from the small town of Chercassy. He attended the mathematical school in Kiev before finishing his education with a degree in civil engineering from the Engineering Institute in Moscow. After working on several building projects, in 1985 he started as a technical consultant to the Research Centre for New Consumer Goods. But he has always been an amateur yacht designer and for the last ten years has been on the Technical Committee for the Soviet Yacht Racing Federation. He explained that engineers make about 300 roubles a month. To put that in perspective half a rouble (50 kopecks) can buy you a beer, 20 roubles a dinner in a 'state' restaurant, 50, dinner in a 'special' restaurant. A TV costs about 600 roubles and a car could be 8-10,000, if you can get it.

Since he had no car, we took the metro, one of Moscow's assets in that it works and is spotlessly clean. The outskirts of the city were bulldozed to the ground during Stalin's time, destroying any village or community atmosphere, and in their place, rectangular blocks of apartments house the majority of the city's population.

'You will see, this is a typical Moscow flat,' he explained to me as we went through into the foyer that looked like a poorly appointed service entrance. His apartment, that he shared with his lovely wife Tanya and 10-year-old son Pavel, was the standard two rooms with kitchen and bath, simple and neat, but the leaky taps and threadbare carpets were not only typical of the Soviet Union, where nothing is new, but were also typical of the life of any yachtsman, of any country, where all the spare household cash goes for blocks, sails and fittings and the yearly sailing holiday. In fact it was very reminiscent of my own home.

In the main room that doubled as a bedroom he had an old stereo, a TV and an impressive library of books with a prominently displayed, signed copy of Dennis Conner's book *Comeback* about his 1987 America's Cup turn-around victory.

Valeri Chumakov and the new skipper-elect, Alexei Gryshenko, also came over and we spent the evening talking, eating and toasting ourselves and the future of the project. I remember quite clearly the simplicity and sincerity of that conversation in the closeness of that small room, a rare evening in our Western world of cheap talk and sometimes inane entertainment.

During the next five days I spent 6 to 8 hours a day inside the Fazis office discussing the boat, the equipment, the crew and what we would do when in England. The big news was they had decided to ship the boat to the UK for completion. Instead of my proposal to put it on a freighter in the Black Sea, they went one better and decided to fly it out in the world's largest cargo plane! They were then negotiating this flight that was to cost 80,000 roubles.

Alexei Gryshenko had been the lead man on the construction and had come up to Moscow to discuss technical details with Vladislav. He had only recently been chosen as the skipper in preference to Anatoly, as Anatoly was, as Vladislav described it, 'a bit too authoritarian'. Alexei came from Kiev and worked as an engineer in electronics, but his real passion was sailing boats. He had built his own 35-foot racing yacht and campaigned it in local races on the River Dneiper and the Black Sea. He was supposed to be one of the most experienced offshore sailors in the Soviet Union.

The trouble was he spoke absolutely no English. He and I would grunt at each other over drawings and specifications lists, break for lunch and grunt at each other in the stand-up café around the corner. A serious man with a perpetually worried brow, he looked like I had always imagined a Russian would (he was in fact Ukrainian); pale skin, solid frame, moonfaced with a shallow chin, but with the strongest stare I have ever come across, giving me the impression he was a hard man – and he was, but every now and again, despite our inability to communicate over some detail, he would break out in a deep laugh, reach out and shake my hand in mutual understanding.

One evening we were invited to dinner at the Union of Cinematographers by the Soviet film producer who would be making the documentary of the project. Before the dinner, there was a lecture by an ex-Red Army General, comparing Western and Soviet defence expenditures. A lot of the audience were falling asleep or laughing at this comical figure; we walked out half way through and got stuck into the vodka toasts at the table.

Toasting is *de rigueur* at any dinner or function. Everyone has to wait until the next person says his piece and then you all down your poison together – in almost a solemn fashion. We toasted the Soviet Union, the boat project, our mothers and wives, America – a lot of simple platitudes, or so I thought. When it was my turn I made the mistake of getting bogged down in things too profound for the occasion like international relations, the possibility of friendship without the military, and a lot of crap conjured up from 1960s Americana, which was all translated by Vladislav, who I think understood what I was trying to say. Instead of the usual nods of approval I received icy stares and almost a snarl from our host, the film producer. I must have misinterpreted what I thought was his disapproval of the General's speech and our premature exit from the lecture. Possibly we were just late for dinner.

On the evening of 3 June we were once again at Vladislav's for the evening and watched Andrei Sakharov on TV, at the new People's Deputies' Congress, deliver a salvo against the government that had the Congress in an uproar. He said in effect that Afghanistan had been not only a mistake, but a crime, and the people in the government who were responsible should be punished. Gorbachev sat behind him near the podium and took it all on the chin.

I fancied I had witnessed something quite historical but little did I realize that this was the start of an incredible chronology that would take place during the following 12 months – the literal breakdown not only of the Communist governments in the Eastern Bloc, but of the Communist system as an institution.

'But what about Lenin, would we ever see his image dismantled?' I asked Vladislav that evening.

'Not now – it is too early. Unlike Stalin, Lenin remains a positive idea for most people. Can you imagine telling the old people out there that they have lived their entire lives in a huge mistake? For the young like us it is different. We can accept that change, but I think it will be only after these older generations are gone.'

'Let's drink to that, *nosterovia!*'

In two days my visa was due to run out. I still had not seen the boat and when I pressed Vladislav about this he thought it was, 'at this stage unnecessary'.

'There's no way I can go back to Europe without seeing that thing, Vladislav. People are already suspicious about what's going on over here and I have got to come back with some answers.'

They finally conceded and the next day my visa was extended for a brief trip in search of the Golden Fleece. That afternoon Alexei and I took a domestic Aeroflot flight to Sukhumi at the foot of the Caucasus Mountains and then changed to a small commuter flight to the port of Poti, flying low over the rich farmlands at the base of the fertile triangle which makes up the Soviet Republic of Georgia.

We were met at the local airport by a delegation of Fazis directors and whisked off in what goes for a black limousine. I immediately felt more at ease as we drove along the rural roads into Poti. Instead of blocks of flats, closer to town there were separate houses, the stucco painted in pastels. Well-kept gardens of flowers and vegetables, some shaded by grapevines on trellises, were surrounded by attractive wrought-iron fencing along tree-lined avenues. The people were dark complexioned and confident and moved with the slow, almost lazy gait of the Mediterranean. A look or a gesture seemed to say simply 'Relax, you're not in Russia'.

The Georgian protocol is to eat and drink first and foremost. We spent over two hours in a restaurant with a group of about 12 hosts, consuming a huge lunch of the local delicacies and drowning ourselves in good Georgian wine, Georgian champagne and Armenian brandy. My enthusiasm and impatience for seeing the boat soon wore off, and after each toast I grew more and more sleepy in the late afternoon heat. This was no time for any righteous behaviour about consuming alcohol in the middle of what was, for me, a working day – and a critical one at that. I just got on with it and would suffer the consequences later.

My hosts, now satisfied they had done their work, brought me down to the waterfront to the Poti Shipyard. Here they manufacture aluminium passenger hydrofoils that are exported worldwide, and here they were building the Whitbread yacht.

The building shed was enormous and dwarfed even the hydrofoils themselves, which were arranged along the sides on a semi-production line. In one corner was the 82-foot hull of the yacht. I wasn't quite prepared for what met my eyes. At first glance it was one of the most radical hulls I had ever seen, with almost no depth at all. Its configuration was more like that of a dinghy than an offshore boat. A raised bow profile and very fine forward sections gave it an almost comical appearance, and for a minute or two I was incredulous. I was reminded of the well-known cartoon that is probably on the wall of every boatyard, in which the builder realizes that one end of his canoe is facing down and the other end up; he holds his head in his hands muttering 'Oh shit!'

The hull was swarming with workmen in dirty overalls, their heads wrapped in rags as they sanded some fairing on the hull and ground bare aluminium. A welder crackled away in the shallow cockpit with an assistant standing by shielding his face with a bare hand. Overhead, the hook of a 40-tonne crane on a running gantry cruised the air nearby.

These were the crew who, in three months, were due to set sail from England on the Whitbread Race! They had been toiling away for the last seven months working seven days a week, 9 to 10 hours a day, building a dream.

I nervously shook strong hands and met Sergeis, Viktors and an Igor. I thought I could recognize a pair of eyes smiling at me out of a face disguised in epoxy dust – it was Anatoly! While he was on his knees, sanding the transom, Alexei walked past with his clipboard. God knows what he was going through.

The deck was straightforward, but down below was a nightmare. Without any headroom, the interior was nothing more than a crawl space, and even without any fixtures or fittings it was already claustrophobic. Nevertheless the achievement was impressive, given the time and place. The boat was certainly modern in hull form and represented some original thinking. It definitely was not the square, box-like structure you would expect from the Soviets who are notorious for their sense of form. Like a well-designed car or motorcycle, it had sex appeal.

Early that evening I was asked to address all who had an interest in the project – the Fazis board of directors, some town officials and the manager of the Poti Yacht Club, who wore a Stars & Stripes T shirt from Dennis Conner's visit. With a scowling portrait of Lenin staring me in the face behind Fazis General Director Viktor Tichov, I told them diplomatically, through an interpreter, that they had so far built a fantastic boat and would amaze people in the West (which after all was the object of the whole exercise) but that they were in real trouble with the schedule. I reckoned it would take a lot of capital and six weeks from the boat's arrival in the UK to the launch, and that was without major hold-ups, which in a situation like this were almost inevitable. The shipping of the boat by air would have to be on time and go smoothly. Without any foundation I promised them that if we could begin work on the boat around 12 July we could make the start – just. I half believed myself, but knew I was really bullshitting.

They assured me all was organized. On 1 July the unfinished hull would be christened and given a celebration launch in Poti, then immediately put back in the shed for four more days of work. It would then be taken by barge down to Sukhumi, transferred onto a truck off a naked beachhead and taken to the main airport. It sounded like a logistical daydream.

Late that evening I met the crew in their barracks-style accommodation nick-named the 'Poti Three Star Hotel' next to the shipyard which serves as a hostel for merchant seamen while their ships are under repair. Some spoke in broken English and others through an interpreter. They asked me all sorts of questions about equipment, sails and navigation, questions that were sometimes naive, but always sincere.

From the back of the room a voice that belonged to a curly black head boomed out in perfect English, 'Do you think this crew can handle such a boat as *Fazisi*?'

34

I looked around. I suspected there was not a racing man amongst them, at least not to my standard – how could there be? 'I think we will have difficulties, but I can see that anyone who has built that boat by themselves will have the common sense to sail it,' I answered. I made a personal vow that I would not let them down. I sensed an air of the wonderfully impossible there; the over-ambition of people who were out to prove themselves, and people who were obviously in over their heads – things that I can easily relate to.

I was due to fly out early the next morning, almost before I had got my bearings. I woke up at six in the Poti Three Star Hotel, dehydrated from cheap wine and suffering a fierce hangover, after a fitful sleep. The mosquitoes were still feeding and outside the window a moth-balled Soviet Naval crew were running around the parade ground making noise while doing calisthenics. Eugene shoved a glass of astringent tea in my hand, the water boiled on the spot with an immersion heater, and gave me a slice of black bread with what looked like a slice of some of the excellent Georgian cheese I had had the day before.

'Here, pig fat,' he said as he pulled on his dirty overalls. It was all I could do not to throw up.

An hour later Mr Tichov and I flew low over the old Phasis River on our way to Sukhumi.

As I came to my senses I started to think about what I was getting myself into. I know what they will all say back home when we don't make the start – or worse – 'Yes, another Novak fiasco, he's famous for these projects and now he's gone too far.'

That afternoon Tichov and I pushed and shoved our way off the plane in the usual Soviet fashion and lined up on the tarmac waiting for the passenger bus to arrive. To my amazement and delight a bus pulled up with Igor the KGB man waving us inside. Tichov and I climbed aboard, leaving our 250 companions standing there, and proceeded out of the gate and onto the street without the usual scrutiny of papers. Tichov, a big bear of a man with an engaging manner, was obviously a heavyweight – possibly a Godfather. We would need one.

4

Shuttle Diplomacy

Nervous businessmen were ten deep on standby when I got to the check-in desk at Moscow Airport that same evening. They were all more than determined to be on that plane – more to the point, to get the hell out of Moscow – and you could read in their faces that another day fighting the inconveniences of the Soviet system would be the last straw. After some aggressive behaviour with the ticket clerk I just sneaked through, and four hours later landed in Frankfurt.

I flew on to Munich in order to visit the Speedwave factory and check on the keel, rudder and steering system. I was then to make tracks for London the next day to meet Herr Wawer to discuss the Pepsi deal. At the same time, Vladislav was making his first visit to England to meet the Whitbread Race Committee and talk to Sparcraft. Apparently the contracts and letters of credit were almost finalized.

Hans Waimer met me at Munich Airport and I spent the night at his home making short work of his brandy supply as we swapped Russian stories well into the early morning. He had instigated and been on the first delegation to reconnoitre the Soviet America's Cup and Whitbread projects with Dennis Conner back in December. His anecdote is worth repeating:

'Come on Dennis, you can't pass up a trip to Russia!'

'But Hans,' Conner answered, 'I can't go to Russia. Aren't those people our enemies?'

After some persuasion he agreed to make what is now considered his historic contribution to *glasnost*.

Speedwave was only working on the design of the equipment on order, and now, since the boat would be shipped to the UK, it was necessary to change the consignment address for the keel and rudder to England instead of Poti. Mrs Waimer was adamant that we had to rewrite the contract to change this, which would in turn alter the letter of credit, or, as she explained, 'We won't get paid!' North Sails and Sparcraft said the same. Another hitch – more lost time.

While checking the specifications, I realized there was not a lot of communication between the Poti Shipyard and Speedwave. Many technical details were either unclear or wrongly interpreted, so with my technical co-ordinator's hat on I tried to put these right so that basic things like the keel and steering system would actually fit the boat when delivered.

A short visit to North Sails on my way back to the airport confirmed that they were in fact doing nothing. They, like the others, had not received any guarantees as yet and were least enthusiastic about taking any risks. With nothing else to do, I grabbed the next flight to London.

That evening I tried to check into the Kensington Palace Hotel. No good. My Visa card didn't clear the £90 needed, and I had no cash. Since the beginning of my involvement in April I had run up a personal debt of £4,000 for expenses and there was no prospect of a solution in sight. I was getting nervous.

Mike Winterfeldt turned up and kept me off the street that night, but he and Klaus had bad news. The Pepsi deal had fallen through. Pepsi felt they had no time to organize the promotion despite ASM's offering to handle all the logistics and public relations. They showed me the famous letter dated 28 November 1988 from Pepsi's president Mr Beebi, promising the Soviets $250,000; $75,000 on signing, $75,000 on launching and $100,000 at the start. All this for only simple name and logos on the boat and one sponsor's day for Pepsi.

But this was back in November, and when Mr Beebi left the company in January all his pet projects went into the waste bin. Perhaps the new president was more interested in golf than sailing boats. ASM could find no other communication between the Soviets and Pepsi until 14 March when a few faxes had been exchanged, and it wasn't until late in April that ASM, now under an exclusive contract with Fazis, had begun to pursue the matter.

In the short term, Pepsi's refusal was a disaster as there was now no foreseeable money for when the boat arrived in the UK. Winterfeldt and Wawer, who were furious at Pepsi's attitude, were determined not to let the matter drop however, citing prior agreement, and they planned to fly to Pepsi International Headquarters in Somers, New York, in ten days time, to meet the brand marketing manager, Tony McGrath, for another attempt. They suggested I come along.

In the meantime I began, reluctantly, to make preparations for the arrival of the boat and the finish of the construction in the village of Hamble, near Southampton. Trucking of an oversize load from Heathrow to Southampton had to be co-ordinated, the boatyard, Hamble Yacht Services, had to be briefed on space required and labour needed, and we had to set up our own temporary office and communications base with a secretary in place. Not least of all, accommodation for the crew had to be found, cars and office equipment rented, and a hundred other details that were all vital in attempting what most people said would be the impossible.

With no contracts, no cashflow and no guarantees of anything down the road, I could only turn to friends for help, making sure they had their eyes open. With his salary indefinitely deferred, I hired on Fazis' behalf my neighbour Jim Saunders to manage the shore operation. A jack of all trades and master of many, Jim could fix your car, wire your house, sail your boat or design and build you a three-piece suite. Whatever needed doing he could organize it, or do it himself if he had to; in spite of spending what some consider to be an inordinate amount of time in The King and Queen he was totally reliable. Hamish Laird, my companion on the Antarctic expedition, ski instructor and sometime boat builder, was also recruited. A native of the Isle of Wight, he was between jobs, dossing on my sofa, and he gladly accepted the risk and the challenge of working for the Russians, with the same spirit as explorer/sailor Bill Tilman used to acquire crew for his epic voyages through advertisements in the paper; 'Crew wanted for sailing expedition, no pay, no prospects, not much fun.'

Another old friend, Jane Redford, the project manager for the Whitbread entry from France, *Operation Cargo*, soon to be renamed *Charles Jourdan*, had been making enquiries for us on and off from her Paris office and she agreed to come to England before the boat's arrival to help set up the office. With Hamble Yacht Services, Jim Saunders and myself paying deposits we might never get back for goods and services, this 'shore team' forged ahead in blind optimism.

On 26 June I flew to New York. Mike Winterfeldt, Klaus Wawer and I drove into upstate New York for the meeting with Pepsi. After 10 days of negotiating it looked as if the deal might be on again. I was asked along to answer any difficult questions regarding boats, boat races and the like, and also to provide some credibility for Pepsi in a crew of faceless Soviets.

I came through with the required expertise and enthusiasm, which could have fooled anyone who knew next to zero about racing yachts, meaning ASM and Tony McGrath. They then thrashed out the contract behind closed doors. By the end of the day they had outlined the deal: for a six-week promotion beginning with the boat's arrival at Heathrow as a media event, going on to the Pepsi launch in early August, a trip up the Thames and through Tower Bridge and then the start on 2 September, we would get, not $250,000, but instead $200,000. (When ASM took off their 25% there would not be much left over for the project.) We all realized the bottom figure was not the issue, but only the hook to land Pepsi on our deck. The tickler was a clause in the contract that gave Pepsi the option to renegotiate a deal for other parts or the entire race as our major sponsor up to $1.8 million. The message from Tony McGrath, a Scotsman and Pepsi 'lifer', was that if we did well, they would look at the rest of the project with an open mind. I was later told that in promotional parlance, Pepsi, from the beginning, had been a 'reluctant sponsor'.

It seemed strange that when I asked for some Pepsi logos,

graphics, flags and stickers for the boat when it flew into Heathrow in 12 days' time, they could not find any. I pressured Tony until he finally struck a shady deal with the person in charge of the flagpole on the expansive corporate front lawn, who reluctantly took down and surrendered the colours. Thanking Tony for his cooperation the three of us left the Pepsi 'cradle to grave' atmosphere and headed back into the fug of New York City.

Mike and Klaus went straight to Hamburg to finalize the contract and budget for the Pepsi promotion (not part of the sponsor's fee) in conjunction with Pepsi UK who, as part of the new deal, would be in charge. Although they would miss the 1 July launch in Poti, they promised to be in England on 10 July and have the cashflow established, the first Pepsi instalment being payable on signing the contract. I took the night flight out of New York, picked up fresh clothes, my camera, some paperwork and the onward ticket from Jim at Heathrow, and was on my way without delay to Moscow.

The foreign delegation was due to meet in Moscow that afternoon – 29 June. I arrived at the Hotel Sport late that evening. This was a hotel catering for visiting athletes and served no alcohol so the journalists I knew and expected to find had understandably gone further afield. A good thing since I was completely exhausted.

Early the next morning our party of twelve departed by domestic Aeroflot for Sukhumi. Invitations had gone out to the press at the last minute and there were no free rides, so the response was not inspiring. Nevertheless, Tim Jeffery, correspondent for the *Daily Telegraph*, looked set to scoop this one for the London dailies. An ITN film crew, on loan from the Moscow bureau, was accompanied by Gareth Evans who would be presenting the TVS Whitbread programmes as part of the British TV pool. A Frenchman, a few Danes and a few Moscow correspondents filled the gaps. Kurt Larson, senior surveyor from the American Bureau of Shipping, came along to make the last inspection of the welding, accompanied by his wife, and lastly, Gerd Budzek, a young West German who had his own sports' marketing company, had been hired by ASM to help us out. He was a fluent Russian speaker, had been to university in Moscow and had been dealing with the people there for years. Today he was our *de facto* tour director. A very bright and understanding individual, he grasped our difficulties and would prove to be invaluable later on.

As before, our arrival in Georgia was fêted with a splendid meal in a local restaurant in Poti. The foreign delegation spent the night in an Intourist Hotel in Kobuleti about 25 kilometres down the coast, while the Soviet journalists stayed in town at a 'Soviet Hotel'. I was billeted with the crew and the mosquitoes at the Poti Three Star.

Phil Wardrop from England and Bruce Deeter from America had been there for a week already. Bruce worked for Barient Sparcraft in California and was advising on the winch installation on the deck (a consignment of deck gear and miscellaneous parts had arrived during the middle of June from Sparcraft UK). Having done his job, he was flying out that same day.

Phil, or 'the Nudger' as he's better known in the business, was representing his own company Diverse Yacht Services, in Cowes. He was supposed to be wiring up and installing the electronics which were all there, but he had come out too early and was not pleased.

A brawny Tasmanian, Phil had followed the boating scene to the UK almost 20 years ago and was one of the more popular figures for his outgoing manner and, like most Australians, his keen sense of repartee.

'Aw mate, I've been sitting on my ass doing fuck-all for the last week. I thought these guys said the boat was ready to wire. Shit eh, they're still welding the friggin' cockpits in! And that Poti Three Star, what a fuckin' beauty she is, I almost chundered when I went into the dumper the first time.'

Phil was still a travelling man and in spite of an overloaded schedule back in the UK he was interested enough to stay for the launch and the shipping out.

'I'll tell you something else you should be aware of,' he said as he pulled me aside. 'There's something funny going on with the crew. Seems like Anatoly's boys from Odessa are still loyal to Anatoly and don't want to have anything

41

to do with Alexei's mob from Kiev. There's a helluva lot of arguing going on all the time.'

Fazisi was being pulled out of the shed that evening and would be loaded on to a floating crane to make a short journey from the commercial port round to the new harbour for the next day's ceremony. She had a coat of flat grey paint over her roughly faired hull and *Fazisi*, written in Georgian script, painted in blue on her topsides.

Before she was cradled on the barge, the crew gathered, apparently impromptu. From amongst them, still wearing their begreased overalls, a lovely Georgian girl materialized with a bottle of Georgian champagne and when the conspiratorial crane driver momentarily dipped the hull in the harbour, she broke the bottle on the bow and christened *Fazisi*. It was a private workers' ceremony, which the Nudger and I were lucky enough to witness.

When Vladislav arrived 20 minutes later he was visibly upset and had some words with Alexei. Either he hadn't known about the ceremony or they hadn't waited for him. The psychologist Nadia was hovering around like a black cloud, pulling people off to the side to try and defuse the situation, but only succeeding in depressing her patients further. With *Fazisi* safely strapped down, the crew returned to the barracks to shower and have dinner.

The 1st of July was the big day in Poti. The Nudger and I had a Turkish coffee or two in the café next to the town square before the noon press conference which was the first event of the day. A Whitbread monument had been erected in the square months before, in honour of Poti's participation, and we took photographs of each other standing in front of it.

Only 10,000 people live in Poti, but it's always been an important sea port and a terminus for trade between the East and West. Today, ships from all over the world take on and discharge cargoes, not only for the USSR, but also for Asia Minor – a recognized trade route since the time of Jason.

The Argonaut Legend is visible everywhere in town, in statues and monuments and in the names of buildings, cafés, restaurants and hotels, celebrating not only Jason and his crew, but also the native Colchians who were guardians of the Fleece. Georgia has a rich history and a culture and language that have survived almost untouched by external influences. As Christians, they have always looked west – not to the Muslim east. They are crafty businessmen, and a large part of the contraband trade comes into the Soviet Union via Georgia. The people there are materially better off, and know it. Georgia grows the only tea and most of the fresh fruit produced in the Soviet Union. Their well known manipulation of corrupt Soviet officials has always given them inflated prices for their goods and in the USSR they are considered rich.

The press conference was well organized, with short speeches by Mr Tichov, Vladislav, the president of the Poti Shipyard, the Communist Party Chief, the Mayor, Alexei and myself. They had the good sense to serve Heineken beer in addition to the obligatory Pepsi, and not the local Soviet beer which is foul and sour. When Vladislav announced that I would be sailing the Whitbread with them as 'Assistant Skipper', I was taken aback. A week ago I had agreed to do the first leg of the race with them if we made it that far – and I was supposed to be called a 'co-skipper'. Terminology aside, I didn't care what they told the Soviet press, but now I would have to deny this new development to the foreign journalists without sounding counter-productive.

Another grand lunch followed, while the floating crane and barge cradling *Fazisi* was moved around to the attractive jetty that served as a public esplanade. The official ceremony was scheduled for eight o'clock.

A large part of the population turned out that evening. There were long speeches by the same people as at the press conference, which might have bored people without a vested interest in this project, but the item on display, suspended by the big floating crane, was so curious that the podium held everyone's attention. Then Nana Alexandria, the Georgian chess master, assisted by Alexei, did the honours over the bows for the second time in two days and *Fazisi* floated free, for the first time ever. A great roar went up from the crowd. Music and Georgian dancing followed for an hour. The day was a great success. Tichov looked satisfied, Vladislav wore a big smile and so did Alexei, but I could see he was already preoccupied with the crucial days to come.

I drank far too much that evening and it is not completely clear how I wound up in the Soviet Hotel with an attractive journalist from Moscow. I do know I am a sucker for foreign accents – and she had a strange one. At six the following morning I was cowering under the undersized sheet from the mosquitoes that were having another feed, when I was roused by a vicious shout. I focused what must have been two narrow slits on to the face of a Soviet policeman who was, I realize with hindsight, screaming at me in Russian to get up and stand at attention. As I didn't move quickly enough for him, I was dealt instant justice with a karate chop just below my ribcage which doubled me over, and I was soon retching on to his highly polished jackboots. Luckily his partner in this atrocity, a waist-high black Alsatian, licked my face in a not unfriendly manner. By then, the woman in the other single bed was screaming hysterically, trying to explain that I was an American and a personal friend of Mr Tichov, who was incidentally the deputy mayor.

Soon more policemen arrived as I struggled to get dressed. All the time they kept asking for my papers, of which I had none. The *babushkas* who guard each floor like stormtroopers were now gathered in the hallway, nodding their approval of the treatment I was receiving, the stool pigeon from our floor somewhere among them. Of course, I was illegally in the Soviet Hotel, but there was an added mix-up. A theft had been reported from another room that night, and I was the likely suspect. A senior officer arrived, dismissed the others and then turned his back on me which was the signal to beat it. Back at the Poti Three Star, my story of Soviet brutality was met only with ribald laughter.

That day was a write-off for everyone, and work didn't resume until the following day. *Fazisi* was brought back into the shed for four more days of welding before 7 July when she had to be on her way down the coast on the barge to Sukhumi to be loaded onto the aircraft.

The Nudger and I did a deal with the manager of the Poti Yacht Club about our accommodation. Jumberi Tsomaya, a tall, good-looking Georgian with a big, scarred nose, said we could stay at the Club on the waterfront. Our excuse was that the Poti Three Star was oppressive, as the windows and doors had to be kept closed to keep the mosquitoes down. At the Club there was more breeze, but more mosquitoes as well, and there was no shower. The good thing was it was close to the good open-air restaurant on the explanade where we could spend time late in the evenings and, we hoped, have a cold beer. But the bad news was that their refrigerator was broken; the beer and the champagne, that Jumberi, or 'Juki' as he goes by, insisted on ordering seemingly by the case, was served warm.

Juki was a man-about-town in Poti. A sports teacher, he specialized in sailing and ran the affairs of the Poti Yacht Club. This was not an all-consuming task, mind you, since the Club only owned about four Laser dinghies, one Hobie catamaran, a 45-foot cruiser which was the flagship, and a small fleet of Optimist dinghies for the kids. They did have a very good clubhouse, though, finished only a few years ago, built by the government as part of the Port of Poti Project. In his office, Juki had a collection of memorabilia on display, including a poster from Dennis Conner and the sawn-off butt of an oar from Tim Severin's re-enactment of the Jason voyage in a replica galley. They had rowed from Greece to Poti and Juki had taken part as one of the oarsmen on the last section up the Reoni (ex-Phasis) River.

I was curious, but not surprised, to hear that Juki would be on the *Fazisi* crew, in spite of his never having done a day's work on the boat in the seven months it had been under construction. There was an undercurrent of grumbling and resentment about this from some of the other crew. Nodari Teneishvili, another Georgian from up-country and a navigating officer from the merchant fleet, was also involved but he had been on the shop floor. Juki was included because the crew needed more Georgian sailors, and to inspect the racing fleet at the Poti Yacht Club is to understand the lack of talent.

Four days were all that was allowed to finish the fitting and welding, a task that should have taken ten. I spent all the time explaining things that were needed that they, with their lack of experience of big boats, hadn't thought of – a

45

few padeyes here, another backing plate there, guards for the steering wheels, bigger cockpit drains, inspection windows in the hull for the propeller and rudder, hatch surrounds. Many things had to be redone, a few things eliminated. I knew that to get the welding and metalwork finished here was essential. The guys were driving hard and were cheap, both of which would be different once we reached the UK, the land of the tea break.

The Paton Institute of Welding in Kiev had specified the welding schedule, including the type of parent metal (supposedly a superior strength alloy not available in the West), the filler material, the method of welding with regard to speed, amperage, number of passes and sequence to avoid distortion. They even supplied the welder, an untiring blond Ukrainian named Viktor Uschenko who flashed away for 10 to 12 hours a day as we came up with the jobs.

The work was going as well as expected, but I reflected on what seven months of this routine must have been like. It was apparent that the crew had done almost all the work, the Poti Shipyard only providing the shed and the use of machine tools and craft shops. Safety standards were appalling; dodgy and broken electrical cables lay in puddles of water, there were no guards on any of the tools, the shop floor was pot-holed and there were no guard-rails around gantries and catwalks. Women were spray-painting with epoxy, their heads wrapped in old rags, and not wearing breathing masks. Most of the factory workers' hands had deep scars from broken equipment and unsafe working practices. I gave not a few thoughts to the *Fazisi* press release about the 'most sophisticated aluminium boat construction in the world'; after all, this was the land of propaganda.

In my travels about the deck, with the crew swarming around like worker ants, I suggested to Eugene that Edgar, the crew member fitting the steering wheel bearings, should use a hole saw to cut the 4-inch diameter opening in the cockpit wall, instead of chain-drilling and filing, an operation that would take him all day instead of ten minutes with the right tool.

'You see this!' he yelled at me, on his hands and knees,

waving a big round half-file in my direction, 'Adjustable system. Different size files. Everything in this fucking country is like this!'

It was true. They had built this boat with hardly any tools except a circular saw, an electric drill, hammers and a bunch of files. There were no shaping tools, no hole saws, no special grinders which would have saved them months of work. I had not noticed this on my first trip in early June, and anyway it was too late by then to have done something about it, but a couple of grand spent on tools at the outset would have made an incredible difference. But Edgar had done a perfect job with the file, and he was cheap.

In addition to the yacht, two containers were being airlifted to England, with the gear from Sparcraft that had arrived only two weeks ago, some of their own equipment, and about a tonne of food for the crew including 200 kilos of Georgian sausage, boxes of cosmonaut food and undisclosed numbers of cases of vodka and Armenian brandy. Anatoly was in charge of loading and writing up the manifest. I came close to getting a priceless photograph of the Russian customs man sitting at his desk in front of Container Number 1 while goods were being loaded – and then hidden – while he slept, his head in his hands. Just as I pressed the shutter a big fist covered the lens – his assistant, obviously corruptible!

Alexei spent the last two days organizing the final touches for the complicated shipping manoeuvre, darting around with clipboard in hand. I knew what he was going through as the man in charge, and it was clear it was not a lot of fun. We were due to spend a night in Kiev on the way to London when he would get a last chance to see his new baby daughter, born in early June, and I'm sure that was also on his mind.

At 4 p.m. on 7 July Alexei turned off the welding set for the last time – in the middle of fitting the support for the mainsheet traveller which was the last welding job on board. We had done well. The last trip out of the shed was well rehearsed and the loading onto the barge went like clockwork. The next day the barge would be moored to a naked beachhead near the airport at Sukhumi ready for the yacht to be loaded on to the truck. The Nudger and I would be off for Moscow with hangovers, he to fly on directly to the UK, I to get my visa so I could then take a night train to Kiev to join the cargo plane before it left for London!

The shipyard threw a farewell party in the yard's canteen that evening. Nodari, their worker hero, was the *Tamada* for the evening. In Georgia the *Tamada* is usually the family elder, the toastmaster and the man with the biggest capacity for drink. Nodari came armed with a 5-gallon jerry can of his family's homemade wine, warm and cloudy. We were all obliged to drink a tumbler-full, non-stop, before giving our toasts. 'Tradition,' said the *Tamada*, with a big smile.

The Shipyard President said his piece, Alexei Gryshenko said his and so on down to the Nudger and me – all the usual toasts; 'The Fatherland, our town, this fine ship, our mothers . . .'

I was getting bored making all these familiar toasts, but I didn't stick my neck out this time. Then, Nodari's wife of three weeks, Elisso, the girl who had christened the boat at the workers' private ceremony, got up and made fools of all of us. She said:

'A Georgian writer said that a man's soul is 100 times heavier than his body. Since the souls of the wives of these crewmembers will be on board *Fazisi*, the boat will run no risk of capsize, as the wives' souls will provide sufficient ballast.'

June 1989 – the *Fazisi* project is unveiled (*above*) in the Black Sea town of Poti by Victor Tichov of Fazis Moscow, Poti's mayor and communist party secretary and the chief of the Poti Shipyard.

Right. Fazisi's primed but unfinished hull and deck emerges from the shed at Poti Shipyard.

Below right. Due to the immense pressure of time, *Fazisi* was flown from the Soviet Union to London's Heathrow airport in a giant Antonov 124 Ruslan, the world's largest commercial aeroplane.

Overleaf. Keeping the halyards and control lines organized on deck was a constant task.

Above. Anxious moments for Fazis chairman Victor Tichov (left) and crewman Juri Doroshenko (right) when a new keel has to be fitted to bring down *Fazisi's* rating.

The scramble at Hamble – five weeks from the Whitbread start major items such as the generator were being installed (credit: Rick Tomlinson).

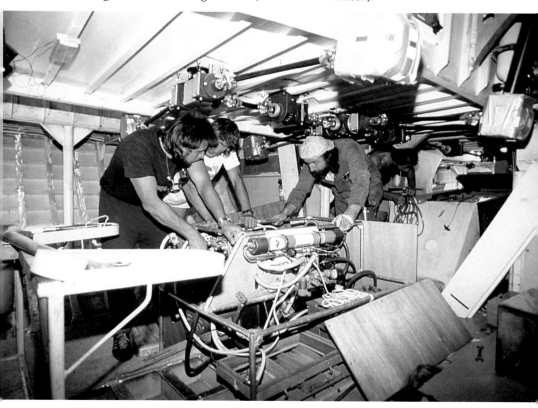

Reaching down the Atlantic on Leg I from Southampton to Uruguay. The crew are clad in Pepsi Cola's colours, even though the US drinks corporation dropped their sponsorship the day after the start.

Long distance ocean sailing calls for much mor[e] than just sailing skills. The Georgian Jumberi 'Juki' Tsomaya treats helmsman Edgar Terechi[n] to the onboard barber shop.

American Brian 'Mugsy' Hancock as the Queen (right) and navigator Guennadi 'Crocodile' Korolkov as King Neptune hold court at the Crossing the Line ceremony on the equator.

Nodari Teneishvili, a Georgian merchant navy officer and Tall Ships sailor, collects rain water in the foot of the mainsail during a Doldrums downpour.

Animated and amiable, Juki prepares a flying-fish supper as *Fazisi* slips through the south-ea[st] tradewinds.

The Duchess of York came aboard during the Leg I stop in Punta del Este, Uruguay. Here, I'm introducing myself, flanked by Nodari Teneishvili, Eugene Platon, Victor Yasykov, Valeri Chumakov and Dale Tremain.

Fazisi's main boom snapped in the Southern Ocean on Leg II, close by Kerguelen Island. We managed to keep the mainsail driving by using the spinnaker pole as an outrigger.

Left. Juri Doroshenko, a Ukranian merchant seaman from Sevastopol, reads an old Soviet newspaper.

Below. With one reef in the mainsail and storm spinnaker set, *Fazisi* could blast along at 23 knots. The bow wave shot passed with the force of a fire hydrant.

The South Atlantic in an unusually benign mood. Here English shore boss Jim Saunders (left) and New Zealander Dale Tremain, who signed up for Leg II, seek out the faintest zephyr with cigarettes.

Right. Fazisi was dubbed the Soviet Submarine. This was our first Southern Ocean storm, water boiling across the deck as we surf downwind in heavy conditions. Survival suits for the on-deck watch were essential.

Edgar Terechin, a 470 and Tornado class sailor from the Baltic town of Riga, was one of the best Soviet helmsmen. *Fazisi*'s rigger also, he's inspecting a new check stay.

Below. Jim Saunders, our shore manager, was a true jack o' all trades. He sailed on Leg II to bolster our big boat experience.

Sailmaker Valeri Safiullin from Alma Ata stitching the mainsail. A Ukrainian seaman, he's spent much time in the Pacific out of Vladisvostok.

With a low freeboard and the steering wheels located near the middle of the boat, the hiss and hum of the bow wave was a constant companion.

With the mainsail well reefed down, the amount of spray flying around as *Fazisi* thunders along on a reach was tremendous.

Having found Cape Horn on Leg IV in a gentle mood, we were greeted by a 50 knot blast a day later as we steered north to Uruguay once more.

In one particularly fierce 50 knot squall near Kerguelen Island, we dropped the chute and ran bareheaded just to keep *Fazisi* under control and on her feet.

Above. Hurtling downwind, the bow would often bury, scooping up tons of water which filled cockpits and knocked your feet from under you until *Fazisi* would rise once more and shake herself dry.

Below. Moments after the 50 knot blast, the boom snapped just by the vang attachment, a problem that struck six of the yachts during the race.

Above. Anatoly Verba, a research assistant from Odessa on the Black Sea, was one of our helmsmen and watch leaders.

5

Strangers in a Strange Land

Just as it was necessary to fly the unfinished hull of *Fazisi* into England, so it was equally important that the arrival should be a media event. Before my last departure for the Soviet Union I had been assured by the Markham Group, the public relations firm that had the Whitbread Race account, that they would organize a press reception for the celebration arrival, and it was obviously in Whitbread's best interest for them to do so. But little did I know, while incommunicado in Georgia, that on the Friday afternoon before our intended Monday morning arrival, the Markham PR girl, who will remain anonymous, decided it was, in her limited experience, impossible to get the press past the Heathrow airport security – so she took it upon herself to cancel all plans and went to the country for a horsey weekend.

Facing a disastrous situation, Jim Saunders, who knows nothing about PR except the obvious, contacted our friend Jock Wishart, a yachtsman and sponsorship executive for Hill and Knowlton in London, who does. To add to the tangled web of PR companies, Hill and Knowlton run the Pepsi UK account and were just coming to grips with the promotion that Pepsi International, via Tony McGrath, had dumped in their laps only days before. Luckily, Wishart, a Scotsman with a sense of enthusiasm that would make the most bubbly of his countrymen cringe, jumped into the fray and spent his weekend in a London hotel room with Winterfeldt, Wawer and Jane Redford, sorting out the press passes with the airport and pulling strings to make the other arrangements at that late hour.

After the Antonov had touched down and taxied to a halt, but before the seal on the big cargo door had been broken, Mike Winterfeldt was standing on the top of a metal ladder outside the passenger exit, handing in a box of Pepsi T-shirts, Pepsi hats and two big Pepsi banners that read 'The Choice for a New Generation'. When the big nose cone was raised into the open position only minutes later, the two banners had been tied alongside the hull and the crew had changed shirts and donned hats – Team Pepsi had arrived in the UK! In the publicity stakes that would make or break us, we had just scraped through, a pattern that would follow for the next ten months, all the way around the world.

We had made a good first impression, but few people knew that the Soviets had arrived in Britain without so much as a quid between them. We still had no cash flow, in spite of ASM's effort to get the first payment out of Pepsi. The operation certainly gave the impression of a big money approach – a maxi boat shipped by aircraft, Marine Movers Ltd standing by with a flatbed truck and 50-tonne crane ready to load the boat and hurtle down the M3 motorway without delay, the team looking smart – and Pepsi obviously paying for it all.

Before the crew was bussed down to Southampton, we gave them a small reception that evening at the Sheraton Hotel near the airport, a token gesture of sandwiches and beer only. When the time came to pay the bill, which was not small change, the management team looked at one another and dug into their own pockets – another pattern that would be followed.

Fazisi arrived in Southampton on Wednesday 12 July. The road into Hamble Yacht Services is a winding country lane, impossible for a wide load, so the boat was unloaded at Moody's Marina, farther up the Hamble River, but easier of access. By 4 o'clock *Fazisi* was being towed downstream to HYS, through the thousands of moored pleasure craft, some with their crews on board getting ready for a lovely, warm summer evening's sail. *Fazisi* had been featured the night before on TVS and BBC South, while delayed on the motorway somewhere outside Winchester, so the incredulous onlookers might have known who we were, with no keel on and floating ridiculously high out of the water, even if they may not have known just what we were.

Hamble Yacht Services was the focal point for the Whitbread fleet for the summer. They provided not only convenient haulage, with their 40-tonne mobile lift and all the usual boatyard services, but they also had space for our shipping containers and temporary offices. The British favourites *Rothmans*, and *Maiden*'s all-girl crew, used HYS as their home base from the beginning of the season, while the visiting yachts like *The Card, NCB Ireland, Gatorade, Martela, Union Bank of Finland, La Poste* and others were moored in HYS's marina next to the haul-out facility. *Rothmans* was out of the water, on 'the hard', as much as she was in the water, dry sailed like a dinghy; she boasted an enclosed compound around her cradle bounded by a double-storey office block and three 40-foot containers. Granted, they didn't have a chain-link fence and guard dogs, but the effect was just as imposing and certainly managed to keep people away.

Fazisi's second critical arrival was well timed. Dead abeam of the haul-out gantry stood the *Steinlager 2* beer tent, the watering hole for the Whitbread crews erected by the New Zealand sponsor and run by publican Tim Rendall of the King and Queen in the village. It was overflowing with Whitbread crews and camp followers after a usual 9-to-5 working day in their well-run campaigns.

Managing Director of HYS, Dick Saint, and Ed Danby, a 'can-do' Whitbread yachtsman, hired by HYS to manage this demanding fleet, were directing the lifting operation in front of a crowd of interested spectators, some smug and cocky, others politely impressed, all on their third or fourth pint. Some of the comments are worth repeating.

'Aw mate, who designed that bloody numba? Looks like a bloody submarine,' asked a strapping Kiwi from *Steinlager*, his brand cradled in the crook of his elbow. 'You gonna sail on her? Better you than me!'

'You think she'll rate 70?' commented, not inquired, a *Rothmans* man (the maximum handicap value allowed).

'God knows,' I answered.

'Well, I don't know what that guy was smoking when he designed that thing – but I want some!'

The start was only little over six weeks away when we arrived on the Hamble. All the other entries had been sailing for at least four months, some for a year. All were now fine-tuning and making last-minute preparations. But we had a boat to build. And the black cloud that hung over us was whether we would be able to pay for it – and not only the fitting out; there was also the race itself to consider. The stopovers in Uruguay, Fremantle, Auckland and Fort Lauderdale, where we would spend three to four weeks with almost 20 people who needed to be housed and fed, let alone the repairs that might be needed, should have been budgeted for and fixed six months ago. But to organize any of these things, deposits needed to be paid. Since we had nothing, we were effectively hamstrung from organizing anything.

Even before the boat arrived we were heavily in debt to benevolent creditors. HYS had agreed to purchase anything we required, in addition to yard materials, albeit for an added 10%. They even paid for the crew's accommodation in a dormitory at Southampton University. The King and Queen did us a cheap deal for lunch in the beer tent, payable 'when we got the Pepsi money'. I put the three rental cars we needed on my Visa card, Jim did likewise for parts and other pieces we needed. Sparcraft and Nudger's Diverse Yacht Services also took their chances in this crazy game of Russian roulette and supplied required parts and service over and above the original contract price, knowing full well they might never get paid – just because they knew they had to. The boat had to make the start (then everything, we hoped, would be OK).

We were all playing a high-risk game that, under normal circumstances in the marine industry, you wouldn't touch with a barge pole – but the *Fazisi* Project was fundamentally different, and although maybe we didn't know exactly why, or even didn't say as much, we all kept it rolling in those first weeks, knowing it had to roll, hoping we wouldn't go broke in an aborted attempt, hoping that the Pepsi deal would come right. I for one did not want to be responsible for the project failing due to any lack of effort, or because I got cold feet about a few thousand pounds. Money made in the sailing business is usually easy-come-easy-go, and is far less important to me than the time already spent by the Soviet crew, who were about to face another two solid weeks of back-breaking labour, fairing the hull with epoxy fillers around the clock – for no material gain, just to be at the start of the Whitbread Race.

Our schedule was so impossible that it became ridiculously simple: build a boat in three weeks. We had set the Pepsi launch date for 2 August, and it was now 13 July. We had a virtually bare aluminium hull with only the main engine and a few plumbing fittings installed below. The main task was to fill and fair the hull, usually done with the hull upside down so all the heavy sanding can be done 'down hand.' Although suggested by several experts, this was impossible because all the other work – fitting deck hardware, running the electrics, finishing the plumbing, installing all the other machinery like watermaker, generator and bilge pumps, and installing the steering system – had to be done simultaneously.

Through HYS we had reserved a subcontracted team of fairing experts and painters. They didn't inspire the greatest of confidence. I let them slide for three days, but they worked in an unorganized fashion, with as much professionalism as a moonlighting 'home builder' on the dole, and borrowing our tools to boot, and it was obvious they would never finish the job within two months. In what some saw as a foolhardy measure, which didn't win any popularity points with Dick Saint and Ed Danby, I dressed down the team's boss in my well-known diplomatic fashion and fired them on the spot. Officially the boatyard should have done this, but there was little time for protocol. My reasoning was simple; with those guys, we couldn't make the deadline; if we couldn't find someone else, we were no worse off.

Once again, an apparent miracle happened. Ian Armstrong and Donny Donnarumma, a freelance, 'do anything', fairing and painting team, had luckily just become available. They didn't muck around. They worked out a schedule down to the final hours before the launch, almost two and a half weeks away; they were fully equipped and supplied everything from their own trailer down to the ghetto blaster and the music that kept their team of 12 workers and *Fazisi*'s team of 12 crew enthused while they worked 12-hour shifts around the clock.

They were not a pretty sight in the morning after a night breathing epoxy dust while lying on their backs, six or eight men sliding a 15-foot PVC tube covered in sandpaper back and forth underneath the hull. Although they got paid well for this, to Ian, Donny and their team we owe our gratitude for an effort far beyond the call of any normal work ethic.

With that storm under control, the Central Committee in the Portakabin office could concentrate on everything else. Jane Redford's sister, Monica Tingay, had been hired to man the office phone and fax machine and keep our burgeoning filing system under control. Hamish was the project's roving purchaser of all the bits and pieces that could not be supplied immediately by the boatyard – odd plumbing and electrical fittings, nuts and bolts, tools, raw materials and heaters for the fairing job – the thousand and one items that make up the whole of a finished racing yacht. Jim was all-round foreman, watch-keeper, and trouble shooter assigned to special projects, like installing the hydraulic system. Vladislav was technical director, looking after the installation of the keel and rudder, and concerning himself with the looming IOR measurement – making sure that we would fit in the handicap system that some said, when the keel arrived from Germany and looked like it belonged to a 50-footer and not a maxi, would be virtually impossible. Since Vladislav was the kingpin of the project – the man who started all of this – he also spent an inordinate amount of time composing long faxes to Moscow trying to explain why we hadn't any Pepsi money yet and why we might need more from Fazis. Alexei was the Soviet crew foreman, consulting with Vladislav in the office over drawings and specifications and then making his forays into the yard to check the work in progress.

My job was overall coordinator, a kind of tool pusher of the schedule, not doing much at hand, but looking for the next fire to put out and then sending in the men. I also had to keep the priorities clear. When the Soviets started to dream about on-board computers and other luxuries that we had neither the money nor the time to contemplate, I would give them another fundamental job, like drilling the keel bolt holes through the hull, to keep their minds off the impossible.

I would also spend many hours – what seemed like all day at times – on the telephone: to ASM in Germany about money and Pepsi, to Hill and Knowlton about plans for the launch and the proposed trip up the Thames into London later in August, to Barient Sparcraft about the mast scheduled to arrive the day before the launch, to North Sails in Germany about the same, and to not a few journalists who had to be entertained, because a big part of my responsibility was to be spokesman for the project – the guy who could tell the story, and getting the story out on the street is what sponsorship is all about. Wearing an overcoat of overall control, I was also wearing far too many hats and this rankled with a few, who were used to managerial positions. Anatoly grumbled about almost everything Vladislav and Alexei decided, and Eugene Platon, the Moldavian, who normally works in applied mathematics at the Institute for Cybernetics in Kiev, obviously resented the hierarchy. Not enamoured with the situation, and fast getting a reputation as one who spoke his mind, expletives included, Eugene was overheard to say, 'Here we are on our backs sanding this fucking boat and Skip's sitting in the office making fucking publicity!'

It was difficult establishing a working routine because every day was different, but we started each morning with a crew meeting in the office at 8 o'clock. Jim, more often than not, had been helping the night shift and came prepared with another list of materials and tools for that evening's work. This went to Hamish so that he could begin his master purchasing list of the morning. All the crew's requests for equipment and materials had to be in to him by 10 o'clock. He would then spend an hour on the phone with the Yellow Pages, and then disappear for most of the morning and afternoon hunting the items down, in an area stretching from Portsmouth to Bournemouth and sometimes beyond. Vladislav, Alexei and I would brief the crew on the work scheduled for the day – who would be sanding and who would be lucky enough to do something else – and then off they'd go with Jim to start them out – but not before Monica had dealt with their domestic affairs. From the moment they arrived, they had had no time to settle in to a new culture.

Dealing with the basics we all take for granted like who could drive and who couldn't (only two had licenses), where they could eat, how to post a letter, or have a beer, all had to be explained to them in a hurry. Because of the language barrier, it was done with loud clipped voices and wild gesticulation. The pantomime and sense of urgency in explaining how they could get their laundry done must have put the fear of God into not a few of them.

Monica is a petite blonde standing about 5ft 2in, but she handled them with the dexterity and discipline of a circus lion-tamer. She had all their pictures, with their names, stuck to the wall above her desk so she could put the names to the faces during those first few days. Quickly earning their respect, Monica became the matriarchal figurehead for *Fazisi*. She would rave to anyone who would listen about 'what gentlemen her Soviets all were', and very soon after, they wouldn't even consider leaving the boatyard to post their mail without asking her permission.

To appreciate the situation it must be realized that not only had the Soviets never been in the West (barring a few who were merchant seamen who had been handled ashore by a Kommissar), most spoke hardly any English. They missed a lot in Vladislav's translations about what was happening next and this was particularly true of their leader Alexei, who was supposed to be in charge. He spoke not a word of English and as a consequence the work in progress and the planning mainly went on without him – simply because there was not enough time to explain things over and over. Both he and Vladislav must have felt the reins of the Fazisi Project were slipping from their grasp. In effect, the management had been taken over by the West – the technical side by Jim and me, the as yet non-existent cashflow side by ASM, the promotion by Hill and Knowlton. For the most part, their opinions were considered, but decisions were often made without them or their input was simply ignored for expediency.

This was never more true than on the financial side. Vladislav had had the notion, back in Georgia, that, to keep the costs down, the crew would complete the boat on the Hamble and we would need only 'a few specialists'. But it was apparent to me we would need an army of specialists – fairers and painters, riggers, mast-makers, sailmakers, electricians – plus the labour of the crew, if we had any hope of making the start. I had budgeted for £220,000 for materials, parts, labour and sundry crew living expenses from the time the boat hit Heathrow until the starting gun fired on 2 September.

Vladislav couldn't see how all that money could be spent. I'm not sure that he ever relayed my budget back to Fazis in Moscow, subconsciously lowballing the figure, while he hoped for a miracle from Pepsi. But he began to see the light when Dick Saint submitted the first boatyard bill, after Day Ten, of £40,000.

Dick cornered me, two mornings later, outside the office after we hadn't acknowledged not only their bill, but all previous accounts. 'Listen, Skip, what's the situation with the Russians? I've already let you guys slide a long way, but I'm soon going to be facing a crisis of my own here. We've got Jim and Hamish in the yard store every ten minutes ordering thousands of pounds worth of gear – and that's fine, but how are you guys going to settle up?'

'Look, Dick, the Pepsi money is due to arrive this week, and when it does you'll be the first to know. I'm in the same situation here; they owe me a packet of money as well. I know it's not looking too healthy, but it will come right.' I believed what I told him, but I didn't let on that the first Pepsi installment of $100,000 less ASM's 25% commission, less miscellaneous expenses already incurred by ASM, wouldn't even cover the outstanding account today, let alone future costs which were increasing exponentially by the hour.

ASM, although not on site, were in touch with us daily from Hamburg, assuring us that the Pepsi money and their logo, now the icon of our salvation, were immediately forthcoming. The Pepsi business aside, there were obvious problems between ASM and Fazis. They had an exclusive contract to find all the necessary sponsorship and run the public relations for the project. So it seemed strange to everyone that they thought they could do it from Germany. To my way of thinking, we needed two PR people in our office, handling the press, making proposals, dealing with the celebration

57

launching, not least of all representing the company Fazis in the western marketplace which was what the whole promotion was supposed to be about. Gerd Budzek had spent a few days with us on behalf of ASM, but he explained he had his own business to run. He would help us later when needed, but could not be full-time. They eventually put their London associate, David Tilley, at our disposal, but London wasn't where it was happening, which was on the Hamble. It was left to Vladislav, Monica and me to promote the project amateurishly from our office, but ASM hadn't delivered the promised *Fazisi* stationery so we could not even write a decent letter! ASM blamed the Soviets for not delivering the boat 'on time', which under the agreement between them stated that Fazis would supply a 'finished yacht' to the starting line. Finding the campaign funds was the responsibility of ASM, the plan being that when the funds found outstripped the requirement of the campaign, this surplus would revert back to Fazis to reimburse their initial investment in building and equipping the yacht – in the order of $1.5 million. That was the ASM version of the story. The Soviets had another, stating that ASM had 'guaranteed' start-up money and had 'assured' them that $5 million would be raised. When I asked to see a copy of that contract to form my own opinion, I was told it was in Moscow, and only existed in German.

After a long heart-to-heart with Vladislav he was finally persuaded that more money had to come out of the Soviet Union by whatever means possible. He sent what must have been a very difficult fax to Fazis, and several days later, a miraculous reply was received that assured us that Valeri Chumakov, due to arrive on 25 July, would bring a cheque for $80,000 that could be drawn on any Midland Bank! This would not pay all our accounts, but it was a positive sign. It meant that the Politburo in Moscow knew the reality of the situation. My only reservation was, after all the financial obstacle courses we had to overcome with the original contracts, how was it possible a simple cheque could be produced for hard currency? It was, as Churchill had once characterized the Soviet Union, 'A riddle, wrapped in a mystery, inside an enigma'.

Out in the yard, other problems were brewing. Because *Fazisi* was built of very thin aluminium plate, in places only 2.5mm thick (the minimum allowed under the American Bureau of Shipping Regulations), the weld distortion due to heat absorption made the job of fairing the hull with filler to get a true hull shape more difficult than expected. In some of the hollows, the filler had to be applied an inch deep. Ian Armstrong pointed out that if we were to go all the way and make it 'right' we would be adding about 800 kg of putty – an additional weight that Vladislav had not calculated for, which was not inconsequential when the total displacement was supposed to be about 22 tonnes.

Not only the weight, which determines how the boat will float, but a raft of other complex measurements of every dimension of the hull would determine the 'rating' or handicap of the yacht. To put things in perspective, an 80-footer was measured down to the last millimetre – a few millimetres out here and there, and a threshold in one parameter could be reached that would tip the balance of the 'rating' in the wrong direction (up) which would mean sacrificing strength in another variable, like sail area or stability (the amount and position of the ballast in lead which keeps a sailboat upright). In our case what it boiled down to was, since the boat was built to measure in aluminium, we had to be careful about changing the principal dimensions when adding so much filler for the sake of a 'fair' hull. The alternative was to go through major structural surgery, now out of the question. Vladislav spent a lot of time checking and rechecking dimensions with Ian, who was reshaping the hull each day as his men laid on the filler, and then, 12 hours later, scraped some off again, all the time trying to stick to Vladislav's data.

Although he didn't show any undue concern, he was aware of the added weight not only of the filler, but also of all the other equipment that was being added to the boat – deck gear, plumbing, electrics and fittings – most of which he had allowed for, but some of which he hadn't thought about in his original weight calculation. This was no discredit to him, as he hadn't the experience of building such a large boat before, and it must be said in his defence that this oversight is one of the most common mistakes made even by designers who do not live in the Soviet Union, and should know better. There was no turning back, however, and the work continued – all thoughts on making the 2 August fanfare launching date.

Vladislav and I went up to London on 28 July for a meeting at Pepsi UK's main office. All the principal players came together in one room with Pepsi UK Marketing Director John Postlethwaite – Winterfeldt, Wawer and David Tilley representing ASM, David Ketchum from Hill and Knowlton and Vladislav with Fazis. We all had the common goal of promoting *Fazisi* via the Pepsi sponsorship package, although it had been made with Pepsi International in New York, not with Pepsi UK, which was fundamentally a problem. If he never said it outright, the brash and at times arrogant John Postlethwaite let it be known that he considered this whole Whitbread Race nothing but a huge pain in his backside, a policy decision that had been dumped on him by Tony McGrath. ASM had made the contractual arrangements with Pepsi International about how the Pepsi promotion money (as opposed to the sum going to the boat) would be spent, but Postlethwaite, who was in charge of the UK promotion, had other ideas. ASM had plans for an all-round media and entertainment programme, which was what the Fazis people had been led to expect. Postlethwaite wanted almost all the money spent on securing television coverage for Pepsi during the launch, the trip up the Thames and the day of the start. This left nothing in the budget even for chartering a boat to take the delegation of Georgian and Russian politicians and dignitaries who were coming as guests of Fazis to watch the start. ASM tried to explain how all these other aspects could be good for Pepsi's image, but Postlethwaite was hard-nosed, and although a minor compromise was made, it was clear the Pepsi sponsorship would not go as we had originally planned. It was David Ketchum's and Jock Wishart's job to do Pepsi UK's bidding, as the public relations account holder, much to ASM's displeasure. It was clear even then, that it would be a public relations war for control of the project for which they would both claim credit if it was a success, but with the convenience of a scapegoat if it all went wrong. This proved to be true; they fought over every detail, from invitation lists, the catering and the printing of posters to what would be done with the Soviet delegation when they arrived.

What made me nervous was that we were guaranteeing to Pepsi that we would be on the starting line when we couldn't afford to get near it. We had proved already that we were a media attraction so we put more pressure on Pepsi and ASM to come up with the first payment. We didn't tell them that, three days before, Chumakov had arrived from Moscow with the Midland cheque.

Vladislav was distressed because Valeri had been given the job of financial controller. I knew we were in for another tough ride when I drove him to the Midland Bank in Southampton to open his account and, I hoped, clear the cheque so we could start paying some bills.

In his poor English, with the added and annoying habit he had of smacking his lips and 'hymphing' as each proclamation, he told me, 'Nyashet, Mawnica receive £600 every month, hymph, I, in Moscow receive 300 roubles only, hymph!' He was trying to come to grips with what he made in Moscow against the going rate for a secretary in the UK – a meaningless comparison – and he was sent over to do the accounting!

We got the cash, placating Dick Saint and a few others temporarily, but my fears about Chumakov's methods proved true. He had brought over a typewriter with Cyrillic script and spent most of his day one-finger typing long accounts and explanations to Fazis – when he was not pestering Monica and Jim about the odd £5 unendorsed chit in the petty cash that he couldn't account for. It was an example of the most liberal of free-market economic principles: we could pay £5 in cash to the guy who threw a quick eye splice that we needed into a bit of rope in his spare time, or pay him £10 by cheque for the privilege of having a receipt (or £20 to the boatyard, to make the point clear). If Chumakov understood this Western phenomenon, he still took his accounting seriously, because he probably rightly assumed the administration in Moscow wouldn't.

I don't think any of us got to know the Soviets at all during those first three weeks. There was no time for socializing barring the odd beer in the *Steinlager* tent or further afield at the King and Queen. The *Maiden* all-girl crew invited our crew to a get-together there one night – and bought the beers, which were backlogged four or five deep per man by pub closing time. I don't know what they discussed, but the rumour was that skipper Tracy Edwards's girls had a wager with a £50 kitty for the first one to sleep with a Russian – and this was paid out soon after. Without going into details, Gorbachev's *glasnost* policy made possible this historic East-meets-West love affair that lasted until Fremantle – a long-term relationship by Whitbread standards.

One Sunday, while waiting for layers of filler to dry, I took the crew to my friends Ted and Sheila Lonsdale for afternoon tea. They have a lovely seaside home on Hayling Island and have been kind enough to host my crews for the last 11 years. Croquet on the lawn, tea and cakes, and a moment to relax in a beautiful setting were certainly appreciated. One of them said that it was the most beautiful home he had ever seen and asked how it was possible that a solicitor could acquire this much wealth – making Ted and Sheila very happy indeed! Ted was just about to broach the drinks cabinet when Alexei broke the reverie and pointed out that it was 5 o'clock and they had to get back to resume sanding the hull . . .

Wednesday 2 August fell in the middle of Cowes Week, a rest day for the Admiral's Cup fleet, so we were assured of getting the press over to the Hamble. *Fazisi* had been moved out of the shed only days before the launch to give us time to instal the keel and rudder, do the final fairing and antifoul the bottom. The boat had been given the final coats of polyurethane paint the morning before – broad diagonal wedges of white and Pepsi red. It looked impressive. The New Zealand designer, Bruce Farr, who boasted four new maxis in the race including three of the four favourites, was known for unconventional approaches to design in his past, but has now gone a bit conservative mainstream. On a Hamble visit he took one look at the hull, another at the keel waiting to be fixed to the hull, and said, 'Well, if she rates [in the IOR] she'll be the fastest boat in the fleet.' A compliment, in a way, but also a warning.

On 1 August Dick Saint ordered the boatyard to be cleared of all debris, swept up and a space cleared for a marquee tent for the next day's celebration. Dick had his own public relations company in on the act and they were not going to miss this opportunity. With the keel on, Ian's and Donny's men worked straight through the night applying the last coat of bottom paint, while two men from McKeon and Company, who produce computer-generated vinyl transfers, fought in the wind and the darkness to apply the 3-metre-long Pepsi logos and the *Fazisi* name on the sides and another smaller version on the stern. When I turned up at the boatyard at 8 o'clock the next morning they were still working. They had three hours to go – the celebration was scheduled for 11 o'clock!

Hill and Knowlton did a great job in organizing the launch. We had Pepsi girls, Pepsi flags and banners visible everywhere, champagne and caviar for the insatiable press corps and Russian singers for a bit of authentic atmosphere. The crew, dressed of course in Pepsi shirts and hats, looked as proud as they could be in front of their yacht as the big travel-hoist slowly lowered the maxi into the flood tide of the Hamble River with 400 fans cheering them on. The paint was so fresh you could still smell the thinners.

Alexei and I broke a Pepsi bottle over the transom (finding an extant glass Pepsi bottle in our world of plastic was another last-minute drama), jumped onto the afterdeck and unfurled our joint venture colours – the Soviet flag for him, the American one for me, and then stood there, forcing smiles, for the next ten minutes for what must have been thousands of the same picture.

That same afternoon, the Barient Sparcraft team had delivered the mast from Lymington and they spent the next 36 hours putting the two halves of the 100-foot aluminium tube together, attaching the rigging and getting it ready for stepping, which we did on the high water of the Friday.

The Fastnet Race was starting on the Sunday and it was critical that we were out on the water as a media draw, in spite of the fact we would not be competing in the Race. Big yachts almost never go together as easily as did *Fazisi* and if we had amazed the dockside pessimists by launching on time, we successfully turned any other doubters into believers by motoring out into the Solent for our first sail, two days later. Unfortunately the boltrope of the big mainsail, the piece of material that slides up the groove in the mast, was too big and much to North Sails's Albert Schweitzer's embarrassment, we could not hoist sail and had to go back to the dock – but there was always tomorrow.

Vladimir Kulinichenko and Valeri Safiullin, our two sailmakers, assisted by the North Sails service loft, provisionally set up at HYS, worked all night to replace the boltrope and by 9 o'clock the next morning we headed for the Fastnet starting line – with the Soviet crew, the Sparcraft team, the North Sails team and about five other pros to lend a hand, and a crowd of journalists to tell this historic tale – a risk we all had to take.

Brian James, who was on board for *The Times*, wrote an encouraging article a few days later about the day's experience. To his credit, he was easy on us, appreciating that this project had more important implications than not a few mistakes made with some ropes and pulleys. However, he didn't neglect to point out the obvious inexperience of the Soviets when he wrote, 'Had other Whitbread boats put a spy on board they would have been in fits: far from going around the world it seeemed a toss-up whether *Fazisi* would ram the Needles or reverse up Southampton Water to run aground in the Tesco car park.'

After some posing around the Royal Yacht Squadron, where we were told the TV cameras would be, we left the starting area early, to beat our way up to the Needles Channel where there were more cameras, who had been given instructions to film us if possible, which was what Pepsi had paid their money for.

The maxi fleet, most of them soon to be our competitors in the Whitbread, passed us in short order, but I think everyone on board was more than impressed with *Fazisi* on her first sail. She was beautiful to handle in the fresh breeze. Thousands of spectators lined the shingle beach around Hurst Castle which marks the northern end of the Needles Channel, and as an encore we turned smartly around, awkwardly hoisted the light spinnaker for the first time – the one with the Pepsi logo of course – and flew downwind through the Admiral's Cup fleet at 13 knots. Normally, these hard-core international pros don't like it when a hacker or a cruising boat gets in their way, but they didn't seem to mind – they just stared at what they had vaguely heard about or had seen as a bare shell only two weeks ago, now charging past them in proud splendour and most gave a wave in acknowledgement, some even a cheer. Yes, we had made it – so far.

6

Send Lawyers, Guns and Money

We had successfully fooled the general public into thinking we had it all together – not so our creditors.

'Any news yet, Skip?' Dick Saint would politely ask when I passed him in the yard, when I couldn't avoid him by taking a detour.

The £25,000 that Chumakov had reluctantly paid HYS two days earlier may have stopped more of Dick's hair falling out (which he seemed to be losing at an alarming rate) but it did little to ease his long-term worry because it represented only a third of what our total bill was likely to be in two weeks' time. After settling up with Nudger (on the principle of pay first those you need now and later) for parts and services on the electronics little was left in the kitty. We still had not received the first instalment of Pepsi money from ASM either, even though the second instalment was now due. And not only the problems with money, but their lack of performance in general was casting serious doubts about ASM's ability to cope with this project.

With the prospect of an unplanned holiday in Siberia looming, Vladislav grew increasingly desperate. He wanted to call Pepsi directly and explain our doubts about ASM, which was the last thing Pepsi wanted to hear, as ASM and Fazis were supposed to be partners. Although completely naive about Western business practices, Vladislav was a fast study. He asked to see a lawyer. We both felt it was time to go off on our own and try to attract another sponsor or sponsors.

The lawyer, who could read German, was amazed at the simplicity of what he considered a one-sided contract, but he assured us that it was good enough to stand up, until non-performance could be proved – a lengthy and costly process. The issue really was, if we worked outside the contract, what could ASM do about it? I could imagine a nasty scenario in which ASM put a lien on the boat, preventing us from starting the race, or worse. After some investigating, however, the lawyer gave his opinion that, under the circumstances, the British Admiralty was unlikely to impound the vessel, and if it went to litigation, the High Court was unlikely to freeze any funds coming to us from another source, beyond ASM's commission which, under the contract, they were legally due.

Vladislav and I forged ahead, in the limited time we had, trying to make other contacts, but they were all shots in the dark and, in a way, counterproductive. We made it a point to explain the situation with Pepsi, that they were committed for the summer only and had an option to continue, but in view of the massive publicity Pepsi was then getting, nobody believed that Pepsi would even consider dropping us – so, in effect, potential sponsors didn't take us too seriously.

If we, and they, had known, what was then happening in America, it might have been different. Pepsi's media exposure was so effective that it created a conservative backlash – the catalyst being Nance Frank, the skipper of the American all-girl crew, who had unsuccessfully tried to get US sponsorship. She was now bad-mouthing Pepsi about their apparently unpatriotic involvement with the Soviet (read Communist) entry.

A hemisphere away from that unsavoury brew, we plodded on. Not only was the rushed boatbuilding exhausting, but so too was the office work, not for the volume, but because of having to switch gears. I recorded what I had done in an especially heavy session on 9 August.

0800 – usual crew meeting
- wrote supplementary contract between Sparcraft and Fazis for Chumakov's accounting
- negotiated free Patagonia clothes for crew with UK distributor
- sorted out hydraulic system installation with Jim and Eugene

- arranged meeting with lawyer for Vladislav, sat in on one-hour meeting
- gave television interview to British Telecom public relations man
- spent half an hour with lady who gave us free duvets for crew
- found another welder to give us comparative quote for bogus bill from other welder
- got cheque for rental cars from Chumakov to reimburse my Visa card
- checked detailing for reef blocks on mainsail
- negotiated free Harken boat shoes for crew from US factory
- many phone discussions with ASM and Hill and Knowlton about Thames reception
- organized for Tower Bridge to open for us at 1200 on the 17th
- talked through the outstanding accounts with Dick Saint
- checked bank accounts for Pepsi money, called ASM again
- wrote letters of invitation for Thames reception to US and Soviet embassies
- 2100 – had an hour's meeting with Vladislav about all our problems

The crew were working just as hard but, I suspect, had little idea of the complexities involved in a Whitbread campaign – like most crews, all they wanted to do was to go sailing. I envied them.

I had always tried to encourage the project to spend what little money we had on keeping the crew in similar conditions to those of the other syndicates. I wanted them to be well clothed, based ashore in comfortable, dignified quarters and with a few pounds in their pockets, so they would fit in with their peer group and not stand out like 'poor Russians'. This, I felt, was all the more important when trying to impress Pepsi that we were organized and presentable. There is nothing worse for a sponsor than an air of poverty. Chumakov, like any bean counter, had different ideas and he tried to keep a tight rein on the crew. For example, rather than eat a decent meal at the pub, they were encouraged to use the tins of food they had brought over from the Soviet Union, and consume them in the austerity of the shipping container in the back of the boatyard. They would often be in there, huddled together like gypsies, brewing their tea and eating out of the tins, or devouring the Georgian sausages they had suspended from the ceiling to dry – like feudal peasants in a living museum. To my way of thinking, the amount of money needed to give the crew a fair deal was insignificant in the grand scheme of our deficit, so why not keep them happy?

They certainly resented the paltry sum they were given as pocket money by Chumakov, when he paid it all, though it was the natural inclination of some not to spend it anyway, but to hoard it for the future. You can buy a lot of roubles for £100 back in the Soviet Union – and the Georgian sausages were not bad either.

What really rankled with them, and me too, was the old Soviet scare tactics Chumakov seemed to enjoy using. One morning, after they had spent a dirty night out on the town, some of the crew didn't show up for their group breakfast at the Southampton Seamens' Mission, where they were now billeted. Sergei Stanetsky and Guennadi Korolkov, known as 'the Elephant' and 'the Crocodile' respectively, two of the more sociable of the Soviets, were famous for going temporarily AWOL. Chumakov, now jokingly known as the Komissar, took delight in indirectly threatening them with expulsion, by reminding them what an embarrassment they were, not only to the project, but also to their country, for their despicable behaviour. I was amused by their antics and actually encouraged what I thought was perfectly normal, which enraged Chumakov even further, turning him into a comical figure at times. It was a great relief to everyone when both he and Vladislav took the train to London on 10 August to visit the American and Soviet embassies.

With Vladislav out of the office, I immediately rang up Mike Winterfeldt in Hamburg. Although I did not tell him that Vladislav had consulted a lawyer, I explained that he was about to blow it by threatening to call Tony McGrath at Pepsi, and there was not much I could do to stop him.

'Please, please, try to prevent him from doing such a stupid thing! As I have told Vladislav repeatedly, I have sent the money. You should get it today. And we are now right in the middle of talking to Tony about extending the sponsorship, which they are looking at very favourably.' He promised to send Klaus Wawer over in two days to smooth things over.

On 13 August we took *Fazisi* out for her second sail, better prepared this time after another week in the boatyard. Unlike the gentle breeze of our first outing, this time it was blowing a solid 30 knots out of the southwest. As usual we had a big crowd on board – our crew, riggers from Sparcraft, sailmaking consultants from Norths, and a journalist from the *Daily Mail*.

We never did get a genoa up, but cowered instead in the lee of a big oiltanker berthed in Southampton Water while we struggled with the mainsail, trying to sort out the reefing system. If the crew-work on the day of the Fastnet start had been an amusing circus, in the strong breeze it was chaos. Halfway up, the flogging Kevlar mainsail jammed when the main halyard, that pulls the sail up, fouled on the winch drum. Viktor Yasykov, a muscular, blond, blue-eyed Russian of 40, who normally has a disposition like a lamb, exploded with such vehemance from his perch in a boatswain's chair three metres off the deck, that the hardest of hard-core yachties along for the ride stood there with mouths agape in shock, while the other Soviets yelled back at him with equal fury. Minutes later, when the mainsail started up again, a loud report like a rifle-shot came from the bow, and we saw the genoa halyard, an 8mm-diameter steel cable, flying aloft and inconveniently wrapping itself around the top of the mast, 90-feet above the deck. It had been clipped to padeye on the foredeck, and when the crew had mistakenly engaged the wrong winch in the cockpit they had ripped the stainless steel eye off the deck as if it was made of putty. More shouting and cursing. Vladislav looked embarrassed, Alexei fraught; I stood at the wheel with my head propped in one hand, unable to do anything about a situation that was too far gone for words. Only one of us was entirely pleased, the journalist, Anne Barrowclough, and she was ecstatic – a ship of fools had come in and she had her story.

'Reds sail in the fun-set . . . but they're all at sea' was the headline of the article that appeared a few days later. After recounting that and a few more *faux-pas* in graphic detail, she went on to say, 'And while *Fazisi* may be doing a lot for *glasnost*, you come away with the uncomfortable feeing that she and her amiable, amateurish crew are hardly going to set the yachting world alight. The shambles on deck is awe-inspiring as the non-English speaking Russian crew struggle to understand the instructions of American skipper, Skip Novak.' She also caught me with my guard down and quoted me as saying, exasperatedly, '"I don't have the time to train the crew. These guys have never dealt with this type of equipment before. They're still trying to work out how to put the sail up," for heaven's sake!'

Motoring back in to the Hamble River, having accomplished nothing except the grim realization of what it will be like trying to sail *Fazisi*, for the first time I expressed serious doubts to Vladislav about my involvement. I told him we needed at least two other pros on board for the first leg. He solemnly nodded his approval.

'I sure admire you Skip,' said Damian Byrne from Sparcraft, just before we made the dock.

'Oh yeah. You mean you think I'm crazy, is that it?'

'Look, what you're doing is a great thing for these guys. I don't know how the hell you keep getting involved in these weird projects, but I think it's great, I really do.'

'Does this mean you'd like to come on the first leg, because there's room?'

'Well, you know, not really!'

The problem was that most of the better sailors with Whitbread experience were already on other boats, and we couldn't have guaranteed them a wage anyway. Jim and I had been secretly making a plan that he should do the leg. He was certainly more than good enough, although he has had little ocean experience, but has sailed and raced extensively offshore in Europe. Another thing in his favour was that he knew the crew, and they all liked him.

Every married man who sails has faced the same dilemma: it had to be a secret, not from the Russians, but from Jim's wife Liz. A yachtswoman in her own right, Liz also ran her own company, Hamble Sailing Services, which was, incidentally, making all the bunk cushions, soft lockers and sail covers for *Fazisi*. She would have been more understanding than most, except for one factor – she was due to give birth to their second child in seven days' time!

In the beer tent later that afternoon, Jim puffed away on

his Gauloises, with a firm hand wrapped around a Heineken. Having given him the green light, I knew I was putting him in a difficult position.

'Well,' he said, clearing his throat, then resuming in his inaudible, nasal way of communicating, 'Listen, I'd love to go and I'll work it out – just give me a few days. Yes, I think I can work it out . . .'

The next day was horrendous, spent trying to get everything ready for the London excursion. All our creditors converged on the office at about 4 o'clock, including Dick Saint who wanted another £15,000. I fended them off for another day. Now, the immediate problem was to get our foul weather gear, with its Pepsi logos, from Musto Ltd for the London trip. Unable to pay for the entire order for the race, we had to cut the consignment in half so we could get our hands on the bare essentials. By the time Chumakov had sorted the accounting out and written the cheque, it was too late for Musto to deliver the goods for our intended departure at 5 o'clock the next morning. Monica had to drive to Essex late that evening and pick up the order, then sort out the gear into piles for each man – oilskins, boots, hats, thermal gear and long underwear. We left just after dawn the next morning, not only because of the fair tide, but also to avoid another confrontation with Dick, whom I had not informed about our departure. His security against £60,000 of unpaid bills, had literally gone down the river.

The forecast was for a southerly gale so we were hoping for a fast reach to the Straits of Dover. Starting out cautiously, with our smallest sails, we flew out of the Solent at 12 knots and by Beachy Head the wind had moderated and we had full sail up by 10 o'clock.

This was our first real sea trial, 400 miles to London and back, and we were testing not only the mast and sails but everything else – the generator, the watermaker, all the plumbing, the electronics, even the meals we would be using for the first leg, prepared by a local girl Lizzie Wallace-Jones, who did all the buying and packaging and was there in person to test it out on the crew. It was an easy and pleasurable sail on one of those cool, clear summer's days on the English Channel, complete with a dull green sea, a washed-out sky and a red and white boat, like a typical Beken photograph. For the first time we could all relax a bit and take stock of the situation.

So far, *Fazisi* had been trouble-free. The primary equipment like the rigging and sails had fitted first time – a credit to the suppliers. She was easy to steer, the balance on the wheel felt right and she was fast! We caught a few waves with the big spinnaker up, in not much wind, later that afternoon, and surfed along at 16 knots effortlessly. She had a lot going for her.

Vladislav spent hours at the bow and stern, like all designers do, studying the way the leading and trailing edges reacted with the passing water. In his case, I think he did a bit of that, but a lot more day-dreaming, because for this man from the Soviet Union, more than for anyone else out there, *Fazisi* was a dream come true.

The Soviets had done well to build *Fazisi*, but it was the Soviets themselves that I was worried about. We were led to believe that these were the best sailors in the Soviet Union. Maybe they were, but they were not racing men, and their sailing skills left a lot to be desired. It is true that in the Soviet Union they don't have modern equipment, and obviously the crew had never sailed a maxi before, but like in mountaineering, the latest iceaxe, or plastic boots versus good old leather don't make a good climber – it is a question of feel.

The crew's habit of continually fouling up the ropes and halyards, and the fact that some even wrapped lines around the winches in the wrong direction – questions of handling – would improve with practice and didn't worry me as much as other subtleties which were alarming. When a boat heels over in a puff of wind, a good sailor immediately eases the mainsheet to relieve the pressure and put the boat 'back on its feet'. Indeed, in a dinghy (and there were supposed to be some dinghy sailors in the crew) if you don't do something, the dinghy capsizes. The Soviets, however, would just smile while the boat buried her rail underwater, until Jim, Hamish or I suggested the ease. Of course, with the language barrier it was difficult to figure out just what they knew or didn't know, or if they were in fact waiting for a command to do what was obvious to us.

Early the next morning we were motoring up the Thames, well ahead of schedule. Too early for the opening of Tower Bridge, we docked impromptu at the Prospect of Whitby, the oldest pub on the river, and had a great lunch. We continued upstream on three pints of bitter each – a fitting end to our first sea trial. That evening, with *Fazisi* safely berthed in the Pool of London, the crew went ashore to explore the town. At midday the next day, we sailed through Tower Bridge, with the Pepsi spinnaker, for a photo call, followed by a champagne reception at St Katharine Dock, all of which went smoothly and made the papers the next day.

That same afternoon we were off on the ebb tide back to Southampton, pleased with ourselves at having accomplished another task in what would, we hoped, be the road to sponsorship riches.

While motoring on the Thames, the crew lazed around the deck in the afternoon sun, reading the London magazines and newspapers they had collected.

'This is amazing!' said Eugene. 'Here is an article about how Stalin took Moldavia in 1940. It's not the history we learned in school. Which one do you think is correct?' he added with a wry laugh.

Jim and Liz had a baby girl on 21 August. Vladislav and Chumakov went to the Moscow Norodny Bank in London to try to get a loan, with the boat as security. Debt collectors were on the phone at precisely 9 o'clock in the morning demanding their money. The last measurement of *Fazisi* was scheduled for Thursday. We all had a lot on our plates.

On the 23rd we went sailing once again, for the press. Even before the first lines were thrown ashore back in the Hamble, I had my bag in hand, jumped off the boat and ran up to the office for another telephone marathon before office closing time. We had a financial crisis on our hands. Cheques that Chumakov had been writing were beginning to bounce; he thought that funds had been wired to his account from ASM, but they still hadn't arrived.

Those were short-term disasters, but the long term also looked very grim and unpromising. I made a courtesy call to Tony McGrath to make sure he was invited to the start of the race and to feel him out for the future. I never got very far.

'Didn't those guys in Hamburg tell you? We've had to make a corporate decision not to continue our involvement with you because we were starting to get some bad PR from our domestic bottlers about why we were backing a Soviet boat when we should have been supporting these American entries, if we were doing it at all. I'm awfully sorry, because you guys have been doing a great job for Pepsi.'

'But Tony, surely you'll get bad publicity because Pepsi will be seen to be dumping on us?'

'Yes, we are aware of that, but we'll just have to ride that one out.'

In view of the events that were to take place in Eastern Europe at the end of 1989, with hindsight, this seems a very unenlightened viewpoint, certainly not, as they say, 'For a New Generation', but, in the hardball world of American advertising, Pepsi didn't want to risk any loss of market share to their competitors. We had been defeated by conservative, middle America, most of whom had never even seen the ocean; it was the end of what could have been a great beginning.

In a state of depression, I made out another list of accounts due for ASM who were now trying to collect the second Pepsi instalment, and who had decided to pay our bills directly, rather than give the money to Fazis. Even if we got the money we still had a shortfall of roughly £75,000. Everybody was panicking. No word from the bank about the loan, no word from Moscow. If the boat didn't start, ASM would be in breach of contract to Pepsi and we would be in breach of contract to ASM. The press were primed and ready to pounce about how the Russians had been defeated by what should have been their saviour – Western capitalism. I could not imagine the ramifications for Fazis back in the USSR. I was losing hope and I told Vladislav and Alexei that as far as I was concerned the jig was up – we were bust.

They said little and left the office to take a long walk in the parking lot. Chumakov, perhaps oblivious to the big picture, interrogated me with minor accounting problems:

'Hymph, Monica no give receipt for petrol for car – hymph!'

'Valeri, just fuck off!' I went to the beer tent to have a pint with Jim; I needed it.

An hour later, when we were well into our cups, Monica called me back to the office. We had received a call from Moscow. Tichov was coming over in two days and had arranged to bring another £70,000! I put Dick Saint's mind at ease, although he had heard it all before. I slept more easily that night; there was hope yet.

Financially we would look OK if Tichov came through – at least to clear our debts up to the start of the race and give some breathing space to find another sponsor before we hit Uruguay. Temporarily turning away from major disasters, we began to discuss comparative trivialities, like the final crewlist. Some of the Soviets would have to sit this leg out and rejoin later. Rami Leibovich Vladimir Kulinichenko Vladimir Musatov and Oleg Byelomiltsev were scheduled to return to the Soviet Union after the start. Vladislav's biggest problem, however, was Alexei and himself. Alexei expressed some doubt about doing the first leg as he was tired, and besides he wanted to spend time with his family, since he hadn't seen them for almost nine months except for the odd day. Vladislav wanted to do the first leg, but could not as he had to stay behind and help look for other sponsors. I told Alexei that, in my opinion, if he didn't do the first leg, he would have a hard time coming back on board for the second, as most of the crew would know more than he would, an impossible situation for a skipper. He thought about it, but was not settled in his mind.

One problem palled, only to be replaced by a far greater disaster. Later that afternoon *Fazisi* returned from Southampton where she had been measured for stability, the final parameter before the rating could be calculated. In this test, the measurer, employed on behalf of the Offshore Racing Council who administer the International Offshore Rule, checks a boat's inclination to tip, by adding lead weights to a spinnaker pole that is extended at right angles to the hull and attached to the edge of the deck, providing, in effect, a long lever. With an inclinometer, he can measure how many degrees the boat will tip with a certain weight and thereby calculate the real-life stability.

This was the measurement that we all feared would be our undoing. Because of what everyone considered to be our undersized keel, it was possible we might be too unstable to fit into the handicap system of the race.

With all the other measurements completed, it took only minutes to feed the stability figures into the computer. An hour later, the rating office in Lymington called us up. We were over, all right, by four feet of rating – which is heaps. Chief measurer Tony Ashmead was almost certain that we would need a new keel, possibly twice the weight of the original – impossible to achieve as there were only ten days to the start, not to mention the expense!

We sat looking at each other in the office. With the realization that we had now finally lost the game came almost a sense of relief. Chumakov produced a bottle of Armenian brandy, poured out four glasses and we toasted our failure and our immediate futures – they, back to the Soviet Union in disgrace and the salt mines, me, on to other disasters more wonderful, hopefully even more absurd.

When we came to our senses we realized that, to save face, we would have to be seen to be trying, at least, to extricate ourselves. I suggested several scenarios to Vladislav and Alexei. In order to make the start we would have to fit an additional lead bulb to this keel, which probably wouldn't work because the keel would not be structurally strong enough to take the extra load. A new keel would take too long to design, loft and build. Possibly we could find a discarded keel and modify it. If that wasn't feasible, we had to build a new one, but would obviously miss the start. We could then either ship the boat to Uruguay, but I was not keen on doing Leg II in the Southern Ocean without a sea trial on Leg I, or (and for me this was the best plan) we could sea trial the boat here and then ship her to Fremantle in time for the less demanding Leg III.

Either way, we had to find somebody to pay for all this added expense, not to mention the fact that we would be breaking the Pepsi agreement by not being on the start line on 2 September. By the time I had got through all these possibilities, the tide of hope had receded, leaving us once again on the rocks of despair. We were in big trouble.

In any case, we needed help. I called up Tony Castro who lives just up the road. An Anglicized Portugese naval architect with an infectious personality, Tony, if anybody, would be our man, not only because he was nearby, but because he was a numbers cruncher – someone who could quickly figure out the problem and suggest the best solution.

He realized immediately what he was being asked to do and said he would come down in one hour, propose a scenario and give an estimate. To sort this out, he reckoned he had to stop all work in his office and put all four of his staff on to it around the clock. In the meantime I got on the phone and fax and put out an all points bulletin for any old maxi keels lying around Europe that we could use.

Tony made his proposal, which was not cheap. He would begin by digitizing the design of *Fazisi* into his computing system. He would have to look at all the design parameters to come to the best conclusion about what kind of a keel we would need. He wanted money up front but as Tichov wasn't arriving until the next morning, nothing could happen in the next 15 hours. From my enquiries, there were no suitable keels in Europe, so it looked as though we wouldn't make the start, unless a miracle happened.

'Well, Vladislav, maybe something will turn up. Waimer is still looking. You never know,' I said, trying to cheer him up.

'No, no Skip. I cannot imagine we will find a keel, how is it possible?'

I turned round to open our office door and there, not 50 yards away, was *Rothmans'* shore manager Dave Powys, pushing *Rothmans'* first-generation keel into a corner with the yard's fork-lift. 'Hey, Vladislav, what about that keel? There's your keel right down there,' I jokingly told him.

We looked at each other. I grabbed a tape measure. If he was still doubtful, my imagination was running wild. Dave said that the keel was due to be picked up the next day and taken to be melted down and sold as scrap lead. We made a few measurements and found out that it weighed

9.2 tonnes (about double our keel!) and had a steel tongue and bolting flange, making for an easy installation.

'Cancel that truck, we may have it! Where's Lawrie?'

By the time I walked down to the village to look for Lawrie Smith, skipper of *Rothmans*, in his Hamble flat, Powys had called him, and he then called the project manager, Mike Pavitt, in London. They agreed to sell us the keel as scrap if we decided to use it, as a gesture of good will. It was made clear, if not said, that it would be used as a publicity exercise for Rothmans. This was another £4,000 to add to our budget, but it was only the beginning of vast expense in a go-for-broke campaign.

Tony and his team began work in earnest on the Friday, eight days to the start. By Saturday they had confirmed that the correct keel would need roughly 3.5 tonnes more lead than the original. We would also need roughly 1.5 tonnes of internal ballast which was far less than the 4.5 tonnes we had before, so we were effectively taking lead out of the bilge and putting it lower down in the keel, which would make the boat more stable. Tony warned that we would also have to reduce our sail areas slightly to get the rating below 70 feet.

Although I have spent most of my life racing sailing boats, I will be the first to admit that I know only slightly more about how this rating business works than, say, a London daily features writer. Ian Wooldridge of the *Daily Mail*, also baffled by rating after a different incident, later in the race, wrote an article headlined 'We need an Einstein to rule on whether a yacht's a yacht!' and explains the incomprehensible better than I ever could. He writes, 'Measuring a yacht is marginally more complicated than explaining the theory of relativity. Brilliant academics, burbling happily, have been carted off in straightjackets while attempting to measure yachts. You might think, for example, that a yacht's measurement could be assessed by its length, width, height, weight, or even by how many people you could squeeze on to its deck at cocktail hour. No such damned luck I'm afraid. Measurement of the 15 maxi yachts in the Whitbread Round the World Race, which is the key to a fair battle, is determined by a formula requiring a certain number out of 248 separate

components of each to be multiplied, divided, square rooted
or raised to the power of a number some antique admiral
once drew in a raffle. Anyway, for the event to be a genuine
test of seamanship, the answer must be 70. Precisely 70
what nobody knows. It could be called 70 dalmations, 70
gallstones or 70 Fergies, but just to confuse matters further,
they call it 70 feet which is not, of course, the length of the
boat.'

Everyone was asking how Vladislav could have made such
a huge mistake, that the weight of the keel should be out by
a factor of two. He blamed it on the weight of the gear above
the centre of gravity, which he hadn't allowed for, plus the
800 kilos of filler, plus, I suspect, a few more inadmissions.
The matter to this day remains a mystery, and is better
left buried in the archives of the Leningrad Shipbuilding
Institute.

By late Saturday we had decided to go with the *Rothmans'*
keel, and also to cast another bulb that might have to be
fitted because the *Rothmans'* bulb was marginally undersize.
There was also the problem of fore and aft trim. Removing
the internal ballast and effectively putting it farther aft in
the keel, would make the boat float stern down and the
remaining 1.5 tonnes of internal ballast might not be enough
to put her 'back on her lines'. So the bulb was designed to
face forward, like the bows of a tanker. Tony was the first
to admit that though a lot of science, and some art, had
gone into this design, there was also an element of 'hit
or miss' and he gave no guarantees that it would be right
first time.

On Sunday *Fazisi* was lifted out of the water and work
began to remove her keel and strip the interior in the
midsection of all internal fittings. The frame structure was
not strong enough for the heavier keel, certainly not strong
enough to pass American Bureau of Shipping Regulations,
so we also had to find a welder willing to work over the bank
holiday weekend, find the right gauge aluminium plate, and
begin a massive restructuring to Castro's design.

Eugene Platon and Igor Mironenko, who were known as
'Technical Services' for their skill in all things mechanical,
were given the task of fitting the *Rothmans'* keel. Thirty new

keel bolt holes had to be drilled from the bottom through 35-mm plate – a back-breaking job. And they were not happy.

'So we will put keel on while designer sits in office?' said a disgusted Eugene, while sharpening the massive drill-bit in the container. 'Maybe designer of *Fazisi* should drill these fucking holes, what do you think?'

Changing the keel and the structure was not the end of the story. All the full-size genoas and spinnakers had to be recut to lose sail area, which meant the spinnaker poles had to be shortened. The luff of the mainsail had to be shortened, and consequently the locking system on the mast for the halyard had to be remachined in a new location; all necessary jobs, one relating to the other in order for Tony's theory to work to get *Fazisi* under 70 feet, or Fergies, call it what you will.

We were now alone in the boatyard because all the other entries had gone to Southampton, to the race compound at Town Quay, for final scrutineering and preparation. But another distraction descended on us when the Soviet delegation of thirty arrived from Moscow on the Wednesday. While Winterfeldt and Wawer were having some serious meetings with Tichov and Kedishvili, and organizing all the outstanding accounts to be paid, Gerd Budzek, our Russian speaker, kept the visitors amused and out of the fray.

With all the work completed by noon on Wednesday, *Fazisi* was relaunched, rerigged and that evening taken back to Southampton for Tony to make his trial flotation and inclination measurements. After an all-night session, the results looked good; we would not need the other bulb. At six the next morning IOR measurer Malcolm Skene arrived to take the official measurement. Measuring a boat, in the water, with a plumb bob and what is effectively grandma's yardstick, is an inexact science if there ever was one, especially when you add to it the effects of wind and swell in any body of water connected to the sea and the results can be arbitrary at best. If Malcolm Skene read the rise and fall of the swell on his inclinometer in our favour, all the more credit to him. At 10.30, Tony Ashmead confirmed that *Fazisi* rated 69.99 feet! Tony Castro and his team of whizz-kids had done it, and they became everybody's heroes.

Fazisi spent all day on Thursday back in the Hamble, loading food, sails and miscellaneous equipment. I had been through this last-minute panic before with *Drum* four years ago, and this time I had hoped to take the last few days before the start a bit easier – go to a few cocktail parties with the other skippers and blow smoke about the vagaries of the Azores High. It was not to be – we had our hands full right to the end.

For example, on the Wednesday, in the middle of the remeasurement, Alexei decided he wasn't going and was taken off the crewlist while Vladislav was put on, along with Jim, incidentally. Twelve hours later, Alexei was back on and Vladislav was off, the law having been laid down by Tichov who insisted Vladistav stay behind and look for sponsors.

Not only was it a matter of getting the boat ready. I was leaving for what could be eight months and I had to get my affairs in order. On the Thursday afternoon I was starting to clean out my desk drawer in the office, packing it all in boxes to go in the container, when Jim dropped a bomb. He couldn't go. Liz had put her foot down, and quite rightly so. How he and I had thought it could be otherwise, two weeks ago, I will never know, but it had not been intelligent thinking.

I looked at Hamish who was standing next to me. 'Well, what about it?' He knew the Russians just as well, and was an action-man.

Possibly he knew them too well. 'Ugh, hmmm . . . I just don't think I'm qualified Skip . . .' was his stuttered reply. I immediately flipped open my address book and picked up the phone. It was 7 a.m. on the east coast of America.

'Hey, morning Skip, how the hell are ya?' answered Brian 'Mugsy' Hancock, shipmate of two Whitbreads, turned slumlord property maven on Cape Cod.

'What's ya up to, Mugs?'

'Oh not much. Property prices are down and I'm actually in the shit financially. I need to get out of here for a while. This place sucks.'

'Good. Now listen, I'm in big trouble here and I can't explain everything now, but I need you for the first leg.

£2,000 in the hand plus the flight. Can you get on tonight's plane?'

'Christ, let me think about it . . . OK, listen I'll call you back in an hour when I've made the reservation. I don't know what I'm going to tell Erin . . .'

That night, east coast time, he called his wife from the airport in Boston and informed her he wouldn't be back until the middle of October. She said to tell Skip thanks a lot and she would deal with me when we next met.

At 4 o'clock in the afternoon, the day before the start, *Fazisi* roared into the marina at Town Quay under full sail, tacked in front of the cheering crowd, who must have numbered in the thousands, and after dropping her sails, took her place in the line of the 22 other Whitbread yachts. In 20 hours time, we would be on the ebb tide bound for Uruguay, over 6,500 miles away.

7

Leg One – Sailing as an Art and Science

Although never recommended, there is an attraction to embarking on the Whitbread ill-prepared. It implies an urgent sense of purpose ('we can relax once we're offshore'), gives cause for serious questioning ('do we have toilet paper on board?') and is a cavalier approach seen less and less in today's planned, professional world ('don't worry, we'll sort out the reefing system on Leg I'). It has the added benefit of amazing and amusing your peers as they watch your struggle against all odds and reason to get to the starting line of an ocean race that there is a high risk of not finishing.

I can hardly remember clearly all the events that took place during those last two weeks before the start on 2 September. But I will never forget that during that time, when the *Rothmans'* crew were vacuum-bagging spare pieces of rigging and their underwear and socks, while the boys on *Fisher & Paykel* were swapping stainless steel deck fittings and fasteners for lighter weight titanium, and while the *Steinlager* crowd moved lazily around Hamble village from the beer tent that bore their name, up to the King and Queen and back again, en masse like Japanese tourists on holiday, we, on *Fazisi*, had to change our keel, change the structure of the hull and recut most of our sails just to comply with the entry requirements of the race.

This panic culminated for me at two o'clock in the morning on the Saturday, while packing my gear for the voyage. Years ago, I used to take great care over this, usually days beforehand, writing lists and making sure I had all that was necessary. Now, I haphazardly shove a few drawerfuls of balled-up socks, hats, gloves and T-shirts into the standard seabag of foul-weather gear, thermals and boots. Cameras and film, suntan cream, two pairs of sunglasses and sea-sick pills complete this impromptu mental list of necessities, all the more surprising in its accuracy since it is usually done inebriated, and distracted by the raucous laughter from the friends gathered around on my last night ashore, the ones intelligent enough to be staying there.

When I arrived at the boat at 9 o'clock in the morning the usual pre-start pandemonium was in full swing. The crowds were thick on the jetty, making it difficult to man-handle my gear on board, all the while being polite to the press in last-minute interviews, and, worse still, having to sign autographs on pieces of blank paper shoved in my face. For all I knew I could have signed my net worth away, or committed myself to an insane asylum, which wouldn't have surprised the crowd that made up this bedlam. Jim, Monica and Hamish were already on board making lists of last requests and taking notes for things to be done in Uruguay before our arrival. They had all been retained by Fazis to run the stop-over there. The crew were also preoccupied – in saying their goodbyes instead of packing away the mountain of equipment and not least the food, that was randomly stacked on the cabin sole, some still in cardboard boxes.

It's always an immense relief finally to leave the dock and motor out to the start. A symbolic umbilical cord to the confusions of the past is then cut, leaving you to concentrate only on the near future, and a smaller, simpler world consisting of the boat and 16 men. Just before we cast off, Vladislav jumped on board to ride out to the starting area with us, having made arrangements with Tony Castro to be picked up in his rubber dinghy.

He was elated that his dreamboat had made the Whitbread, but melancholy that he would be left behind in its wake and, I suspect, more than worried that if he returned to the Soviet Union he would never be allowed out again. Although we hadn't discussed it much, we both knew that the keel change, for whatever reason, was his responsibility, and had cost the project well over £50,000 (if you consider the price of the original keel as a throw-away), a sum that Fazis could ill afford. Mr Tichov had conjured up a £300,000 loan from some undisclosed source in the Soviet Union, enough to clear up all our debts and get us as far as Fremantle. By then, we were sure a new sponsorship deal would have been made.

The designer of *Fazisi* and I stood side by side at the port steering wheel while hundreds of spectator craft escorted us out into the Solent. 'Well, Vladislav, I am sorry you won't be with us, that I can tell you. I for one could really have used your help, not least of all in translating.'

'For me it's terrible, as you can imagine. Yes, of course it would be better for me to go with the boat, to check crew and check performance, but then who would look for another sponsor? It is now decided with Mr Tichov. In two days I will go to Germany to meet with ASM and hopefully work with them from their office, then to Moscow for one week before meeting you in Uruguay. If all goes well and we find some money I will join you for the second leg. And, Skip, please, be careful and take it easy on the guys, try to be a little softer sometimes. Goodbye and good luck!'

The dinghy came along side 20 minutes before the start, with Tony Castro gesticulating wildly for Vladislav to jump in. He had a short chat with Alexei, then the crew waved him goodbye. A few then turned to Mugsy, a stranger, who was still standing there, and who they must have assumed was a friend or a journalist and would also be getting off.

'By the way, this is Brian Hancock, 'Mugsy' we call him. He is going to Uruguay with us to give a hand. There was no time to tell all of you yesterday. Eugene, can you translate to the rest of the crew?'

Five minutes later, a motorboat came close by and tossed us a bag full of coffee mugs and a few charts! Jim had come through with the last items on the shopping list in the nick of time – the charts we could probably do without, but I didn't relish having to drink our coffee and tea from flat dinner plates. As the ten-minute gun fired and we began to take position, I wondered what else we had forgotten in the confusion.

At precisely 12 o'clock the starting gun on HMS *Ambuscade* fired its salute to the 23 yachts lined up more or less north/south across the Solent, with a few disorientated stragglers in the rear, and in the moderate northerly breeze we reached quickly towards the Needles Channel.

We made a good start, high at the windward end of the line, with clear air and second across only to Peter Blake's big red ketch *Steinlager 2*. We had the rail well underwater, and in the wash made by the spectator fleet that was dangerously close, big seas were cascading into the leeward cockpit where I was steering, keeping an eye on *Fisher & Paykel*. Every so often a wave would submerge me for a second, much to the amusement of the Kiwi crew on her weather rail, now slowly but confidently steaming past us through our lee.

I think we were seventh through the Needles Channel. It's here that most of the day-trippers turn back and only a few support vessels of well-wishers linger on out into the English Channel, leaving the fleet to settle down to some serious racing. We had spinnakers up soon after, the wind went light and more easterly, and by dark the fleet was spread out and invisible save for the odd navigation light or the beam of a torch reflected on a sail.

If the light weather was not the best conditions for *Fazisi*, it was ideal for the crew to settle in slowly to the new routine. Alexei and I split up the watches, and while he and Mugsy came to grips with some nighttime sail changes, I went below and surveyed the situation. The two navigators, 'Crocodile' and Nodari, were muttering in Russian over the chart of the English Channel. They were on opposite watches, each navigating for his watch, and it looked like they had things in control. The bearded Nodari was calculating the time and distance for the tides, and he pulled out a slide rule, something I hadn't seen since my high school days. I introduced him to the NC 77 navigational calculator, but he said, 'Slide rule is very, very good! I do quickly as calculator.' And he could, at least for that calculation.

What concerned me more was the galley and how the first dinner was progressing. Surrounded by plastic rubbish bags of food, the cook, who doubled as the doctor, was totally bemused. None of the bags was marked, and there were no instructions on how to cook any of it. It was mainly freeze-dried food – a substance which I assumed would be unknown to a Soviet. Alexei Drosdovski was the doctor's name and to avoid confusion with Alexei the skipper, he was always known as 'The Doctor'. The Doctor had only joined the project during the last days in Georgia, and had only come to England a few weeks before the start. Since he had not participated in the protracted construction, that fact immediately set him apart from the others.

On my first visit to Moscow, in April, I had insisted that the boat carried a doctor, contrary to Vladislav's and Chumakov's judgement. 'Fine,' they said later, when the decision was made that I would be sailing on Leg I, 'You can have your doctor, but he can also do the cooking.' Because he was too busy trying to sort out the medical kit, he took no part in the food preparation in England. When I had instructed Lizzie about the menus I had said, 'If you misjudge the quantities, err on the plus side.' And she did. Each day's menu, down to the sugar and tea bags, was packed in a daily food bag. We had 30, but each could easily have fed the crew three times over. The bulk was enormous and the bags seemed to be stowed everywhere.

While the doctor successfully identified a bag with spaghetti bolognese, and put the water on to boil, I propped myself up against one of the 15 bags of sails we had on board that almost filled the main cabin up from sole to deck head, leaving only a crawl space to manoeuvre in.

There was not a lot of free living space for 16 people for a voyage which would last 28 days. Sixteen pipe cots in total lined the sides of the boat two deep. Under each cot, and part of the bunk cloth, was a soft locker for each man's personal gear. The foul-weather gear and boots were stowed forward in a big hanging locker by the main hatch. The sit-down galley and the generator box, which also housed the watermaker and water pumps, and the toilet cubicle, known in marine parlance as the 'head', were in an amidships console and dominated the main living area. Hanging from the overhead and protruding into this was the underdeck winch drive system with gear boxes, connecting shafts and universal joints, like the parts found on a combine harvesting machine. You were unlikely to lose a limb when all of this came to life unannounced, but getting your hair caught up in this unprotected machinery could certainly be painful. Back aft was the chart table and eight bunks, which is where I slept. We had had no time to insulate the deck head in England, so bare aluminium frames and stringers were the decor, complete with sharp edges and rough-hewn corners.

By comparison, the other boats were spacious and well finished. Those crews who had seen the interior all agreed it would be pretty rough living on *Fazisi*. Cornelis van Rietschoten, twice winner of the Whitbread in his celebrated *Flyers*, in 1977 and 1981, a man well known for impeccable organization and one who realized the value of a few creature comforts for his crew in what was obviously a successful formula, was, to put it mildly, shocked. While on a nostalgic tour of the fleet the day before the start, Mugsy had shown him below. After he bumped his head on the underside of the deck once too often, he fell back into the safety of a bunk, looked around, looked at Mugsy, and silently took his head in disbelief.

Not so Eric Tabarly, another Whitbread veteran who for the first time since it all began in 1973 was missing the race. Tabarly is the well known French hero/sailor who became a role model to a generation of yachtsmen, but was famous for his austerity in matters of comfort and his suspicion of refinements for their own sake. During his visit, two hours later, he nodded his approval of the simple deck layout, but it wasn't until he went below that this man of few words really became enthusiastic and said, '*Oui, très simple, c'est bon!*' which, coming from Tabarly, was tantamount to a blessing. Aspiring to the Rietschoten formula, but admiring Tabarly's, my main concern was for Mugsy and myself. After all, the Soviets had no yardstick, so for them Hotel *Fazisi* would be just fine.

After an uneventful night we passed through the Chenal du Four that separates the Isle of Ouessant and the Brittany mainland, luckily with a full, fair tide. As expected the big four, *Steinlager 2*, *Fisher & Paykel*, *Merit* and *Rothmans* were substantially ahead, but the good news was that we were in the middle of the remainder of the fleet and holding our own. Our next 'mark' of the course was a dog-leg to Cape Finisterre on the northwest corner of Spain, about 400 miles away, and then it was a straight shot, down past the Canary Islands and hopefully into the North East Trade Winds.

Well across the Bay of Biscay we sailed alongside *Fortuna Extra Lights*, the Spanish entry, another lightweight maxi very similar to our own. Under light spinnaker, with the wind on the rise, we were able to sail away from them and lost them completely by nightfall. In spite of the fact that almost none of the crew knew anything about how to trim a sail, or even what it should look like, we were doing all right. The light but steady winds made the manoeuvres for changing sails easy, and like a sailing school, which in effect we were, we had a discussion on how to do it before each change.

The next evening things piped up, however, and by 2100 it was blowing 30 knots and *Fazisi* started to surf at speed in the conditions that she was designed for. Blasting down medium size waves at 20 knots, submerging the bow and filling both cockpits with water regularly, *Fazisi* was still a joy to handle and felt incredibly safe in spite of her 'submarine'-like qualities and the strange noises coming from the deck as the sheets and guys loaded up – a real-life test of all those new fittings we had installed only weeks before.

When any vessel gets into a big sea for the first time, there is always a measure of apprehension. Each padeye, winch and piece of wire is scrutinized for its integrity as it creaks and groans, and grim thoughts run through the minds of the crew; ('Is the traveller base strong enough?' 'What about that dodgy genoa tack fitting? I knew it should have been made stronger,' 'Will the carbon fibre spinnaker poles go the distance?') It's like a nightmare; a thousand and one relatively inexpensive fittings, fasteners and pins, if not specified and installed correctly, are waiting to lay waste to a project worth millions. But after a few hours of this mental torture, those creaks and groans settle into a routine, as you realize they won't break (at least not yet) and some days later, their familiar cadence actually helps you to get to sleep.

In these conditions, that are described as 'marginal', it was not just a question of steering for speed, but steering for safety. One false turn of the wheel, one bad wave to which the helmsman doesn't react quickly enough, and we could broach or gybe and lay the boat flat on its side. When this happens, damage to sails and maybe the rig, not to mention the crew, are a real risk. If it was apparent in the light weather that we were weak on natural helmsmen, in a blow it was now disturbingly clear. Only Edgar Terechin, a dinghy sailor from Riga in Latvia, had any feel for it at all. Anatoly was not bad and certainly confident, but the others, including the co-skipper Alexei, were mechanical drivers and very nervous and wouldn't be much good without a lot of practice in easier conditions.

By midnight the wind was still coming from east of north, blowing in the general direction we wanted to go. Because we couldn't steer directly down wind, and had to favour one gybe or the other, we stayed on port, out of convenience. First of all, we didn't have any tactical plan with regards to a long-term weather forecast, so for us there was no clear direction to favour. But more significant was that we had never gybed the boat before in any kind of a wind, so I made the decision to hang on as we were through the night – we cleared Cape Finisterre by 25 miles – and by first morning light things would clarify. Understandably I was nervous about trying a heavy air gybe, which would have been a new and therefore risky manoeuvre.

As expected, the wind eased early the next morning and by the noon position we had run 305 miles in 24 hours which was not bad going. After plotting the fleet's positions at the 1100 GMT interyacht radio schedule, it became painfully apparent that it wasn't good enough. During the night, west was the way to go, and those who had gybed to starboard, the 'smart money', like *Merit* and *Steinlager*, were even further ahead, having carried the strong breeze well out into the Atlantic. They had reported 40 knots of wind, but this short-lived first gale had also taken its toll; *Merit* had torn off a base to one of her mast spreaders and was making a running repair, and *Union Bank of Finland* also had an undisclosed rig problem and was heading for the island of Madeira to pick up a replacement part from a dispatched support crew.

By the afternoon we were ambling along at only 9 knots in a light breeze. In easy weather once again, we continued to make some alterations to *Fazisi*. During my four months with the project, I had drawn three plumbing diagrams for our two mechanics Juri Doroshenko and Oleg Byelomiltsev (Oleg was sent home from England, never to return). Despite this, they had succeeded in connecting the seawater foot pump, the seawater pressure pump and the freshwater day tank all together so they came out of one tap in the galley sink. As a result, back pressure from the seawater system was tainting the fresh water. This became apparent with the first cup of coffee. Even worse, the toilet discharge which should always be isolated, was connected by a T-junction to the galley sink outlet, providing an easy path for microscopic bacteria to wander up into our sink where The Doctor washed and stored our dishes. It was only a matter of time before dysentry would strike.

Eugene was also worried about the water supply. He claimed that the only two water tanks that were integrally built with the hull, and which carried a combined 300 litres, were undrinkable due to the fact that the aluminium manganese alloy would contaminate the water with dissolved metals. Under the race rules we were required to carry 9 litres per crewman for every 1000 miles we had to sail, which meant for Leg I, 6,281 miles, we had to embark with about 900 litres and then keep sufficient supply for the miles remaining. With an embargo on two tanks, we were slightly illegal.

I felt that the water issue was exaggerated, but I had to respect Eugene's opinions. He was undoubtedly the brightest guy on board and very quickly grasped some basics about how a big sailboat works. He also knew a thing or two about environmental pollution and was making it clear that he was not going to have any forced down his throat.

Certainly Eugene's command of English endeared him to me more than the others. He was a cut above the others academically and he knew it. A Moldavian by birth, he went to Moscow in his teens and graduated from the Moscow Technical Institute in the Department of Control Science and Applied Mathematics. Since 1982 he has been working in Kiev at the Institute of Cybernetics, doing research into algorythms for parallel computers, apart from a break at the Ministry of Electrical Power, in the computer division, working on operations research for the electrical grid of the Ukraine. All this aside his biggest attribute, so far as I was concerned, was that I could have a conversation with him, complete with innuendo, and get at least one honest viewpoint of what it was like in the Soviet Union. He was a radical at heart, deeply anti-government, which was not surprising, but what also set him apart from the others was his desire to say so.

Because of his connections with the university community in Kiev, he had found out about the Chernobyl nuclear reactor disaster a day ahead of the public announcements, which were made two days after the explosion. Thinking quickly, he had the sense to move his three-year-old child 800 kilometres away, to where his wife's grandmother lived. A week later he volunteered for the clean-up during the aftermath of the fire. He spent a month on site directing personnel cleaning up nuclear waste in and around the reactor. For his effort, his hair is now falling out, as are Viktor Yasykov's teeth – another Chernobyl veteran who volunteered during his time in the Army.

'That's why, Skip, it has been scientifically proven that one of the most effective antidote's against radiation sickness is to drink a lot of red – not white – wine, which we did every day before going into that reactor.' His command of the language was so good I couldn't make out if he was serious or just pulling my leg.

During the next week we fought, in even lighter airs, to get back to the west, but the wind was again directly behind us, making it difficult to decide not only which gybe to be on but also what course to steer, relative to the wind direction. Below about 16 knots of true wind, the technique is to 'head up' and reach, rather than run dead downwind. Because you go faster, you cover the increase in distance more efficiently. Though this is a well known vector problem,

93

it was unknown to the Soviets and they would insist on steering the wrong angles, giving us endless ground for discussion and argument. I would tape a piece of paper to the deck near the steering wheel with the correct wind angle to steer for every knot in true wind speed and most would mechanically follow the instructions – for a time – until, for example, Anatoly would be caught steering dead down wind in almost a dead calm. Although his command of English was improving by leaps and bounds, he would always recite his litany to defend his theories of yacht racing, some of which I have also put into practice, but on Lake Michigan during the weekend races almost twenty years ago. Like a broken record, he would say, 'In the Black Sea Cup, on my yacht, we have won three time championship'.

Racing techniques aside, Anatoly was having a difficult time within himself. It was obvious that he coveted the skipper's position and it was clear he considered himself more experienced than Alexei. In this I would have to agree. He was certainly more approachable, felt more at ease and seemed to be enjoying himself, consequently he was generally well liked by the crew.

Alexei, by contrast, was not a communicator and didn't even have much of a rapport with Eugene and Igor who had crewed for him for years on his boat in Kiev. I had felt very early on that he realized he was in way beyond his abilities out on the water, and he was not comfortable as the co-skipper, when the crew looked to me for most of the answers.

When Mugsy or I tried to explain something to him we had to have Eugene translate for us. If he wasn't around, the others, like Igor, who had enough English, flatly refused to relay information to him. I quickly concluded that it was Igor's ingrained respect of Alexei as his skipper, an irreproachable icon, which made it unthinkable to suggest an alternative way to the method they had been using on Alexei's boat in the Black Sea for the last five years. To name one case in point, Igor was obstinate that we were doing too many sail changes, although I tried to convince him that the other boats were probably doubling our average.

In the Soviet system, where crewing positions are few

and far between and therefore not to be taken lightly, the skipper is always the best helmsman, his opinion on all things is gospel, and if a crewman thinks otherwise he had better not say it, or he might find himself ashore – for good. This outdated method may work on shorter, day races, because when the racing is over the protocol is dropped until next weekend's outing, but on the Whitbread it is different because you have to live with the people in a give-and-take environment.

Alexei struggled to come to terms with this but his antiquated Soviet ways were causing him to become more and more isolated. I continued my role as neutral Yankee advisor, and *de facto* skipper, and Anatoly assumed the role of first mate and father figure for the crew, which, on some of the more successful boats, is what the role of Whitbread skipper has evolved into.

On 10 September we passed between the islands of Hero and Palma in the Canaries – in dead last position in the maxi fleet. Nodari called the local VHF radio station there and miraculously made a connection to his house in Georgia. His wife said that *Fazisi* has been reported to be 60 miles in the lead! Nodari was so happy, he presented me with his only copy of Shota Rusteveli's *The Knight in the Panther's Skin*, which is the romantic Georgian classic.

Nodari and Juki are the two Georgian 'representatives' on board, or that was now it was explained to me by Fazis, indicating they were chosen as a political move, and not for their sailing abilities. Juki had come right in England despite not having done any work on *Fazisi* while in Georgia. I can only assume that toiling like a slave was above his station in his home town, and it was a Georgian custom to enjoy this supremacy over the 'Russians', when you can. But without cover in England he worked his heart out alongside Nodari, and they, almost alone, faired the hull. In spite of that effort, there was no mistaking the discrimination they suffered at times from others in the crew, who referred to them, behind their backs, as 'Georgian Monkeys', while The Doctor called them 'Niggers'. I found them both incredibly easy going company, by far the most outgoing and happy of the crew, which Juki said was part of their national character. 'All

Georgian people friendly, Skip. No Russian people same, blah!'

Juki was one of those rare individuals who could hold a meaningful conversation with only a handful of words and a rich repertoire of body language. He had other attributes, too, like the ability to bake a decent loaf of bread, learned from his father who opened a bakery in the port of Poti, after a lifetime spent in the Soviet merchant marine. He would frequently stand in for The Doctor at breakfast, and instead of The Doctor's sometimes strange concoctions of pasta and warm milk, he would turn out a proper omelette, a fresh loaf, or maybe a mess of fried flying fish harvested from the deck the night before.

The crew seemed to argue continuously, but in spite of this the atmosphere on board was very relaxed, at least for them. Not so for Mugsy and me as we tried to instill a sense of urgency in manoeuvres and a general attentiveness commensurate with a race, not a cruise. I had the impression that, with a few exceptions, most of the guys had envisaged the Whitbread as more like a Tall Ships Rally, where they would be lounging around the deck, smoking pipes, singing sea shanties and speculating on their fortunes in the next port of call. Although I knew they didn't know much about sail trim, or the nuances of boat speed, they didn't seem keen to learn and were quite content to take the usual losses and the infrequent gains of the position reports all in their stride. 'Look,' Mugsy said to me one exasperating day, 'It's obvious to me, these guys are rooted from that construction. They're on holiday now – just glad to be out here, and not back in the Soviet Union.'

Anatoly, one of the more aggressive crewmembers, in his own way tried to change the system. He declared *perestroika* a failure, and said that *glasnost* would be indefinitely postponed, at least on *Fazisi*, because the crew had failed to grasp a democratic reform and organize themselves into an efficient team. He was right, of course, but my system of openness in letting everyone have a go at steering, trimming and working the foredeck, was necessary simply because they all needed the practice. Instead, the central committee, meaning Anatoly, temporarily scrapped reform in favour of a regimented hierarchy.

While he spent two days below working out a complicated and unworkable schedule of who would trim the genoa, steer, grind the mainsheet, and when – down to the half hour, the rest of us faced another water crisis.

Juri announced that we were using more than 6 litres per man per day and was blaming it on The Doctor's sloppy handling of the water in the galley. He, in turn, blamed it on Juri's plumbing, already exposed as less than the optimum system. For an unexplained reason, our big forward 600-litre tank up forward was already completely empty, even though we made 25 litres a day with the watermaker. I suspect most of the crew had been using and wasting more water than they were allowed. I was confident that only Mugsy, Eugene and I actually understood the rules. I asked Eugene to once again translate for me, but having made the enquiries he looked at me sheepishly. 'Well, what did you find out?' I asked him.

'Nothing. It's like when I tell them to trim the sails; they say I talk too much.'

Alexei, in one of his rare moments of taking control, conducted a crew meeting on deck to sort it all out, the results of which were never disclosed to me, but it seemed to solve the problem.

Two days after Anatoly posted his crew roster on the bulkhead we were back to normal, the crew having realized immediately that Anatoly should not be steering for four out of every six hours on his watch, that it was impossible for Nodari and Crocodile only to do the navigation and that even Juki would get fed up only grinding the mainsheet.

I left Eugene on the wheel in the early hours of 13 September. Although not a natural, he was becoming one of the best helmsmen, simply because he could coordinate the information on the sailing instruments into a pattern of helming – a necessity even for a natural helmsman, in light air. We were 40 miles away from the northwest group of islands in the Cape Verdes and could pass between any three of the little islets that were generally on our course. Nodari, who was slowly being weaned off his slide rule in favour of the calculator, was left as the navigator in charge. I left instructions with Mugsy to wake me up when we got close.

Four hours later I was shaken in the pre-dawn darkness by Anatoly who mumbled, 'Please to look at island'. Still half asleep, I peered over Nodari's shoulder; he was whimpering over the chart, his eyes as wide as dinner plates. The radar screen, set at 1 mile range, was nothing but a solid green reflection – ground zero! I jumped onto the deck and shouted to Mugsy, 'What the hell is going on here?' He was sailing dangerously by the lee, risking an accidental gybe as he tried to sail low to avoid the shoalwater underneath a cliff edge that now towered above us, dead abeam in the darkness.

'This is a real fuck-up, big wind shift – too complicated to gybe. Did you check the chart?' he shouted back.

'Never mind, it's too late, if we're going in, we're going in.' I braced myself for the impact, but we made it – just. Then the arguing started. They were all jabbering at once in Russian, and Nodari seemed to be taking the brunt of the criticism. Because he was the navigator, he became the obvious scapegoat for an episode when we came dangerously close to losing the boat.

Nodari had completely lost face, and like Tariel, the Knight in the Panther's Skin, who realizes his lover Nestan-Darejan has been banished from him forever, lost all hope and, like all Georgians then and now, wept, with 'Tears overflowing the eyes and moistening the fields and the meadows'.

It wasn't until 12 degrees North that things changed in our favour. The Trade Winds had never materialized, and in the fickle breeze we had fallen even further behind most of the boats that were still out to the west. Our only hope of salvaging an embarrassing situation was the Doldrums – the area of low pressure just north of the Equator, where skill and cunning play a role in a bigger game of chance.

Of course, the leaders of the fleet hit the light weather first and as expected we began to regain a lot of the lost miles, but we expected we might lose them again at the other end when the leading boats were released – maybe. On the morning of the 15th, the hazy sky cleared, giving a visibility that was limited only by the curvature of the earth. All around towering cumulo-nimbus clouds began to develop, with dark, slanted rain-showers issuing from underneath. With her light weather sails slatting listlessly in zero wind, *Fazisi* slowly heaved up and down, moving almost imperceptibly, in the oily sea. We threw our dice and waited for our first chance encounter with a wind cloud.

The day time temperatures were now unbearable, and down below the deck head was too hot to touch. Later that afternoon, relief finally came when the wind increased from 5 to 25 knots in a matter of minutes and we had a panic to change to the No. 3 genoa and reef the mainsail. Off we went, on the leading edge of a big black cloud, at 12 knots. Now the trick was to stay in it and not let the cloud overtake us or veer away. The Soviets were disconcerted when I ordered them to steer 90 degrees off course for 30 minutes, but it worked, and we continued with our private wind for a full three hours before the gods outsmarted us. 'We sure got through that one in good shape, eh Mugs?' I said to my staunch companion, who had just had a rough watch trying to get the crew to speed up critical sail changes.

'Yeah, we sure did, like a bunch of Ukrainian farmers. I can't figure out what's with these guys. That last spinnaker set was a total nightmare. They had Nodari up on the foredeck and he hooked the after-guy up inside the lifelines, and instead of fixing it they just shat all over him. We got Alexei steering all over the ocean, and Viktor shouting his guts out at Igor about the pole hitting the headstay. I was running around like a blue-ass fly, and the problem is nobody will listen to me when I tell them to do something. Trouble is nobody communicates on this boat.'

In spite of the diabolical crew work, which, strangely enough, was not getting any better, we played this game with every squall that came our way. The results were astonishing. In four days, by the 19th, we went from fourteenth to eighth position and were only 40 miles behind the fifth boat! We were truly back in the race.

We crossed the Equator on the afternoon of the 19th. I was still frustrated, but in better spirits because we were doing well. Anatoly organized the King Neptune ceremony and the King, his Queen and two assistants gave the 'right of passage' into the Southern Hemisphere to nine Soviet seaman. The Doctor cooked a celebration meal and Juki, the *Tamada* on board, produced a few bottles of Armenian brandy and made the toasts. In spite of our difficulties in communication and awkward attempts at trying to race *Fazisi* we were as friendly a group as was possible under the circumstances and it was clear the Soviets were more understanding of my behaviour towards them than I was to theirs.

Two days later Eugene started to complain of stomach pains ('from Doctor's cooking') just as Nodari announced he had a toothache. The Doctor's bedside manner was now called upon for the first time. He had just spent two years in the army in Afghanistan, severing limbs and patching up big holes in bodies, so you can almost understand his lack of sympathy for minor ailments. He dished out some medicine to both patients. Eugene's stomach cleared up, but Nodari got worse, so the solution was to stop all treatment. The Doctor was convinced it was a psychological disorder, 'cabin fever,' he called it. Nodari spent the next week below in what seemed like abject pain, totally useless, with one of those cartoon bandages wrapped around the top of his head and under his chin.

I liked The Doctor, but I distrusted him because of his double standards. He and I had struck up a sense of cama-raderie very early on and I sympathized with his problems of food indentification – like when he thought he was giving the crew powdered mashed potatoes, and it turned out to be powdered egg. I even let him steer every day in the hopes of keeping him sweet, and in fact he was not a bad helmsman. In return for these privileges he called me 'my Captain', with an almost grovelling, reverential tone of voice; he frequently bribed Mugsy and me with extra candy bars and oranges, and gave us special tea, 'Admirals' Tea', he called it, which meant it wasn't the Soviet tea which was astringent and undrinkable. When Mugsy had cut his finger, the Doctor was all over him like a cheap suit, and if I hadn't known that he was married (he showed us a photo of a beautiful woman on a beach in Odessa, that incidentally looked like it was cut out of a fashion magazine) I would have said he was slightly bent. Very early on he expressed a desire to get out of the galley and work the deck instead, his theory being that if he did a bad job in the galley he would be liberated.

He certainly followed this concept enthusiastically. His cooking had never been inspired, but what really annoyed me was that the galley was a complete mess, disgusting and a health hazard, in spite of all of our complaints, which only seemed to make things worse. Nothing was ever put away; he kept the cutlery in a bucket that doubled as his footrest and the plates and bowls were perpetually greasy and wet, and were stored between meals in the sink, which was still connected to the head discharge because Juri didn't have the parts to change it.

But nobody got dysentery because the head, a Blake marine toilet, the best in the world, had broken down. I pointed out to the crew that I had never had to repair a Blake before, they were so reliable. They just smiled at me with their mouths full of gold and stainless-steel false teeth. Some people would feel inconvenienced and embarrassed about 'going over the side', but luckily not this crew, and they were quite correct – like the gaucho in the book *Southern Cross to Pole Star*. A. F. Tschiffely, during his celebrated horse ride in 1925 from Buenos Aires to Washington DC, had politely asked where the *baños* was in a despicable café somewhere in the Andes. '*Señor*,' said the gaucho as he kicked the back door of the café open, to reveal a starry night illuminating the naked windswept landscape, 'You have the entire universe at your disposal!'

On 23 September we had reached our zenith in the results, after fighting the variable weather conditions down the coast of Brazil. Tied for fifth place, we had *The Card* virtually abeam of us just one mile away – only a week out of Punta del Este.

When another boat is in sight it is hard not to sail aggressively. Every sail change, every mistake becomes apparent in the relative positions. We had been fighting with *The Card* for the last 24 hours since they appeared on the near horizon inshore at dawn of the previous day. And we were holding our own, which was surprising because we were carrying full sail on a reach which should have favoured the bigger ketch.

At 0945 I woke up to the sound of a flogging Kevlar sail and some familiar voices – Igor cursing, Edgar braying like a donkey and Alexei giving some terse commands. When I made the deck, I was shocked to find us steering 90 degrees to our course while trying to drop the reacher, and aiming directly at *The Card*! They had been changing the headsail 'bald headed' instead of using the more efficient system of sliding one sail up the twin grooves on the headstay inside the other before letting the old one down. In this way, no speed is lost and it also saves wear and tear on the sail.

Incredulous, I immediately flew into a violent rage as *The Card* happily cruised on by us and was a mile ahead by the time we got the No. 3 genoa up and were back on course. Alexei was driving, but Igor was obviously the culprit; we had had this argument before. 'Damn you. I told you not to do bald-headed changes. Christ, look at *The Card* for fuck's sake!'

'No worry, Skip, not your problem, we make sail change, I sail for fifteen years on Black Sea!' said Igor, looking at me through his thick machine-shop style glasses full of salt spray, trying to defend himself from the vicious onslaught.

'Igor, you are an asshole, do you know that, an asshole! All you guys are stupid! What the hell was Alexei doing running off for?' I asked Igor to ask Alexei for an explanation, but as usual he refused. I stormed below, cowering Russians making way for me, and sat down for a late breakfast. I was so worked up, the Doctor's omelette stuck in my throat more than usual. After his trick on the wheel, Alexei came below and sat down on the cabin sole up forward and stared at the bilge for what must have been an hour. He must have felt totally abused by my outrage. I felt terrible, and angry, not with them, but now with myself. Once again, I had let my temper get the better of me. 'What can I say to the guy,' I said to Mugsy. 'He wouldn't understand me, I'd have to get a translator fer Christ's sake.'

Mugsy and I have sailed over 60,000 miles together, so we knew each other pretty well. He came and sat down next to me on a wet sail bag, aware of the dilemma that I had created for myself. 'I don't know, Skip. These guys are a strange bunch so I wouldn't worry about it too much. I can't believe they're making the same mistakes after sailing over 5,000 miles. They just don't seem to give a shit. You know I like these guys individually, but as a group they are worthless. Look, it's not your fault.'

A day and a half later, we turned the corner off Brazil, but not before a southerly squall put us on the wind in a bad sea. We beat against the wind all the way to Punta del Este, sailing with determination all the way, 'whether the crew liked it or not'. Despite my feelings of remorse at my behaviour towards the crew, my ego had taken over and I was determined to do well, or as well as we could – if not for them, then for Mugsy and myself. 'Sailing school is over, to hell with being an advisor,' I told Mugsy as I grabbed the wheel with provocation from Anatoly one evening.

With three hundred miles to the finish we had *Gatorade*, *Satquote British Defender* and *Martela* all in sight, all just behind us. We could easily be sixth or ninth. Mugsy, Edgar and I steered all the way to the finish – and trimmed the sails too – while the Soviets casually muttered amongst themselves and occasionally argued – about what, I never asked. In the dead of night at 0035 GMT on 1 October we crossed the finishing line in Punta. We beat the other boats – by minutes only – and came in an impressive sixth place, with a boat that was late to the start, underfinanced, and carried a crew of amateurs. Fair and square, *Fazisi* had beaten some of the better-run campaigns in the race, but we would find out shortly that this insignificant victory was paid for at an exorbitant price.

8

One Man's Solution

We had surprised everyone with our results, so much so that the race committee, with the tacit approval of the other competitors, had given *Fazisi* the number one dockside position near the arrival pontoon, alongside the leg winner *Steinlager 2*, who had beaten *Merit* by a staggering margin of 12 hours. They had good reason: it was the beginning of the holiday season in Punta del Este and wealthy Argentinians who flock to this exclusive seaside resort, in the otherwise pastoral, third-world atmosphere of Uruguay, would appreciate the attraction that *Fazisi*, with her curious crew of Soviets, would certainly provide.

During the next week, the other 17 entries slowly filled the length of the concrete jetty that serves as a seawall against the Pampero winds in the Rio de la Plata Estuary. The leg had been an easy one, so there was little damage in the fleet, save for the collapse of *Fisher & Paykel*'s mizzen mast only days from the finish, and a curious problem with *Martela*'s keel which had started to fall off. She was immediately dispatched to Montevideo, 60 miles down the coast, for an emergency inspection and repair.

Punta del Este (point east, in Spanish) is a sandy spit of land that points due south from the coast and separates the river water of the Plate to the west, and the Atlantic Ocean to the east. To an errant navigator, the skyline could be mistaken for Miami Beach, or possibly the Costa Brava in Spain – tall, featureless apartment blocks on a low-lying foreshore. A closer inspection ashore would reveal a surfeit of restaurants, shops, cafés and nightclubs and little else, and like the other two holiday havens, the people behind the counters, who take your money with abandon, speak Spanish. Unlike the other two, it's redeeming quality is that it has an unfettered beach on both sides of the point that stretches east and west as far as the eye can see.

In winter it is a ghost town, the infrastructure maintained by an indigenous Uruguayan population from the adjacent town of Maldonado, whose only other claim to fame is that Sir Francis Drake spent the winter of 1577/78 there before he ventured further south, also on an around-the-world tour. It's in the four months of the austral summer that Punta del Este comes alive, and the population swells close to bursting, like an Argentine teenager's bikini. The regular annual visitors who own a flat, or some of the more upmarket properties in the woodlands behind the esplanade, so the story goes, have all invested in real estate here as a hedge against the roller coaster economy of Argentina. Surprisingly, Uruguay is stable by most comparisons.

Hotel accommodation was easy to find for the crews because the tourist season was not yet in full swing. Monica and Hamish had made a good deal with the Spanish-style Palace Hotel, which was only one block from the Race and Media Centre and the fleet's shipping containers that were arranged in the yacht club's carpark. Each boat had one or two sea-freight containers that provided them with a workplace and gear storage.

At the Palace, in the back of a lovely open courtyard, they had set up our office and communications base with the outside world in a rented room. The fax machine was 'on line' and already disgorging reams of paper from the press giving their congratulations and asking for interviews, from ASM who said they were still trying to find sponsors, from Jim back in the Hamble who was scheduled to do the second leg and working frantically to fill all the orders of equipment and spare parts that I had asked him for over the radio while at sea – and of course from Fazis in Moscow, hailing our good result and safe arrival.

Vladislav and Chumakov were due to arrive in two days' time, coming directly from Moscow to Buenos Aires on the Aeroflot flight. Aeroflot was one of our sponsors and was providing all air tickets free to their regularly scheduled destinations.

Luckily, a quick inspection of *Fazisi*, including the entire structure, the mast, the steering system and the hull below the waterline, declared her in perfect order, which was a great relief, as the list of jobs outstanding from England was still formidable. For example, we had to insulate the entire deck head and the side of the hull against condensation. Hamish had alredy offloaded the sheets of one-inch foam from the container, and by the third day in port the crew, under Alexei's direction, divided up areas of the boat and began to glue it in place, a job that would take all of seven days. Eugene and Igor set up a workbench on the dock, following the lead of the other crews, and began to completely strip every winch and block, cleaning all the parts, re-lubricating and then reassembling them. Viktor Kamkin was busy working in the galley, finishing the storage for the galley utensils and the food, while Valeri Safiullin and Edgar took all our sails to the derelict cinema that was the North Sails' temporary service loft. We had no sail damage, but some modifications had to be made and every stitch and seam double checked.

Once again, Hamish was the buyer. He had been to Punta before, two years ago on his way to the Antarctic, so he knew the lie of the land, was used to the inefficiencies of South America, and, because he had met his present girl-friend there, now a nurse studying in B.A., he spoke reasonable Spanish. Every two or three days he would drive the two hours into Montevideo with a long shopping list; a bit of plumbing for Juri, a piece of aluminium for Igor, more tools, a bigger cooking pot for The Doctor, a fuse or a switch for the Elephant, who was still finishing the electrics – the 'wish' list was endless.

On his arrival, Vladislav and I discussed the plan for the next leg. I made it clear from the start, that I was not happy with the performance of the crew. 'There seems to be a general lack of motivation,' I told him in private, 'and the communication is terrible. If I ask them to do something, of course they will do it, but if I tell Edgar to ask the Crocodile to do something, he immediately says, "*tos gesagt*? Who said it? Did Skip say it, or is it you? If it's you, what do you know about it?'' And as far as safety goes, we defnitely need more downwind helmsmen, at least three more. Mugsy has to go home, but Jim is on standby and so is a New Zealander I've sailed with before, who did the race in '82. I'm very adamant about this.'

'OK, let me talk to the crew so I can get more information. Anyway, do you know that Alexei has definitely decided to go home from here for a rest, and then join us in Fremantle? I know this man, and he is very tired.'

I didn't try to dissuade Alexei this time, but I knew that if he went home now, that would be the last we would see of him. It was clear he was not enjoying the Whitbread Race. I assumed that Anatoly would take over as Soviet co-skipper. I thought to myself, 'Well, that's fine,' and then went on to contemplate the new line-up.

We would have to lose three crew in order to keep our number at 16, including the four non-Soviet pros I decided were necessary, at least for my peace of mind. I'd been having a recurring thought about the grim scenario should Mugsy or I fall overboard on Leg I, and the Soviets be unable to turn the boat around because they were arguing about how to do it – the Georgians with the Russians, the Ukrainians with the Latvian – as the helpless victim blended into the far horizon. I didn't want to do the second leg without more help. For the first time in my life, on the eve of an ocean passage, I was running scared.

With Mugsy and Alexei leaving, one more would have to be dropped. It was the general concensus that Nodaria was the weak link and headed for a forced repatriation. When we hit the last remnants of the Falklands Current, and it got a little chilly during the last three days of Leg I, he was only able to sit on deck with his head buried in the neck of his foul-weather gear jacket – like a tortoise and about as useful. His toothache, curiously, cleared up just before we docked, reinforcing The Doctor's amatuer psychoanalysis. In fact, in the sunny weather, of Punta, the tooth didn't seem to bother him at all.

I had Monica find a dentist and we booked him in, just in case. Sure enough, he had an abcess. I had been assured by Vladislav that all the crew's teeth had been thoroughly checked before they left the Soviet Union. 'What about that?' I asked the Elephant. He made his deep, infectious laugh that came from the depths of his chest and said in his baritone, 'Yes, we were checked. But nothing was fixed.'

I told Monica to book them all in for full mouth X-Rays and to have whatever was wrong taken care of. Two weeks later the bill came to $2,280; the score: 49 fillings, 5 extractions and 6 root canal repairs!

Alexei had seemed happier than usual on Monday morning of 9 October. I remember Monica commenting on it when she said, 'He's in a good mood this morning, he even smiled at me in the courtyard'. He knew he was going home, his ticket was booked for the 16th, so we assumed he was getting more and more relaxed, all the while doing his job of directing the crew through the worklist.

Vladislav, however seemed more on edge. ASM was still procrastinating about new sponsors. All other leads in London were obvious dead-ends, in spite of our good results. To finish the boat and fill the equipment list, including three more down-wind sails, a spare mainsail, two new spinnaker poles (the carbon fibre ones broke) and survival suits for the crew, would cost more than $200,000. He probably realized he would miss the second leg too and have to return to Europe – or worse – and continue fundraising. That same morning, when one of the crew had asked him about some detail, he snapped back, 'Ask Alexei, he is in charge of the worklist!'

That morning was the last we would see Alexei alive. Cancelling his dental appointment, he told The Doctor, 'Since I'm returning to Kiev, I'll have the work done there'. He didn't turn up for the standard crew lunch at the Blue Cheese restaurant, nor for the afternoon crew meeting, nor for the crew dinner at El Metehon up the main street.

I was not very concerned about this, especially when it was pointed out to me that he had done this before, going AWOL for an evening in the Hamble, and apparently taking a siesta on the beach one afternoon while in Georgia. I believe every man should be given at least 24 hours slack, with no questions asked, in order to do whatever he has to do. Then again, it was strange. He was not the type to frequent a bordello, and the one in Maldonado was pretty awful, or so I'm told. Plus he didn't speak a word of English, or Spanish for that matter, so it was unlikely that he was ensconced in a café, afloat on cheap red wine, discussing world politics with some newly befriended peon.

Vladislav, however, was immediately concerned and he told me that evening, 'I think something bad has happened to Alexei'.

An accident was possible, but certainly not the defection that we had joked about in the office – where and why would he possibly go?

The logical first step was to contact the police station and the hospitals in the area. But I didn't want to raise an alarm because of the presence of the ever-voracious press corps. I called the Race Committee Chairman, Rear Admiral Charles Williams, and caught him in his hotel just before he was going for his evening meal. Charles Williams was a Navy type in dress and protocol, but he was absolutely approachable and almost a father figure in the fleet. I had no qualms about disturbing him, there were no 'after hours', we were all 'on watch', as it were. I was confident he would know what to do.

'Right! Let me call one of those big-wigs at the yacht club. They know the police chief and hopefully we can keep a lid on it. You don't think he's defected?' He had to ask the obvious. 'Come and see me in my office in the morning.'

In spite of our caution, by midday on Tuesday I was besieged by telephone calls from around the world about the 'disappearance of Mr Gryshenko'. This was South America; the story had been leaked by the *jefe*. Of course, after the first night had come and gone, and Alexei hadn't shown up, we were all seriously worried. The joking was over.

Vladislav called the Soviet Embassy that morning. The ambassador knew about us; in fact, he was due to come to a barbeque in our honour that was being hosted by Franco, the owner of the Palace Hotel. His peons spent all day in the courtyard, digging up the lawn and erecting the grill for the *asado*, jabbering away in Spanish with big smiles on their faces, as a South American *asado* is always a fun, social affair even for the hired help. The ambassador arranged to alert all the prefectures in Uruguay, effectively putting out an 'all points bulletin', on Alexei. There was nothing to do but wait. Vladislav and Chumakov drove up and down the beaches looking for him, hoping he would be asleep on a sand dune. I stayed in the office, getting increasingly more nervous as I waited for the inevitable telephone call. As the time went by, it was becoming more and more obvious he hadn't had an accident, and we knew he hadn't defected.

Wednesday morning it came. Charles Williams called me to the race office. Without ceremony he came right out with it, 'Your chap's been found – hanged himself in the woods'. Although I had expected this, I was devastated by the reality itself. I sat down and looked out of his window, out to a benign sea. 'I know this is not the time to mention it, but you'll have to issue a statement soon, you know what the press will be like. It will make things much easier for you and the crew. Our press officer can help you when you're ready . . .'

I went back to the hotel and told Vladislav and the crew. It was one of the hardest days of my life. I was caught between remorse and still having to function to keep the project afloat. I issued a short statement later that morning, to the effect that we didn't know why he had committed suicide, but the pressures of the project had obviously been a contributing factor; how this man had taken it all so seriously, which was hard for us to understand. It all sounded so ridiculously simple – to sum up a man's life in 350 words.

The story spread quickly, as these things do. I went back to our office. The peons, now silent, with their heads hung low, were dismantling the *asado* and laying the turf back into the courtyard lawn. You could almost imagine a church bell tolling, but there was only the sound of a lifeless rain that began to fall.

'The poor devil, think of what he must have been going through,' said Hamish. He and I sat in the office looking at each other with red, watery eyes, but I was looking through, not at, him. I was lost in thought, as we all probably were, every one of us who had known him. 'Why wasn't I more kind to him? Why didn't I try to learn more Russian? It was obvious he had been adrift in his own ship. Why didn't I try to communicate with him the day of that damned sail change?'

Vladislav was of course shattered, and no doubt had similar memories, maybe of pushing Alexei too hard during the building, of putting too much on his shoulders. The crew to a man, must have felt the same, remembering isolated incidents of conflict or misunderstanding that all came flooding back, the revelation of a man silently crying out for help.

After The Doctor had sedated Vladislav, he and I went to Maldonado later that afternoon to identify the body. Hamish was sent off to the restaurants frequented by the crew to have the televisions taken down and put away. It was more than unfortunate, it was outrageous, that the media had been tipped off and had arrived at the scene before the police. They screened a full TV report, showing Alexei hanging from the tree. Of course, with the Latins' fascination with *la muerte*, this story ran for two days in Uruguay. Out of courtesy for the crew, we made an effort to shield them at least from the TV coverage. Syndicated on the wire service, the story went all around the world that afternoon; most countries only reported the death, but in the Soviet Union the TV ran a full documentary, including sailing shots of *Fazisi*, an interview with Alexei speaking about his 'life's dream' – and then Alexei hanging from the tree. All of this was seen by Alexei's wife and family in Kiev.

The press from four continents were now on to us almost without respite. The ones I knew were sympathetic; others I didn't seemed immediately crass and abrasive. 'Listen, tell me something about this guy Gryshenko. What kind of a guy was he, I need to do kind of a profile, follow me?' Or the woman from AP, 'Is this Mr Novak, the skipper of *Fazisi*?' 'Yes it is.' 'How do you spell Novak?' 'N O V A K' 'Where are you from in America?' 'Chicago' 'Now about this suicide . . .' I suddenly came to my senses, 'Lady why don't you . . .' – before I said it, I hung up the phone.

I suppose they were only doing their job, trying to search for a new angle. There was none. 'We didn't know why he committed suicide, but we certainly could assume that the pressures brought to bear by the project, by the rushed and often confused construction in Georgia, the panic in England where he spoke not one word of the language, his lengthy absence from his young family, all must have contributed to his illness. In his planned return to Kiev, possibly he saw himself as a failure.' If I said that once, I would repeat it hundreds of times over the next five months.

Apart from a man's death, which was an end to a story, we still had to deal with the future of the project, which was now in question. The crew got together and decided that they wanted to continue, but there were outside pressures bearing down on us, not from our peers, nor from the race organizers, nor from the Soviet ambassador, who was wholeheartedly behind our carrying on.

Instead, it came from the Soviet Union itself. 'Of course, we told you so,' 'You are all amateurs. We gave you *glasnost* and *perestroika*, and look what you've done with it – made a mess. The *Fazisi* project should come home!' One old Soviet circumnavigator was quoted in a newspaper as saying, 'Well, they didn't ask my help. They thought they could do it themselves. Obviously they could have used more experienced people who understood round the world sailing – like me!' Anti-*glasnost* hardliners, hard-done-by Black Sea sailors who had been overlooked in the crew selection, and anybody holding a grudge – all had a field day.

This was, in effect, idle talk, because nothing they could say could force Fazis to recall the project, but it could be stopped by an inquiry. And that was what some people in Kiev, friends and family of Alexei, were calling for. They didn't believe it was suicide and wanted a full investigation, which in South America would be measured in months, not days. We were due to start Leg II in two weeks' time.

On Thursday we had a wake for Alexei in the courtyard. His picture was put up on the wall above some flowers and a eulogy, written in English by Eugene, that read:

> The Love of Life
> Is burning, not smouldering
> Forward to the Flame of Life
> (N. Ostrovskii)

Our Captain, Alexei Gryshenko, captain of the yacht *Fazisi* is not going to start on the second leg of the most difficult race around the world. He disappeared in a flame of love for sailing.

For 22 years an experienced amateur yachtsman, he built himself two yachts with poetical names, *Gorobokonek* and *Gonta* on which he sailed more than 20,000 miles. On *Fazisi* he was the main builder, the main manager, the main technician, main engineer and captain, simultaneously since October last year.

During an around the world race one year condenses five years of normal life. Being in love with sailing and the best example of responsibility, he adopted long before the official start this high tempo – a crazy gallop of preparation for an around the world race.

Alexei won! He condensed the time and made a fantastic volume of work and as a result our boat started.

Unfortunately for victory we have to pay. The payment is our health and life. The life strings of Alexei were overloaded. The first leg is also the last for him.

Sleep quietly, our friend. You will be in our minds and we will finish this marathon together.

Crew of the Yacht Fazisi

Almost every yacht in the fleet sent representatives. Although the Irish from *NCB* were present, it was not an Irish affair, but very solemn and quiet as one by one, the visitors drank the red wine, read the eulogy and went on their way.

Almost immediately, the crew, for the first time, were mobilized into working as a team. Without myself, or Vladislav and Chumakov, they organized an all-afternoon meeting on the Friday. They drew up a lengthy document, edited by Anatoly, listing the many grievances they had with the Fazis administration and signed their names to each section before faxing it to Tichov in Moscow. It was kind of a sailing-man's Magna Carta, and could have been written by Fletcher Christian himself. They wanted more communication from Fazis, a direct say in all things concerning the project. They wanted a rest – either to be sent home in turns to see their families, or to have their families come to one of the stopovers. They wanted fair pay for a fair day's work. They wanted Chumakov out! They wanted me to skipper the boat, with no Soviet co-skipper, at least for the next leg. A lot of what they were saying could be construed as an indictment of Alexei's suicide, laying bare the past failings which they didn't want to see happen again.

Meanwhile, we all became preoccupied in getting the

green light from Fazis, who was under considerable pressure to reconsider our continuing. The ambassador sent positive memos to the government, Charles Williams and the Whitbread people issued a statement saying we had to continue as an act of international goodwill, and Vladislav started to draft articles for the Soviet newspapers rebutting their attacks. Once again, he was put under an immense burden, with his credibility under direct attack back home.

That evening Igor got on the phone to Kiev to talk to Alexei's friends and family to try to put the fire out and convince them that he did in fact commit suicide. The Doctor and I were scheduled to appear the next day at the Maldonado police station to make an official statement, in hopes of putting the whole question of foul play to rest.

Alexei had left a suicide note, which didn't say anything more profound than that he asked forgiveness from his mother, wife and baby, and said 'This is the best way out. I've been away from home so long'. The Doctor and I had to verify his hand-writing, which was easy to do as his last message was written in the notebook he kept for working on the boat.

The magistrate then appeared and escorted me into a little room, leaving The Doctor waiting in the lobby for his turn. The magistrate was a woman. This was made clear by her black leather skirt, fishnet stockings, ruby red lipstick and a see-through chiffon blouse. I was relieved when a weedy little clerk came in with a high-school kid as interpreter, not that they could help me if I was attacked by this black widow spider. From the way she crossed her legs, it was obvious that, like most South American civil servants, she was corruptible. While seductively sipping her Coca Cola through a straw, she started to work on me through the interpreter: 'How well did you know Mr Gryshenko?' 'Who was in charge of the boat?' 'How was your relationship with Mr Gryshenko?' *ad infinitum*. I was asked to recognize Mr Gryshenko, not from the many photos available while he was still alive, but the one showing him hanging from the tree. 'Yes that's him,' I answered, starting to become a little nauseated. It was when she brought out a brown paper envelope and asked me to identify the rope that I became really disgusted. I didn't know whether to answer 'yes' and become paranoid or 'no' and pretend that I didn't recognize the old braided rope cover from an afterguy that we had been using as a sail tie. The 'inquiry' ended, and I can only remember it as being not only quite extraordinary, but totally unnecessary.

After another week of speculation, Fazis gave us the official go-ahead. The Kiev faction backed off and things quietened down. Alexei's body was dispatched back to Kiev with help from the Soviet Embassy, and the crew returned to work, with a week lost from the schedule.

On 12 October, nine days after his death, we observed the orthodox tradition of having a farewell dinner 'with' Alexei. Valeri Chumakov, Juki and The Doctor cooked a big meal in the hotel kitchen, to which only the crew and close friends were invited. Juki made several speeches and toasts, so did a few of the others, and it was a more light-hearted affair than the wake – especially when Monica, thinking it would be cordial to change her seat to the other end of the table for dessert, sat in the only empty chair, complete with an untouched place setting. With a wry, and not an unfriendly smile, Eugene said, 'Monica, you have just sat on Alexei's lap. I think he probably would have enjoyed that.'

The week before the start our back-up team arrived: Dale Tremain from New Zealand, veteran of the Whitbread in 1981/82 on *Outward Bound*; Jim Saunders from England, and Roland Jourdain, 'Bilou' to his friends, a veteran of the Whitbread in 1985/86 on *Côte d'Or* skippered by Eric Tabarly, and for the last four years a prime mover on the French Grand Prix multi-hull circuit. Without any speeches or time to settle in, like the professionals that they all were, they immediately got down to work and took up the slack to complete the worklist.

Again it was a panic to get it all done. Four new sails arrived at the eleventh hour. The new mainsail, a $35,000 investment, was hoisted on the Thursday, but the locations for the reef reinforcements were in the wrong place! This was a major problem as our halyard locking system would not work with this sail, and without it the mast becomes marginally unstable as it relieves the downward compression load of the halyard.

North Sails were highly embarrassed, but there was no time to change it before Fremantle. We decided to carry it as an emergency spare and use the old main which, after one leg, was showing normal signs of wear and tear.

Vladislav and Chumakov were also busy successfully negotiating the impossible – a sponsorship deal out of Uruguay. The Otegui Wool Exporting Company in Montevideo gave us $15,000 in return for some signage on the hull and flags, and a publicity spot on television. The offer would be repeated when we returned in March. The bigger picture, back in Europe, was not looking hopeful, however. ASM came up with nothing, as expected, and other independent agents like Jock Wishart also drew a blank, understandably after Alexei's suicide. Everyone was waiting for things to clarify.

On the Thursday before the start the Duchess of York, while on holiday in Argentina and Uruguay, visited a few of the yachts. She was on loan to Whitbreads to present the prizes, which she did on the Tuesday.

We were informed of her intended visit days in advance. Unnecessary tie straightening and unusual shoulder wagging by Rear Admiral Williams and the Whitbread directors were always good indicators that someone from the royal family might be lurking about. We were informed of her intended visit to the fleet days in advance; the covert operation was run with the efficiency of the D-Day landing. 'Right, the Duchess will be on board at 1110 sharp and stay for 10 minutes. Have your boys looking smart!' he said the day before.

I repeated my orders to the crew. I didn't have to chase them on this one. Anatoly took over and had the crew completely clean the boat, inside and out. On the day, they were there on time, anticipating her arrival, all in clean white *Fazisi* shirts – even Igor, the arch nonconformist, who, if he will wear the crew uniform at all, then it will be sure to be begreased and torn.

The Duchess stepped down to the decks of *Fazisi* from the heights of *Steinlager 2* which lay alongside. Resisting the temptation to look up her skirt as I led her down the companionway ladder, the crew and I gave her a proper tour of the Russian Submarine. I think she was most impressed that we had all survived the living conditions below decks.

No doubt she told Peter Blake the same on *Steinlager*, but this time I think the platitude was said in all seriousness. (The Official Secrets Act prevents me repeating what she really said.) She graciously posed for the pictures, the crew standing around her with big smiles, proving that these Russians are more white than red, while the Rear Admiral fidgeted nervously on the dock – she had been on board for 20 minutes and his troops ashore were under fire.

Two mornings later we were in the starting area, making ready for the 7,500 mile bash through the Southern Ocean to Fremantle, the toughest leg of the race. Vladislav, Chumakov and Nodari waved us good-bye from a motorboat. So did Hamish and Monica. She was going on to Freo, but Hamish was off to Antarctica for another expedition, declining the offer of continuing on as our shore manager. He is a man of the mountains and the sea; possibly the indignity of my last request that he run down to the corner kiosk and buy me four pencils and a camera lens cap, made his mind up for good. I can hardly blame him.

Most of the journalists come to the stopovers only for the arrival of the fleet, writing their stories of what happens offshore. After three and a half weeks in Uruguay, the real-life stories began to emerge and not only the suicide on *Fazisi*; the fact that *L'Esprit de Liberté*'s project manager had disappeared with all the project's money and the crews' passports; the dismissal of *Satquote British Defender*'s skipper for incompetence; the death of Janne Gustafsson from *The Card* in a motorcycle accident; an uncomplimentary internal memo from the skipper of *NCB Ireland* to his syndicate leaked to the Irish press. There are close to 600 sailors, administrators and press people, some with families, who travel around the world with the Whitbread for almost one year. It is a world of itself where people come and go, some die, get married or divorced, not doubt a few births are conceived along the way too.

Ian Wooldridge from the *Daily Mail* had the wisdom to come to Uruguay late in the stopover, and says it better in the first paragraph of his article on 17 October: 'If Frederick Forsyth were to cram his next blockbuster with the following cast his fiction would lose all credibility.'

9

Leg Two – War and Peace

By popular request, I was asked to play a lower profile on Leg II. I agreed, for the sake of the continuity of the project, and besides, I had Jim, Dale and Bilou to take up the slack. So for the first time in my sailing career I chose not to stand a watch, to do less work – effectively letting the Soviets sail *Fazisi* themselves. I would come up only for the heavy weather sail-changes and tricky steering conditions and otherwise stick to the tactics and the radio work. In case this system proved to be a success, I brought along Tolstoy's epic to pass the time, a book I was still struggling to read.

The skipper of *Rothmans*, Lawrie Smith, had sparked a controversy in Uruguay when he accused Peter Blake of cheating on *Steinlager*'s rating. He threatened to protest when they got to Auckland and have the boat remeasured. Although it was a preposterous accusation that the crown prince of the Whitbread could be fiddling anything, Smith had cause to complain because once again, within a matter of hours after the start, *Steinlager* was substantially ahead of the fleet in the light airs, apparently unassailable by the other, better, sloops and even the other ketches.

A feeble northerly blew for the first two days and we consequently dropped behind, having difficulty steering as low as the others. They also picked up more wind a bit further south and sailed even farther away from us. That, however, was not our immediate concern. Far more significant than the results was the fact that, only a day out, we faced the prospect of sailing the entire leg without hot food because the gas regulator packed up. The Doctor said, 'My Captain, cooker not working.'

'OK, let's try the spare regulator,' I said.

Twelve moonfaced Soviets could not tell me where it was, but finally Viktor Kamkin admitted to me, 'In container'.

Our survival was not in question; cold porridge oats and muesli can be palatable; but the prospect of cold powdered egg and freeze-dried rice all the way across the Southern Ocean to Fremantle was very grim. Luckily, Igor and Viktor, mechanical wizards, working with matchsticks and sawn-off bolts, contrived to jury rig it – and it worked, at least for the first few days.

Eugene was now a watch captain with Bilou for assistance, opposite Anatoly who had Dale and Jim. For the first three days I hardly came on deck and things went incredibly smoothly – which may have meant something that was not lost on me.

On the afternoon of 30 October we celebrated Viktor Yasykov's 41st birthday with brandy, vodka and tea in the cockpit. Raw cloves of garlic, standard fare for all occasions, were popped straight into the mouth like candy, certainly leaving a more lasting impression of the event than would the traditional cake or biscuits. It was a calm evening and the fiery sunset colours were paling out in sombre tones that suited the sad Russian music echoing from the tape player below. We swapped stories and jokes well into the dark. I was more at ease than I had ever been on *Fazisi* and can remember feeling very happy to be there. Even the recalcitrant Igor and I were striking up a pleasant rapport.

Viktor was one of our mastmen, opposite Edgar. He was more quiet and contemplative than the others, his misty blue eyes often staring out to sea through a crop of blond hair, while the others were jabbering away about trivialities. He told me he dreamed of sailing in the 'northern seas' with his home-built 30-foot wooden cruising boat. He liked the cold and had Arctic experience, having worked in the fishing fleet for a while near the Kamchatka Peninsula, north of the Sea of Japan. A loner, he admired the single-handed navigators and treasured a signed copy of Robin Knox-Johnston's book *A World of My Own*, given to him when he met the author in Southampton. He was a keen photographer and had traded his home-ground rigging knife with a carved wooden handle, a work of art, for Mugsy's Nikonos IV underwater camera during Leg I and was forever after on the lookout for a good photo.

For all of these attributes, and in spite of having the physique of an 18-year-old gymnast, he was pronounced as having psychological problems by The Doctor, a few days later – 'cabin fever' again – and was temporarily sedated, like the political prisoners in Solzhenitsyn's *Cancer Ward*. I was later told by several of the crew that, like a lot of them, he was suffering from the conflict of wanting to go home to see his family, and also wanting to continue in the race.

The reverie of the birthday party came to an abrupt end when a southeasterly filled without warning, forcing a panic change to the No. 3 genoa, with one reef in the mainsail. Immediately the boat came to life, sliding along the old swell while hacking her way into the new head sea. In minutes, water began to cascade across the decks and pour down hatches that should have been closed. We were rail down, fully pressed, with the prospect of a tough night ahead.

The abrupt change was, in a word, miserable. Although only 40° South, it was already getting cold. I woke up around midnight feeling violently ill, a combination of The Doctor's food, the motion, the diesel fumes from Juri's experiments with the heating system, and not a little anxiety. After a desperate struggle with the hatch dogs, mouth already full, I just mounted the aft companionway ladder before exploding on the afterdeck. No one saw what might have been an embarrassing situation, and the next green wave that combed the entire deck cleaned the mess away.

By late the following morning the wind had eased and gone more southerly, and once again we were reaching just south of east, but by this time well behind most of the fleet save for *Belmont Finland*. Our tactical plan was not to go below 50° South, the idea being that any easterly travelling depression near that latitude would put the southern contingent into the wind. We would still be running downwind just to the north while in the westerly winds which always rotate in a clockwise direction around low pressure systems in the southern hemisphere. The gain in going further south was a closer approximation to the Great Circle course – the straight line between two points on the globe. Fewer miles, but more risk of headwinds, is therefore the effective tactical trade-off in any Southern Ocean passage.

As usual I had been harping on about boatspeed (part of my job); how a loss of only a tenth of a knot in speed due to bad steering or bad sail-trim loses 2.4 miles per day. During the frustrations of Leg I, I had even written a multiplication table on the boom in marking pen: 0.2 knots=4.8 miles per day, 0.5 knots=12 miles per day, and so on, with the addendum 'THINK BOATSPEED!'

While in Uruguay, the Soviets had got to know some of the other crews, and how they operate. On 1 November I came on deck to find they had devised a similar multiplication system of their own, obviously intended for the management: a 350 mile day=$600 per man, a 325 mile day=$440 per man, etc. 'Well,' I said to Jim, 'if the Soviets don't win any prizes for sailing a boat around the world, they will surely realize what makes the world go round.'

That same day, *Creightons Naturally*, one of two British maxis in the cruising division, reported they had to turn back for Punta to make repairs to their mast. The all-girl crew on *Maiden* also reported trouble with an unwieldy steering system, and I overheard skipper Tracy Edwards verbally castigating their all-male shore crew for 'changing the gearing'. They also had troubles with cooking gas. They reckoned it was dirty gas, and had temporarily solved the problem by inserting a cigarette filter into the regulator, a clever solution which even impressed Igor. Our gas was again failing intermittently, but the cigarette trick didn't seem to work and we had a cold lunch that day while another solution was sought.

The next day Edgar had to go aloft twice in the boatswain's chair to the very top of the mast in order to fix the halyard locking system. Apparently Anatoly's 0400–0800 watch that morning had broken the trip line when they took a reef out. While Edgar gripped the thin topmast pole swinging in wide arcs across the sky, Eugene sarcastically reviled the crew. Now that he had a command position, he was quickly

121

losing patience. In an ironic tone of voice, as though he was lecturing me, 'There are only three kinds of halyards on this boat, the main halyard, the spinnaker halyard and the genoa halyard. They are all different colours. It is not too difficult to figure it out!' He told me later, 'If I tell the Crocodile, for example, you know, the navigator, to lower spinnaker halyard, he is completely lost – after 6,000 miles sailing!'

The Crocodile was the playboy of the crew, tall, the best looking, and the only one with a good set of teeth. He was obviously a well bred Russian, and educated in an academic family. His mother works as a researcher for the space programme and he has 'priviliged citizen' written all over him. If he wasn't too astute on deck, he was, however, a good ambassador for *Fazisi*, always friendly, with a big smile for everyone, never afraid to test his amusing style of English on anyone who would listen. He was proud to have learned all the Kiwi slang and wouldn't pass up a chance to yell at them, about nothing at all, 'She's a beauty mate! Da Da! She'll be right!'

A merchant ship's navigator, he had been to Cuba on an Atlantic tour, and had also spent eight months on a Soviet Tall Ship in Europe. I'm not sure how much he knew about modern navigation, but when he identified Jupiter in the crescent of a waxing moon, I had to challenge him. Not to be upstaged, as one who was educated on the sea before the time of satellite navigation, I hastily claimed it was the star Kaus Australis. We bet £30 on it, his lead not mine. After a detailed investigation in the *Nautical Almanac* it turned out to be Saturn, so we were both wrong – a good thing for the Crocodile because he could hardly afford to pay me on Chumakov's meagre subsistence salary of $16 a day – the Soviet standard for people overseas. It was also good for me because it saved total embarrassment.

Communicating with the shore was becoming more and more infrequent the further south and east we went. Besides giving interviews and press reports I was frequently in touch with London about the financial situation. With every mile sailed closer to Australia, the nearer we were to the inevitable crisis of insolvency. We had spent a large portion of the loan before the start of the second leg and I was sure there was not enough left to pay for the Fremantle stopover.

'I'm working on this company in Moscow, via the Pencil Group who are another PR company here in London,' the scratchy radio voice of Jock Wishart said to me. 'We can't tell you who the company is yet, but if I mentioned the name, you would recognize it, it's one of the biggest in the Soviet Union. They've got over the suicide business, and anyway, it's the only lead I've got.'

'Have you heard anything from Fazis or Vladislav?' I asked him.

'Nothing at all. Very difficult to get a fax through to Moscow. Look, don't worry about all of this, just sail the boat, there's nothing you can do from out there.'

I was getting bored with the light weather, and recorded as such in my diary, recounting a typical day. 'Sleep to 0800 to catch a late breakfast, listen to the 1130 GMT radio sched, plot the positions, calculate the gains and losses. Lunch is the high point of the day which takes place at 1330, then it's a fair pull to the 1620 weather map from Buenos Aires, now out of range! The dinner at 1930 (Doctor having gone sour) is not so exciting and the 2330 radio sched is my last chore of the day before turning into my bunk for a fitful sleep jammed underneath the deck head, like on a One Tonner, a boat I have always refused to sail on. I have not spent any time on deck, save to relieve myself, in two and a half days, my all-time record! (Soon to be extended as a miserable rain has started in a weak low and associated front).'

Fisher & Paykel had stolen the lead from *Steinlager* and was now 80 miles ahead of her rival, having gone further south. At 50° 40' south, it was an extreme position, but so far it had paid off. *Martela* and *Gatorade*, spread out behind her, were also deeper south and it was not surprising that these three were the first to see ice on 5 November.

In what I thought was a discreet tone of voice, *Rothmans* was informed by *Fisher & Paykel* that they had earlier passed a big iceberg while travelling in the fog, and it was now only four miles dead in the tracks of *Rothmans*' reported position! The Brits had been sailing in the New Zealanders' wake, and both Roger Nilson, skipper of *The Card*, and I speculated over

123

the radio that it might be a ruse to make *Rothmans* nervous and play conservative for the night. The next morning *Union Bank of Finland* came on and reported that they had seen the same berg, and almost immediately *Fisher & Paykel*'s skipper Grant Dalton came on the air. 'I want an apology from Skip Novak and Roger Nilson!'

I immediately answered him. 'OK Grant, I apologize. But next time tell the rest of us, LOUD AND CLEAR!'

Some time later all doubt was dispelled as *Gatorade*, *The Card* and *UBF* also sighted other icebergs. A wave of alertness and maybe not a little paranoia descended on the fleet and although we would see only two icebergs during the rest of the leg, there were so many reports of icebergs from the fleet further south that I got fed up and stopped writing them down.

The fog persisted throughout 5 November and into the 6th. Even the many kinds of albatross and petrels, perennial voyagers in the wastes of the Southern Ocean, who follow passing ships by circumscribing wide ellipses from bow to stern, were sometimes lost in the soup. We had crossed the Antarctic Convergence, a boundary so apparent it might as well have been signposted. Within a few hours we left the relatively warmer sub-Antarctic water and crossed into the colder thermocline that dives below it. Here, where warm water meets cold, the Antarctic krill support the base of a pyramidal food chain with the great blue whales perching precariously on the top. And it's cold! The sea drops to 2°–4°C, and when the wind blows from the southerly quarter, it snows instead of rains. In extreme weather the moisture-laden air can lay inches of heavy ice rime on decks and rigging, adversely affecting the boat's stability. A westerly gale completes the scenario: this is what sailing in the Southern Ocean is all about.

Up until now we had been complacent. If these easy conditions persisted, it would be hard to justify having four Westerners on board for the next leg, as the Soviets were doing fine. But there will always be wind in the Southern Ocean, somewhere, sometime. The morning weather map from Pretoria in South Africa showed a gale on the way, developing from a deep low to the southwest at 60° South.

As early as mid afternoon we started getting it. Whether the Soviets cared or not was unclear, but the four of us were itching for a blow.

Late that evening the big heavy spinnaker was up in a 35-knot northwester. Without any damage we rounded up twice before I called for the 'storm chute'. With the smaller, stronger sail, and a reef in the mainsail as well, we were right back on footing with the wind gusting to 38 knots.

We had no control problems. Bilou, Dale, Jim, Edgar and I did most of the steering, in superb surfing conditions, although *Fazisi* spent most of her time underwater and not on it. The survival suits we had ordered from Helly Hansen in Norway, at great expense, were now worth their weight in gold, as it was impossible to stay dry with even the heaviest of foul-weather gear. Similar to a diver's drysuit, they are worn over fibre pile thermals, have rubber face and wrist seals, and pyjama feet that go into sea boots – very effective for keeping out the water that was coming on board as though sprayed from a water cannon. By midnight even the storm chute was too much, so we dropped it and flew a 'reaching genoa' on the spinnaker pole, a good safe rig for the night, which also gave the other guys a chance for some of the fun driving.

We crossed the Greenwich Meridian the next morning. It was also a holiday in the Soviet Union to celebrate the anniversary of the great October Revolution. The two Communist Party members on board, Edgar and The Doctor, were not fêted by the others, nor did they preach the party line, but Eugene was pleased to hear on the BBC that the Moldavian Popular Front had staged a mass protest and disrupted the celebration. They were put down by the Soviet police, but their desire to reunite with Romania was believed to have grown stronger.

For the next two days we struggled through the westerly storm – changing spinnakers, packing spinnakers, taking reefs, shaking them out again, and making repairs to an unending supply of broken fittings and chafed pieces of rigging and sails. The good news was that we were going fast, averaging over 360 miles per day for three days in a row and slowly gaining lost ground on the fleet from 13th to 9th position. We were doing damn well, but there were still 4,000 miles to go and a lot of room for error.

It came the next evening. Earlier, I had dictated my weekly article to the *Daily Telegraph* over the radio, bragging about how we had run 195 miles in 12 hours, aspiring to the sought-after 400-mile day, without major damage. It was spectacular sailing, especially in the half moonlight, ripping white furrows down some of the biggest and longest waves any of us have ever seen.

I had just finished an hour of steering, cracking off 25 knot surfs, and staying on the waves for what seemed like minutes. I was disappointed to have to go below to do the 2300 GMT radio sched. I gave Edgar the wheel, with Dale backing him up, but as soon as I was at the chart table, I felt less confident as the boat violently heaved and buffeted, not like a boat on the ocean, but with the motion helpless airline passengers experience when flying through the turbulence of a thunder cloud. I just had time to tune the radio in, when at the bottom of a wave, *Fazisi* banked sharply to port and stalled in full flight. We had broached badly, side on to the wind and sea. Immediately, the Gatling gun report of the flogging spinnaker and the unpleasant list of the hull at 70° to the horizontal made it clear to anyone who has experienced this before that we were in for wholesale damage.

Minutes went by as I struggled to get back into my foul-weather gear and harness, while we lay on our side. Then, just as suddenly as we had broached, a wave caught the bow, pushed it downwind and we righted level, only to go off on the next wave at speed, but not before the spinnaker pole had bent itself double, and the spinnaker had inconveniently wrapped itself around the headstay and braided itself into the spinnaker net, a device designed specifically to prevent all of this.

I was sure that we were in for a four-hour spell of 'down time', when you have to untangle everything, pick up the pieces and then summon the nerve to put up another sail – in a pitch black night of a howling gale. Miraculously, with Dale and Jim's quick thinking, they got the spinnaker and net down before it knotted and jammed, cleared the decks and had the 'chicken chute', the smallest downwind sail on the boat and one that described our present state of mind, ready to hoist within an hour and a half of the disaster. We checked everything, preset all the sheets and guys. The sail was 'stopped', that is, bound up in a sausage with woollen thread so it could be hoisted to the top with no risk of opening prematurely.

I put our best driver, Bilou, on the wheel. We hoisted the spinnaker, checked that our life harnesses were all clipped in and the foredeck was clear.

'OK, bring on the sheet!' As soon as the first wool broke, the sail unzipped itself, with no further encouragement, and opened with the shock of a parachute at terminal velocity, promptly knocking most of us off our feet into the bottom of the cockpits. Almost immediately, we were surfing again at 25 knots.

Anatoly took over from Bilou an hour later and was so intent on steering that an hour after that he had to be physically thrown off by Jim. He collapsed in a heap in the bottom of the cockpit which still was half full of water from the last wave. You would think he would have been angry, but he only looked up at no one, smiled and said 'Fantastic!' Even if they didn't say it, most of the Soviets were enjoying this battle.

After twenty hours without sleep, when first light was just breaking, I went below after we had changed to the poled out 'reaching genoa' again as the wind was topping 40 knots and the sea was giving even Bilou, Dale and Jim control problems. With this rig we all could relax a bit; we all needed it.

Thirty minutes later I was pinned almost upside down in my bunk, and struggling to get out. The Elephant had broached! It lasted only for the time it took for the wave to pass, but unfortunately the wire guy that holds the spinnaker pole in position broke, the pole then careered into the headstay, doubled over like a piece of spaghetti and shattered the plastic headfoil into a thousand pieces. Current score: 2 useless spinnaker poles, no headfoil (impossible to hoist a genoa in the short term), miscellaneous broken pieces of running rigging, two torn spinnakers and what must have been a tonne of water sloshing around the cabin, accumulated from far too many waves coming down the hatches.

I ordered all hands up to make repairs: Eugene and Igor set up a make-shift machine-shop in the forepeak and repaired the poles, drilling the rivet holes for the aluminium joining sleeve by hand, as we had swamped the 220 volt inverter which drives our power tools. Valeri, Edgar and Juki repaired the sails, Anatoly respliced new afterguys and sheets, and since we had no spare headfoil ('In container' again) we had to use carabiners as hanks on the genoas. Juri and others pumped the bilges, rearranged the sails and straightened up below. It took us 24 hours to get the gear back in full order and by then the wind had finally died, swinging back in the north. We had run over 2,000 miles on the strength of one major depression! We had also survived.

Eugene will never forget that storm, because it was almost the last thing he ever remembered. Just as the wind was beginning to ease, on 10 November, when everyone was beginning to relax and let their guard down, a freak wave came aboard over the starboard beam and laid the boat momentarily on its side. When she righted, Eugene was hanging on to the end of the boom, half in, half out of the water! He had been changing positions from spinnaker sheet to the wheel, his harness had not been clipped in and he had been washed clean overboard. As the boat took off on another wave, he grappled himself, hand over hand, back along the 20 feet of mainsheet until Bilou and Edgar could hoist him up and over the lifelines. We had been close to losing him. When he was back on the deck he seemed OK when he declared 'These survival suits are perfect!' but later on, when he had a chance to think about what had happened, he became visibly shaken. He asked The Doctor for a cup of tea, a reasonable request under the circumstances. The Doctor, becoming increasingly unpopular for a variety of reasons, said to him, 'Help yourself'.

The next evening we were back to full strength and ready to enjoy the evening meal in peace, the hacksaws, hammers and drills now laid to rest. If the tinned spam, made in the People's Republic of China, which I called Chinese Dog and was fit for Russian cats, was not as appetizing as it could have been, served uncooked afloat in a lukewarm soup, the ambience made up for it. Comforting steam issues from the pressure cooker announcing the countdown to another thin gruel; Vladimir Vysotsky bellows away on the tape player and Juki produces another contraband bottle of Armenian brandy. We sit on the sails, plates in our laps and discuss the carnage wrought by the last storm – how, in minutes, thousands of pounds worth of equipment were reduced to useless rubble, what must be, to a Soviet's way of thinking, an incredible waste. At these times, the atmosphere below reminds me of those Russian cafés, when you can find them – small and steamy with a feeling of togetherness, the plates and spoons a bit greasy and the food produced without ceremony, but always with a home-cooked flair. It was always after these trials in heavy weather that I have the fondest memories of the crew, trials of survival that bring people together and not insignificant 'discussions' of sailing technique, or for that matter discussions of significant politics, that usually pull people apart.

We were pleased with ourselves, but even happier when we heard the damage reports that the rest of the fleet was now admitting. *NCB* had broken a boom and was running without a mainsail, *The Card* had slowed right down with broken spinnaker poles, a damaged headfoil, several blown spinnakers and a crewman's broken arm. *Fisher & Paykel* reported broken blocks, padeyes and running rigging, while *Steinlager 2*, never giving any information away, was overheard on the radio to New Zealand as saying, 'We are now up and running again'.

Anatoly admitted to me that the Soviet crew did not have the experience and were not good enough to steer in extreme conditions, evidenced by the fact that all our broaches were committed by those they thought were the better drivers. In his usual methodical fashion, he showed me engineering sketches he had made to refute Edgar's opinion on the correct direction to turn the wheel in a broaching situation. Edgar had had it all wrong and Anatoly had the proof!

Dale, Bilou and Jim were given Anatoly's seal of approval. Dale was incredibly laid back, never getting riled in spite of the most frustrating situation. He was therefore well liked by the Soviets – though if that was the pattern, it doesn't say much for my popularity at any time. Bilou, on the other hand, was more aggressive. Having just come from grand-prix multihull racing in France, he was used to sailing with the best; in fact, Bilou was the best. But he was young, and took it to heart when the Soviets slacked off in the lighter weather after the storm.

'Look, *mon cher*,' I told him when he stormed below after having a row with Igor. 'I went through the same thing. Take my advice, appreciate this ride for what it is – a cultural experience – and try to relax.'

'*Oui, oui, Chef*, you are right, *mais c'est incroyable, incroyable, bordel!*'

Jim was somewhere in the middle ground. In addition to being an asset in every department (to the extent that one day he volunteered to go to the top of the mast in a gale to sort out the halyard lock) his saving grace with the crew was that they probably could never understand his muffled accent when he shouted at them. Apart from finding Anatoly the chief bane of his life, he was enjoying himself immensely, working the deck on a submarine in the toughest leg of the toughest race around the world. His only real concern was that the Soviets were acquiring a taste for his Earl Grey Tea Bags that he guarded religiously in his private locker.

Not so his wife Liz, who was back in England, reading the papers, seriously concerned about Jim's safety. On radio sched on 13 November we were informed that two crewmen from *Creightons Naturally* had been lost overboard during a violent broach. One was recovered, suffering from hypothermia, after 20 minutes in the water. The other, Tony Phillips, was recovered after 30 minutes, but could not be revived. Both men had lifejackets on and were equipped with personal flares and locater radio beacons, but had not been clipped on with their harnesses. By 16 November, there had been reports of seven men swept overboard. Miraculously all were recovered.

The press back in Britain were having a field day with these stories. Quite a few were released to the media second- and third-hand, with the result that fundamentally inaccurate stories were being published. The Race Committee issued a notice to the fleet on 16 November, via Portishead Radio, with this in mind:

To All Whitbread Competitors

With the numbers of crewmembers being swept overboard and recovered increasing, it is essential that these incidents are reported to Race HQ by the yacht concerned. This should be either direct or through the duty yacht. By this means, Race HQ will be able to deal with rumours originating outside the Race organization, thereby reducing unnecessary alarm to dependants and the public.

Charles Williams

After this spell of high drama, we settled down, although briefly, to contemplating domestic affairs. The diesel heater was always a big topic of speculation – whether it would continue to work until we left 50° South and started to climb north. Juri had coaxed it through several flooding episodes, rigging a makeshift exhaust after the original was washed overboard, and suffered the inconvenience of being woken up at any time, without pity, when it mysteriously turned itself off. Without our heater, which ran 24 hours a day, we had no dry locker, which meant no dry clothes. In *Fazisi*, which was a veritable sponge below, they were about our only creature comfort.

We had been at sea almost three weeks, cooped up in a yacht that was more like a damp sardine tin, so it was understandable that our living conditions could only be accurately described as despicable. Even Bilou was disgusted and for a Frenchman that was saying something. Granted he was from the young generation and we were using the old French system as regards tidying up – meaning we didn't. The lack of space, the fact that we had no bilge (rather we lived in it) and The Doctor's strange attitude to cleanliness in the galley, which, after all, is the heart of any vessel, made any clean-up operation futile.

Until Viktor Yasykov took over one day in desperation. He cooked an attractive omelette with chopped raw garlic on top, a breakfast that was, to borrow explorer/sailor Bill Tilman's description, 'fit for a glass case'. He then proceeded to clean and sterilize the entire galley, the work surfaces having been covered with a liberal layer of smeared butter and

131

grease impregnated with spilled coffee and sugar. He even organized the food stuffs that had become a hodgepodge of half-opened freeze-dried food bags, rotten cabbages and partly used tins of Chinese Dog. Without anyone having to say it, we all realized, as probably did The Doctor, that he had earned his ticket home.

We were holding on to ninth place and trying to decide whether to pass north or south of Kerguelen Island when the next storm hit us on 16 November. Kerguelen, a little known outpost in the middle of the Southern Indian Ocean, boasts a meteorological station and had been predicting storm force winds ranging from another deep low travelling to the south of the fleet. Kerguelen was also a turning point – a *de facto* mark of the course, where most of the fleet would leave the 50th parallel and begin to head north to Fremantle, which was still 2,300 miles away. But unlike the big orange inflatable buoy they use in the America's Cup, this mark was 60 miles across and therefore also became an obstacle to avoid.

We changed our mind twice on the approach, but finally opted for the northern route, as did *Fisher & Paykel*, *Fortuna* and *UBF*. Struggling in the wind that was still slightly north of west, we found ourselves only 20 miles off the rugged northwest tip of the island late that afternoon. Then the front came through and the wind went sharply into the southwest, blowing with such ferocity that to change directions we had to take down the storm spinnaker and tack the boat through the eye of the wind rather than risk the gybe. Before long it was blowing a sustained 50 knots. Then it started to snow. Then it got dark. We stormed off northeast with only a reefed mainsail, unable to hoist anything forward because of a horrendously bad sea condition from the effects of the island. We had been going the fastest we had ever gone, so we had no desire to push our luck.

At 2200 Eugene came below down the aft hatch. Dripping icy seawater all over the chart, he ripped off the hood to his survival suit, shook his head like a dog does after a bath, and said to me mockingly, 'You know the spare mainsail? That was tied to the deck back aft? Now overboard, lost!' It had not been tied down well enough. Fine. One wave, $35,000 later.

In the early hours of the morning we put the reacher genoa up on the spinnaker pole and began to hurtle down the waves even faster. The sea was still irregular, a bad cross sea from the front made steering difficult, and in our efforts to steer as high as possible we were dipping the end of the boom in the water with alarming frequency. We were aware of this and had the hydraulic ram that holds it down fully released and the preventer line that keeps it forward quite slack, giving it as much free movement as possible. Still, one too many times and the boom snapped, like well seasoned firewood, about one third from the inboard end.

The crew of *Fazisi* are called a Soviet crew, but like all things Soviet, they are really international. The Georgians never see eye to eye with the Russians and the Ukrainians are always arguing with the Moldavian and the Latvian. All this bickering is carried out with far more righteousness than, say, an Englishman would contest the price of a bottle of whisky with a Scotsman. The differences run fundamentally much deeper.

So if the boom breaking was unfortunate, it had the benefit of getting everyone in the crew, including the 'Central Committee' of foreign advisors and the 'Supreme Commander' himself, to pull together for a change, one of the few times in *Fazisi*'s history. There is nothing like a disaster to focus effort, nothing like simple hard work under trying circumstances to keep otherwise wandering minds occupied – and I certainly include myself in this category.

It took four hours for the 16 of us to square this new mess away. First we had to arrest and secure the two pieces of boom which were flailing dangerously across the deck which was rolling rail to rail, still in the height of the storm. Then the mainsail had to be lowered inch by inch, which was an incredible struggle as the force of the wind had it plastered like *papier mâché* against the mast. With the main folded and stowed, the booms were then dismantled and lashed to the deck. A storm trysail was hoisted in place of the mainsail, but 8 hours later the wind was on the way down and we were down on speed due to our lack of sail area. We then began a painful repair to the foot of the mainsail which had been torn, working barehanded with needle and thread along the side deck which was frequently underwater.

The effort paid off, however, because within 12 hours of the damage, just as the wind was dropping again, we rehoisted a loose footed mainsail and began to rig an outrigger with a spinnaker pole. It wasn't perfect, but we had the sail area back on her, and were back at speed.

Eugene and Igor reckoned the boom was irreparable, based on a mathematical extrapolation of how long it takes to drill a hole by hand through so many millimetres of aluminium multiplied by the number of holes required to make the join. From the length of time it took to repair the spinnaker pole, they calculated it would take four days of constant drilling to fix the boom – and we only had five or so to go.

The bad news was that during the storm, and partly because of the boom failure, we had run too far to the north too soon and by the next day we were on the edge of a massive high pressure system that was ridging in our direction. Clearly we were in for light weather. If we could have gotten east we might have been in fifth or sixth place, but now we were a safe tenth, if we could stay ahead of *Belmont* and *Gatorade* who had made the same mistake, and *Satquote British Defender* and *NCB* who had also broken booms.

We would spend the next week in slack conditions, struggling to get east, struggling with the unwieldy, but effective outrigger to fly the storm-battered mainsail. Just as a storm can focus the mind, the light and variables let the mind wander again, and more often than not it is away from the collective business of racing and more about personal matters – in my case whether the water pipes were freezing at home, or about that overdue credit card payment.

If the 'foreign four' at least pretended to be racing, most of the Soviets unashamedly slacked right off, and it was hard at times to control my temper when coming on deck to find them asleep or lazing about in the warm sun reading old Soviet newspapers, the mainsail hanging listlessly and the spinnaker in need of trim, with Bilou at the wheel, sailing the boat alone.

'I don't think the cause of this is a lack of interest in racing, or laziness, because they're not lazy,' Jim said to me while he tested the direction of the non-existent wind with his cigarette. 'It's something far more complex and probably goes right to the root of the Communist system.'

He was right, of course, but I could not help lending a thought to the atmosphere on the four lead boats, battling head to head into Fremantle over three hundred miles away. I was envious as hell. The Soviets, on the other hand, didn't care that we were not going to win this leg, and even less whether we came ninth, tenth or eleventh.

After all, the results of the Whitbread will not cure the economic problems of the Soviet Union, nor speed up the process of *glasnost*, nor materially improve the lifestyles of the crew when they go home – unlike how the results might affect skipper of *Rothmans* Lawrie Smith's ability to afford a new BMW – a ludicrous comparison, but one that highlights the question often asked, whether the Soviets, with their economy in the state it's in, should be playing this 'game', at all. Eugene, more sensitive to this issue than most, astutely pointed out, 'We have no condoms in Soviet Union. You can build a nice condom factory for 2 million dollars'.

During this leg, which is about as far as you can get from Europe, we had heard about the resignation of the Politburo in Czechoslovakia, the fact that East Germans were pouring into western Europe and that the Berlin Wall had finally crumbled. I suspect that our crew may feel they have missed out on a bit of history back home, events far more important than the shape of the Light Number 1 genoa in 10 knots of breeze. I would be disappointed if they didn't.

On 27 November, the day we arrived in Fremantle, I finished Tolstoy's *War and Peace* after 27 days at sea.

10

Leg Three – Great Expectations

Leg II had been one of the toughest legs on Whitbread record: an early spring passage with two vicious storms, damaged gear on every boat, seven men overboard and recovered and, sadly, one man lost.

The ruthless extent to which most of the boats were pushed in extreme conditions caused many respected competitors to question the validity of a competition that had a fleet of yachts running at speed, below 50° South, at night, in ice, for over two weeks. Ludde Ingvall, skipper of *UBF*, admitted that he took his spinnakers down at night in high winds and said to do otherwise was foolish. For the next race he was advocating a change of course, farther north into gentler weather. Harry Harkimo, skipper of *Belmont Finland* and a BOC single-handed race around the world veteran gave a TV interview, and said the same, but more profoundly, 'Most of the guys, when they do one Whitbread Race, they have to come back down here [the Southern Ocean] again. I think it's stupid – once is enough.'

Again, *Steinlager* came through in the final stages of light weather and beat *Rothmans*, *Merit* and *Fisher & Paykel* to the finish by minutes only. *Fortuna* had run the longest day, of 405 miles, but this obviously aggressive racing had cost one man a badly broken thigh-bone and another a broken arm. The girls on *Maiden* surprised everyone, especially their detractors in the UK, not merely by having made it, but by winning their class. Five boats had broken booms, sail damage was common and everyone had stories of near misses. The crew of *Gatorade*, the Italian entry, who finished

136

a disappointing eleventh place, said at the press conference, 'We are just nice Italian guys, racing around the world and trying to have fun,' which was apparently an excuse for not pushing harder in the heavy going, but was also a comment on just how tough it had been.

In spite of these and other exciting stories, most of which had been broadcast by radio or published in the press before the fleet arrived, none of the welcomes into Fremantle were that inspiring. Our arrival, two days behind the leaders, was at midnight which didn't help matters, but one would assume that Fremantle, the scene of the famous 1987 America's Cup that launched yacht racing for the first time into the international media limelight, and a formerly decrepit port town that owes its long overdue renovation to the event, thanks to Alan Bond, could have done better than the handful of people there to meet us, most of whom were the Race officials and our own support crew.

Without an Australian national entry, it was clear that the Australian stopover would be little help in lifting the profile of the race, and if this was not of consequence to the other entries, or even to Whitbread themselves, it could have serious ramifications for us.

Our European connections had again drawn a blank on new sponsors. ASM had dropped out entirely and Jock Wishart was still talking to the mysterious Soviet company that Vladislav didn't believe existed. In Fremantle we had to put in a make-or-break effort; we had only $50,000 left in the kitty, and we needed $100,000 to get us clear. We were reduced to appealing to the public for help. Mr Tichov was due to arrive the Wednesday after our arrival to make some policy decisions on the future of the project, which at that point did not look promising.

Most people who are vaguely aware of the Whitbread Race and those familiar with local, yacht-club racing must imagine that after each leg the crews go on a month-long bender in port; being wined and dined in the evening, lying on the beach drying out during the day and telling each other sea stories in the local boozer in the afternoon – and extension of the cocktail hour after the Sunday afternoon races.

In the early Whitbreads, in the days of adventure sailing,

crews were equally adventurous ashore. As in the days of working sail, after hitting the dock, they would immediately disappear into the hinterland for an indeterminate period, only to turn up later hungover, always broke, sometimes blooded and possibly married, or well on the way. Instead of the posh media centre and race office we now have, Whitbread policy was discussed in the local yacht-club bar, where protests were heard and then fought over, unrehearsed publicity stunts staged, not for the press but for ourselves, and the tactical planning for the next leg was carried out over a pint of beer with no secrecy at all.

Times have changed, and Whitbread life has changed with them. By the time most of us returned to the harbour after a short lie-in on the Monday morning, *Merit* had unstepped her mast and was out of the water, *Rothmans* was also being hauled and the crew of *Fisher & Paykel* were cheerfully breaking down and servicing the winches in anticipation of the next leg.

With Jim's and Dale's help, I made an attempt to get our crew into the swing of things by offloading the sails and rigging and giving the boat a good washing-out below, but I was met with something less than enthusiasm.

'I think now we have small holiday,' Igor said to me, in a way that made clear if I tried to suggest an alternative plan, it would be dangerous to my health. I was too tired to argue, an fair enough. They hadn't had any time off since they started to build *Fazisi* almost one year ago, and I suppose, in their shoes, I would have reacted the same way.

Possibly the Soviets would have fitted in better back in 1973 or '77, when we all had the backsides out of our jeans and were known as Whitbread sailors by our unkempt beards and the mad look in our eyes by 6 o'clock – not by brightly coloured rugby and polo shirts with monogrammed sponsors' logos which are now *de rigueur*, and make the crews look more like comical tribes of warring Indians than deepwatermen.

In this age of professionalism in all things, conformity is expected and deviation avoided, so the disparity of the Soviet crew of *Fazisi* in a place like Fremantle was obvious and disheartening, at least for those of us who considered them more than just a mild form of amusement. The other crews are paid professionals for the most part, had money in their pockets to buy a round of beers or pay for a meal, and they looked like a team. The Soviets were dead broke, the original crew shirt had chafed off their backs and they were, no doubt, self conscious about it. They had to suffer the indignity of having their first meal ashore in their hotel rooms, eating cheap food bought by Chumakov – while Dale, Jim, Bilou and I, not in solidarity, went to a good restaurant and had a big steak. I wasn't very happy about all of this, but I do admit to enjoying the steak, accepting this obvious flaw in my character.

When Tichov arrived on the Wednesday Vladislav and I were heavily into a fundraising campaign in Fremantle, which even if it was only tokenism in the big picture, looked good in that we were once again trying everything. I had gone on TV and radio making an appeal for charity and we met with some results. The Rotary Club had donated a sum of money to cover food for the crew in port and was arranging supplies for the next leg, a shipping company was paying to have the boat hauled, restaurants and bars invited the crew to free meals and local ad agencies were trying to put together sponsorship deals.

Though he appreciated all this effort, Tichov was still adamant. We had either to call it quits or detune the budget and turn the trip into a cruise, rather than a race, around the world. Fazis would not – could not – put up any more money he said. This would mean leaving the hotel and moving aboard *Fazisi*, no new equipment or sails, and an end to help from people like Jim, Dale, Monica and myself.

I liked Tichov a lot. He brought clarity to these situations and had the ability to make decisions, because for all intents and purposes he was Fazis. But I also felt sorry for him. I had no idea what he had been told to expect when Fazis decided to sponsor a Whitbread boat. There was a certain amount of euphoric discussion in the early stages of the project about how Western companies would be falling over each other to give Fazis money for what was an ideal media story, and an act of goodwill on the wings of *glasnost* and *perestroika*. Instead, his company was in massive debt, with a non-profit earning 82-foot sailboat entered in an international competition that he hadn't heard of one and a half years ago, and the responsibility for 18 people about to be thrown out of their hotel for not paying the bill half way round the world in Western Australia.

We tried to figure out a way in which we could get to New Zealand on the money we had. There, or so I tried to convince him, we could perhaps raise enough money to get to America, due to the enthusiasm of the New Zealand people for sailing. But to do this, we had to do the third leg right – not just to make it there, but to stay in the race and do well. That meant another new mainsail (another $20,000 expense), new running rigging, our shore team left intact, and Dale and me on board. With the other expenses like meals and lodging and shipping, no matter how we cut it, we had to have more cash from somewhere.

I'm not a businessman, but I do know a little about 'the art of the deal'. Fremantle was not the place to give up. If a company had the ability to borrow half a million, they could always get another 50 grand. Tichov was in a no-win situation. Like some businessmen must do, I felt uncomfortable putting the screws on him, but when he finally caved in after two days of bargaining and agreed to come up with another $50,000, like all businessmen surely do, I felt good about it. Tichov also seemed to accept what had always been the obvious solution. We were in the West and, being a Georgian, he understood the system better than most Soviets would have. He must have known and appreciated the well known Russian joke, 'A student asks an instructor of Marxism-Leninism to explain the difference between capitalism and communism. "That's easy, under capitalism, man exploits man, under communism, it's just the opposite."'

It was decided that, to expedite this plan, Vladislav would be sent to Auckland the following week to make some contacts. Chumakov would continue to manage the money we had, while Tichov, on his return to Moscow with the unhappy Crocodile (who was replaced by Sergei Akatyev) and The Doctor (replaced by Rami Leibovich), would organize the transfer of more funds to Fremantle. Dale's brother

Clive Tremain and his girlfriend Margie Gray had, in fact, already started a publicity campaign in Auckland. On their own initiative they began to produce and sell *Fazisi* T-shirts, with the profit going to the project. Jim continued as technical shore manager with Dale, and Bilou returned, not unhappily, to France.

Meanwhile, after one week ashore, the *Fazisi* crew began to blend into the Fremantle scene, with a few bucks in their pocket now that the budget was eased up. Following the usual confusion of how to get to the harbour and back, and the *modus operandi* of feeding themselves in yet another strange environment, the Soviets settled into a routine like the other crews, one that would be more familiar to a stockbroker or a lawyer than a yachtsman.

To commute to the 'office' they are picked up by bus at 8 a.m. from the hotel. Working until 12.30, they break for an alcoholic lunch, followed by a less productive afternoon. After work they debrief with the opposition and the secretarial pool at the 'local' down the road before facing the 'family'.

There are, of course, differences. The 'office' is the haulout basin at the harbour, and the secretarial pool may be an Aussie 'Sheila' or two in the Norfolk Pub, the yachties favourite – if they're lucky. With 300 strapping sailors in town, the conditions are understandably tough going, tacking and gybing in the lifts and headers in an effort, as the old timers used to say, 'to get in the lee of bum island'. The family is, of course, Valeri Chumakov.

At the weekend I was off for a week to Queensland to visit my girlfriend, Julia, having temporarily exhausted all short-term leads on sponsorship. Like Igor, I needed a 'small holiday' too.

Four hours before I was due to get on the plane for Brisbane I ran into an old acquaintance from Auckland, Paul Smitt, who was in town visiting his mates on *Rothmans*. During the Whitbread, four years earlier, Paul had owned the Leopard Tavern in Auckland which was the favourite after-hours watering hole.

We were standing in the lobby of the Esplanade Hotel. I was late for another appointment and dead tired after

141

another gruelling day on the telephone, having talked in the same way to ten other people explaining once again the pathos of our project. Sensing my apathy, he said bluntly, 'Listen, mate, no bullshit, I think I got a guy that can help you bail out your Russians. Call me in Auckland in two days.'

I took his number and thanked him for his interest. At that stage he was just another lead, leading to another lead.

Four days later I disappointed Julia in Queensland when I flew to Auckland, at the expense of Radio 89 FM. Barry Everard, the President of the station, a yachtsman and part of the in-crowd of Auckland, had already heard of *Fazisi*, but it wasn't until his mate and ex-business partner Paul Smitt explained the hook that it all became clear.

In four days, we had outlined the plan: 89 FM would guarantee us a certain amount of cash, giving them the sponsorship rights to the project while it was in town. In return the station, through its marketing and publicity departments, would run a fundraising campaign that we hoped would net in excess of $150,000 NZ.

Formerly an Auckland lawyer, Paul turned 'homegrown' entrepreneur when he manufactured and marketed the new wave of skateboards and later was the first to manufacture windsurfers in the country. With his experience ranging from publican to big business investor (profits from which have allowed him to semi-retire at the age of 40) fundraising for Fazisi was a piece of cake. He set up an office at the station and got to work.

Then things just happened – not in days or weeks, but in hours. To watch Paul Smitt work the telephone is to realize the value of good contacts. Then the people started coming out of the woodwork. A mutual friend and another all-rounder Bob Houston set up a round of breakfast and luncheon talks for me at local Rotary Clubs, Rugby Clubs and even the American Chamber of Commerce. A hotel manager, part-time lay preacher and community councillor, he, like Paul, seemed to know everyone who was worth knowing, and he was instrumental in advising us on setting up a raffle that would be our biggest-money spinner. Auckland boatbuilders McMullen and Wing offered hauling and service free of charge, the local Lada car dealer, Brian Franklin Motors, offered cars for our use. Complete strangers were calling up saying, in effect, 'I think this is great, this is what I do, what can I do to help?'

By the time I left Auckland on my second trip there (feeling less guilty about my Queensland holiday in between) we had drafted a month's schedule of activities for January. Yachtsman Mike Clark, who manages Coutts BMW, donated a car for the first prize in the raffle. Fisher & Paykel donated appliances and Continental Airlines threw in a trip to Fort Lauderdale for two as secondary prizes. We had firm plans for several fundraising dinners, fundraising parties, an auction, a fashion show and plans for a public-awareness campaign with donation boxes in every pub and public place in the city. The Prime Minister of New Zealand, Sir Geoffrey Palmer, America's Cup helmsman Chris Dickson, radio personality Larry Keating and even skipper of *Fisher & Paykel*, Grant Dalton, all went on the air encouraging their countrymen to get behind the underdog and support *Fazisi*. 'Let's put the wind in their sails!' was the slogan. And they would. It was a perfect sponsorship approach, good for *Fazisi*, good for the Radio 89 FM, and something the people in Auckland could get their teeth into.

Almost immediately money began to flow into the *Fazisi* Fund, mostly in small donations. The one that brought a tear to my eyes came from an old-age pensioner who sent in $10 from his weekly allowance with a note that read 'I have fond memories of some Russians I met during the war. Good luck to them'.

When I arrived back in Fremantle on the Thursday before the Saturday start, the crew were still in the middle of the worklist – 'storming' at the end, like Soviet factory workers trying to fill their quota at the eleventh hour. I was aware that North had still not released the new mainsail. ASM were supposed to pay for it, with Pepsi money, directly into the North Sails account in Germany, then the Australian North loft would give it to us. I spent all the remaining time to the start on the telephone to Europe. We finally got the sail at 7 o'clock on the Friday night.

A new sail, especially a mainsail, never usually fits

143

completely right first time. You can imagine my anxiety then, at 10.30, the morning of the start on 23 December, when we tried to hoist it for the first time, sheltering in the container port; it was blowing 25 knots outside in Gage Roads. Viktor Yasykov had decided to go home from Fremantle, so I decided to replace him with a Kiwi. Mark 'Herbe' Hauser, a young New Zealander, looked aloft from under his yachting visor at the mainsail halfway up the mast while the Soviets had another round of shouting about how something had fouled.

At the age of 25, Herbe was a top New Zealand sailor and had already done the last Whitbread. He was now used to the professional quietude of America's Cup campaigns. He frowned at me, while I passively stood holding the wheel, as though I thought it was normal that a five-minute job should take close to 30. He said, 'I'm not sure what I let myself in for here.'

'Well, Herbe, if I had told you too much,' I said, 'You wouldn't have come, and now you can see why I need you. If you survive you'll be a hero in Auckland.'

The mainsail fitted and at midday the starting gun fired for the third time and we thrashed our way out of the inshore water and around Rottnest Island before reaching off down to the southwest tip of Australia and Cape Leeuwin.

Vladislav had finally been allowed to do a leg with us and Vladimir Kulunichenko had taken over from Valeri Safiullin to repair the sails. With special permission from the government, he brought with him an icon of St Nicholas which he attached above his bunk. It was worth in excess of $5,000 in the West and had to be returned. He only smiled disapprovingly when I untactfully joked that it might be worth a few bucks when we ran out of money again.

It was a rough start, blowing a near gale out of the west and we lurched our way south in the middle of the fleet. Rami, struggling in the gallery that was bucking like a bronco said to me, 'This is not a very good place to learn cooking. Normally my job is a waiter in Riga.'

'When did you find out that they wanted you to be cook?' I asked him.

He smiled and said, 'When we got on the airplane Mr

Keeping the boat moving at her potential means constant trimming of the sails, no matter that the Whitbread is a 34,000 mile race not a 30 miler. Here Edgar Terechin trims the mainsail.

Auckland opened their hearts to the *Fazisi* crew. Here crowds line Princess Wharf at the start of Leg IV (credit: David Branigan/PPL).

Part of our promotion in Auckland was with the 89FM radio station, whose colours were carried on the transom as we headed back into the Southern Ocean.

Sergei Borodinov, a former Flying Dutchman European champion and Soviet Olympic squa sailor, joined *Fazisi* in Auckland. Helming here he's watched by Valeri Alekseev, who later became co-skipper.

On the first day out from Auckland we had a tacking duel with *The Card* off the Coromandel Peninsula. *The Card* had been my project originally before being taken over by Roger Nilson from Sweden.

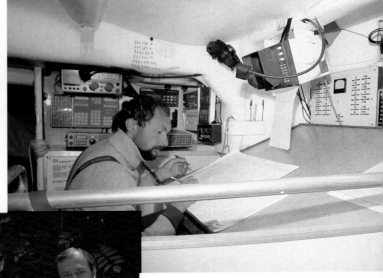

Sergei Akatyev from Kiev became *Fazisi*'s navigator from Leg II. No stranger to cramped surroundings, he's a former Soviet Navy navigator aboard the 145m long K Class nuclear missile subs.

Original co-skipper Alexei Gryshenko (centre committed suicide during the Leg I stop in Uruguay. Here he's flanked by myself (left) a project manager Vladislav Murnikov on launc day in Poti (credit: Tim Jeffery).

Blast reaching in the Southern Ocean with *Fazisi*'s on-deck crew receiving their usual quotient of flying water.

Down in the high latitudes the air and sea temperatures hovered just a few degrees above freezing point. Keeping hands and, especially, feet warm was tough.

Ice! One of the many bergs we saw on Leg IV from Auckland to Punta Arenas. Their blue hue scintillated on ink dark sea.

Sight of our first bergs brought off-watch crew members up on deck to marvel at their beauty and scale. This one's about 80m long and 40m tall.

After a spinnaker is set, the old headsail is lowered and folded. Sails have to be packed on deck before being taken below in long sausage bags.

Another day in the Southern Ocean. The leeward rail scoops up the ocean as *Fazisi* charges on under a press of sail.

Flaking the big Kevlar headsails into concertina folds so that they could be bagged was a regular chore after sail changes.

Igor Mironenko from Kiev and Eugene Platon drill new holes ready to accept *Rothmans'* old keel which we put on just before the start to solve our rating troubles.

Below. The constant motion chafed and split the mainsail repeatedly. Here Vladimir Kulinichenko from Odessa applies sticky-back fabric from the bosun's chair.

The Moldavian Eugene Platon catching up on Gorbachev's progress in *Time* magazine. Opinionated and independent, Eugene works at the Kiev Institute of Cybernetics on the missile defence programme and was involved in the Chernobyl clean-up.

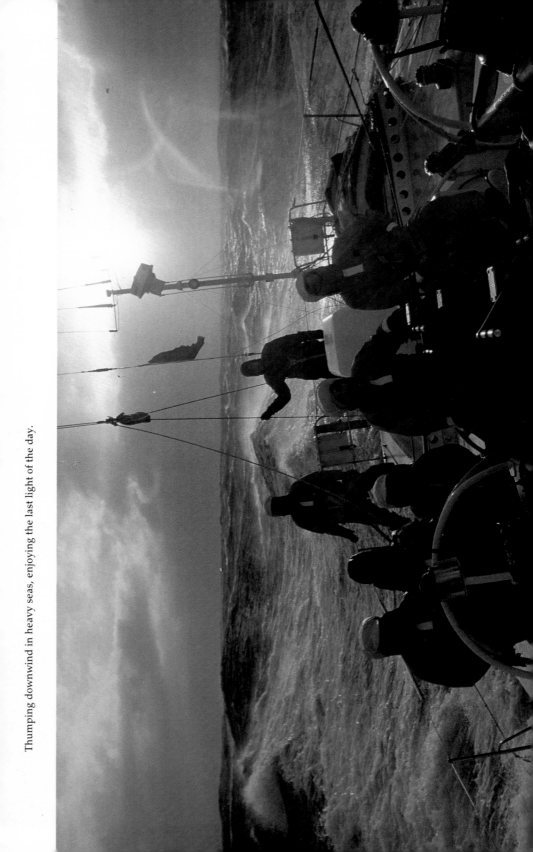

Thumping downwind in heavy seas, enjoying the last light of the day.

Cape Horn, seafaring's most emotive landfall, was unusually docile for our rounding. We did all the usual things nonetheless: toasts of champagne and vodka, and clowning for the cameras.

Historic moment as *Fazisi* heads for the finish line off Fort Lauderdale. Valdimir Kulinichenko steers surrounded (right to left) by Juki, Valeri Alekseev, Edgar Terechin, Viktor Pogrebnov and Sergei 'The Elephant' Stanetsky. French journalist, Thierry Rannou, who sailed Legs IV and V, stands aft.

Just north of the Falklands on Leg IV, the mainsail split at night. We had three reefs in when *Fazisi* broached, scooping up so much water in the belly of the sail it just ripped apart. I'm directing repairs with the aid of a potholer's lamp.

Above. The Genoa was hoisted in place of the damaged mainsail while repairs were made.

Bolt upright and with not a whisper of winds in the sails, *Fazisi* was becalmed off Argentina three days from the Leg IV finish in Punta del Éste.

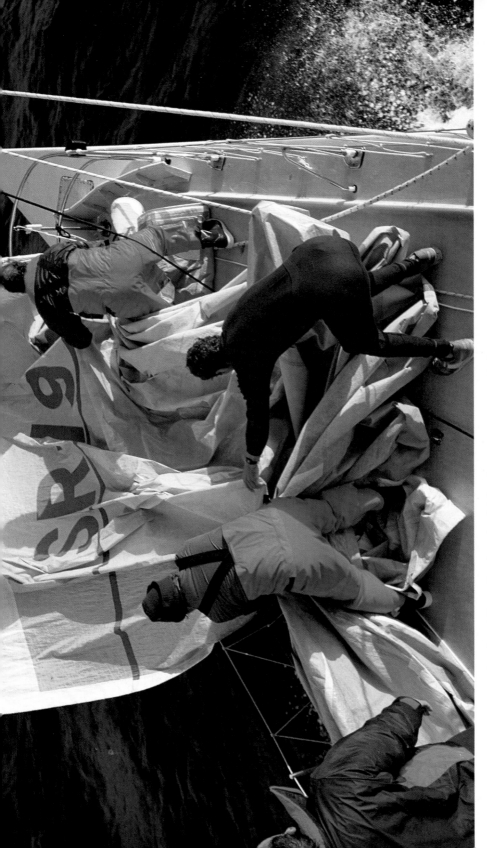

The Kevlar headsail is clawed down after the spinnaker has been set.

Rami Leibovich, a Jew from Riga in Latvia, was a waiter by profession but proved a successful cook. The Elephant pounces on some fresh cut oranges.

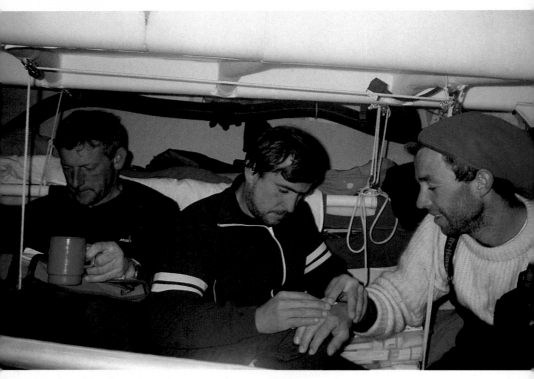

Jim Saunders (left) is seemingly uninterested as Doctor Alexei Drosdovski stitches a cut in the hand of Roland 'Bilou' Jourdain, a French specialist helmsman brought aboard for Leg II.

Guennadi Korolkov, 'The Crocodile', was *Fazisi*'s navigator for the first two legs.

Above. Leg IV did not provide so much of the heavy downwind surfing we experienced on the other earlier Southern Ocean leg, rather there was more blast reaching.

Fazisi's rig casts a shadow on the South Atlantic as the yacht heads for Punta del Este.

Tichov asked me if I cook. I said not really. And that was the end of the discussion. And here I am.' He then joined Sergei, the new navigator, and proceeded to throw-up into a plastic garbage bag.

Sergei the navigator hadn't come to England because he had still been trying to get his visa since he was, at that time, still a security risk. I therefore didn't know him at all. After we settled down on the heavy reach that would last five days until our turn north at the southern tip of Tasmania, I casually asked him one day, 'I understand you were in the Soviet Navy, Sergei. So what was your last ship?'

Like a bell tolling for World War III, he answered me equally casually, 'Russian nuclear submarine'. He said he had spent seven years as one of three navigators on a 'K' class tactical missile sub, lurking under the Arctic Sea for three months at a time. 'All our missiles were programmed on American cities, like Chicago.' I was from Chicago, and I knew he knew it, but I was astute enough to recognize a wryness in him that would make my own cynical sense of humour pale in comparison.

It was Christmas two days after the start. The biggest present of all was the BBC news that the Romanian dictator, Nicolai Ceacsescu had been arrested and executed. The East was still crumbling, and even Edgar, ever so slowly coming out of his Communist shell, showed signs of enthusiasm for the future.

That Christmas means different things to many different people could not be more true than on *Fazisi*. For a start, it was difficult to get any straight answers out of anybody about what went on in the USSR, until Eugene, in his blunt manner, pointed out, 'It wasn't that long ago that anyone caught celebrating Christmas could be thrown in jail'. That shut me up for a while, but after further inquiry I learned that in the Catholic areas, like the Baltic, 25 December is observed, while in the Orthodox regions, it is celebrated on 6-7 January. 'What about Santa Claus, then?' I asked. 'Oh, he comes on New Year's Eve,' explained Eugene, which I suppose was the institutionalized celebration allowed when the religious one could not be observed. So far as merriment, special foods and drink went, I soon found out we were to celebrate all three.

After one of our holiday meals, Vladislav and I settled back on the sails below and talked about things other than fundraising for the first time in a long while. I was glad he was on board to see first-hand the crew-work, or what I considered the lack of crew-work. Their inattentiveness towards racing, the endless discussions and arguments that never seem to have a result, the fact they couldn't yet gybe the spinnaker on their own and – which rankled most of all – the lack of initiative. 'Look,' I said to him, 'These guys are getting the chance of a lifetime to exercise some democratic principles, and they just won't do it!' I felt like Tolstoy, who had difficulty in trying to free his serfs in 1856, simply because they didn't trust the word of authority.

True Bolshevism depends on workers willingly co-operating, which was clearly not the case on *Fazisi*, and Vladislav, like Lenin in 1917, realizing the great revolution had failed in principle, opted for a harder line.

'Russia,' he answered, 'was always a democratic society, even in feudal times. By that I mean people are used to discussing everything, maybe too much. It is our history and you can still see this in our crew. Maybe you should impose more of a tough discipline on them. Maybe we should put these rules in their contract.'

'No, I'd rather continue as it is, and at least keep the crew together and relatively happy and easy going. I am certainly not going to force people to sail. After all, this is a voluntary sport. If it was the army and we were fighting a war, then it would be different. I just think this whole Whitbread Race, and the lifestyle they see, must be an incredible culture shock, making it difficult for them to focus on something as trivial as a boat race.'

Vladislav explained that for years he had read many books and articles and seen plays about life in the West, but it was not what he experienced when he finally went there. 'The Soviet people have one of two opinions about the West; everything is all good, or it is all bad. Of course, it is neither.'

'But what's your opinion?' I asked him.

'My opinion was "all good" but now I'm not sure. Here, people smile at you about all things, but are less sincere in their feelings than people back home. Especially about money! I really feel Soviet people are more pleasant sometimes, more comfortable to be with. But I know that the future is with the West and Western ways. Our people must not only read about it, they must experience it.'

From the limited time I had spent in the Soviet Union, I felt what he had just said was correct. I thought back to all the discussions, all the promises made and the blind optimism of those who were supposed to be helping us, and became ashamed and embarrassed.

On 29 December *The Card*, after having made an incredible tactical blunder in going too far south in the beginning of the leg, passed us, purely on superior boatspeed. This surprised the crew, who lounged about the decks in the sun as though they were on the beach at a Black Sea resort, washing their clothes in buckets of seawater or reading old newspapers. It didn't bother me that much any more, as I was resigned to being in the tail end of the fleet once again. I contented myself by stealing and reading the up-beat articles in the stock of *Playboy* and *Penthouse* the Soviets had brought aboard, leaving them to devour the rest. But Herbe was having a sense of humour failure.

'I thought the Japanese were bad [whom he had sailed for] but at least they know they're bad and want to learn, but these guys think they're good!'

There are some advantages in being at the back of the fleet. This is certainly true during a New Year's Eve at sea, when it is good to relax and improve the atmosphere, which may have faltered through being at the back of the fleet in the first place. Most of the guys were preoccupied with the coming festivities and the dinner, as Rami's cooking was proving far better than we ever could have imagined – and he didn't scowl at you when you asked for the salt.

This slackness is never found when you're up front with the leaders, when a little light-hearted foolishness would be severely frowned upon. Grant Dalton, the hard-driving skipper of *Fisher & Paykel*, when asked by a New Zealand radio interviewer how they were going to celebrate the last day of 1989, tersely put this in perspective when he said, 'Nothing, we'll celebrate in Auckland' leaving this eavesdropper with the distinct impression he meant 'victory' and 'to hell with your New Year's party'.

On *Fazisi* the atmosphere was indeed different, the solution to all problems seemed to be like in the satirical Ukrainian song that played endlessly on the tape deck, and translates: 'A girl is walking along with a bucket of water filled with radioactive protons and neutrons. A boy drinks the water. Now he can only LOOK at the girl. But later she makes a miracle and he can become erect. So the moral is for Ukrainians, make miracles and everything will be OK.'

About the time *Charles Jourdan* was holed by a sperm whale off the North Cape of New Zealand, and *UBF* lost her mast, the two race leaders, *Steinlager 2* and *Fisher & Paykel* staged a command performance in Auckland harbour, having sailed the entire leg neck and neck, right down to a 6 minute margin at the finish. Peter Montgomery, flamboyant radio announcer for Radio New Zealand, who had done a running commentary on this horserace continuously during the last day from the North Cape, had the country in pandemonium. It was a fantastic New Zealand success story and for Peter Blake a hat trick.

Montgomery interviewed us the next day, still some 200 miles behind and fumbling in light airs, with *Gatorade*, once again, in sight. 'Any messages for the people of New Zealand?'

'Yes, Peter, stand by.' I had Elephant and Eugene ready at the microphone, 'THE RUSSIANS ARE COMING!!!'

11

'Let's put the wind in their sails'

After shaking off *Gatorade* in a squall only 40 miles from the finish, we ghosted through the islands of Hauraki Gulf, under the cover of darkness. Several motorboats escorted us through Auckland's expansive natural harbour to the midnight finish at Orakei Wharf. Before we could see the thousands of people there to greet our arrival on a balmy summer's evening, we could hear the dull roar of the crowd.

When we got closer we could see three decks of warehouse balconies on Prince's Wharf jam-packed with well tanned New Zealanders, cheering us on as we flaked the mainsail and rigged the new boom cover that said '89 FM Radio, Auckland's Music Leader,' before making for the arrival pontoon. We hadn't won the leg, nor come second or third; we were placed 10th – but this was New Zealand, where almost everyone, if they haven't built their own, has surely some interest in boats and the people who sail them.

Rear Admiral Williams was standing by with the world's press, ready to present us with the standard bottle of cheap champagne. Served warm by design, it is intended not for drinking, but for spraying into the crowd. I knocked the head off the bottle with a winch handle and passed it around instead. In minutes our waterline had gone down by a foot when what must have been over 100 people came on board to greet the crew. The photographers sated, we cast off, with the customs and immigration men still below filling out forms, and motored round to our permanent berth on the other side of the pier.

Our sponsors, 89 FM, had organized a welcoming party for us that lasted until dawn. The crowd, well out of control, quickly trampled underfoot the nicely prepared food baskets of delicacies for the crew, the cockpits became a quagmire of chicken bones, potato salad, bread rolls and sausages and the decks a minefield of empty champagne and beer bottles.

Clive Tremain presented the crew with their new uniforms the next day. With bright red Canterbury trousers and multi-coloured rugby shirts they were now unmistakeable, sticking out like a troop of circus stuntmen perpetually on the way to their next big top performance. I felt the uniforms were overdone, certainly not my style, and my suspicions were confirmed that very evening when Barry Everard and I were waiting outside the upmarket Brandy's Wine Bar on Customs Street for the crew to arrive for their first promotional fundraising event, having hardly been given a chance to get their bearings.

And there they were! Twelve men in red, mustered by a short blonde, none other than Monica the lion-tamer. Unfortunately Neil Cheston and Patrick Banfield from *Rothmans* were coming down the street the opposite way, and as soon as they saw me I knew I was in for a good dose of their well known sarcasm.

'Well, it looks like Novak and his Flying Kalashnikovs have arrived at last,' said Patrick as he doubled over in ribald laughter.

'Surely you haven't forgotten the dancing bear,' said Neil with a deadpan expression.

I tried to be blasé. 'Look,' I said, 'If you promise not to tell anyone you've seen me, I'll get them to stand on their heads and juggle beer mugs for you.'

'Seriously, Skip, the Commonwealth Games are in town, and there are some fairly strange people walking around, so the Soviets should blend right in with the Tongans and the Ugandans.'

Making the Soviets stick out in the crowd was, of course, the whole object of the exercise, the pay-back, if you will, for Auckland's charity. 'Come meet the Russians, tonight, down at Brandy's Wine Bar,' said the radio ad. Perhaps I was being over-sensitive, but I couldn't help but remember the revulsion I felt as a boy, at a travelling carnival in Wisconsin, where for a dollar you could go into a tent and watch the dwarf show for a good laugh. 'Little people, Little people!' shouted the barker, 'They talk, they dance, they will play you a tune, little people, little people . . .' We entered the wine bar, my mind in a turmoil, somewhere between my boyhood in Wisconsin and my manhood in Auckland. 'Come see the Russians, the Russians, the Russians! . . .'

'G'day mate!' said the big Kiwi barman to Juki. 'Whatya drinkin'?' My fears were temporarily allayed as the crew blended into the evening crowd, at least as well as 12 orangutans would in a family of chimpanzees. They had gone through this before, in a limited way, in Fremantle, but here it was more organized. Some, like Juki, the Elephant and Eugene were better at socializing than the others, who sometimes stood around dumbfounded, almost suspicious of people who could be this friendly. Their handler Monica, assisted by the unabashed Carol Tremain (who was repairing our sails, from North's travelling loft) would then prod them into life and introduce them around.

I try to imagine myself doing the same, trading places with Victor Kamkin who speaks not one word of English: I am in Outer Mongolia and speak nothing of the language. I am taking part in a project I have dreamed about for years, but there is never any time for myself, because to stay in the project, not only do I have to work all day, but at night as well. I have to go out and attempt to be friendly to perfect strangers, who are, for the most part, very nice, but sometimes they look at me strangely and say things that I don't understand to their friends who are laughing most of the time. Every morning, I'm told through a translator where the next evening's function is and I have to be there without fail, even when I don't feel well (in fact still hungover from the previous day's function, because to be courteous I must eat and drink everything that's put in front of me). If I don't go, I may be sent home. I imagine myself, instead of Victor, trying to do the same, and I know I wouldn't have the strength of character, nor the courage.

151

The next day we were better organized. Barry had the whole crew come up to the radio station for a general meeting. He explained how the radio station works, the ideas for fundraising and the general schedule of events that they would be expected to attend, beginning that evening with a fundraiser at the Nag's Head Pub in Parnell, which had adopted the crew for the duration of their stay. To keep the continuity rolling, it was decided that Monica would conduct a crew meeting every morning in her office and make sure they understood the day's events, in addition to discussing their own worklists on board. Every week they would have another meeting at the station where they would receive their *per diem* allowance for the coming week.

We then led them on a tour of the station. The atmosphere was exciting and infectious, young, get-up-and-go people bustling around to the beat of rock music that played in the offices all day. A young 48-year-old, Barry had taken over the station in 1985, when it was at the bottom of the charts, and in three years they were number one in the city. In his spare time he had produced two feature films, *The Leading Edge* and *Never Say Die*, with his company Triple M Ltd. To all appearances he looked like an able captain and ran a happy ship.

I felt good about the station's involvement. For the first time in six months I felt a great weight taken off my shoulders. They would run the fundraising, do the publicity and accounting and pay the bills; they were, in effect, the management company we never had.

While the crew trooped off to the boat with Jim and Dale for the day's work, I went downstairs to Paul's office to give him a hand. Paul Smitt was clearly enjoying working the fast track again and doing what he does best: applying leverage in a way that made it hard for the most entrenched institution to resist his powers of financial persuasion, which at times had the subtlety of a bulldozer. He was in his usual position, feet up on a desk full of memos, his ear wrapped around the telephone, just concluding another difficult extraction. 'Mate, can I expect that cheque tomorrow? . . . Good. Listen, you're a champion!'

He hung up the phone, wheeled around and said to me, 'Got some more good news for you, my son. Terry Cookson is going to rebuild the cracked rudder-blade gratis with all the materials supplied free of charge by High Modulus, and . . . look at this: a cheque from Fletcher Fishing for five grand, so far the biggest single cash contribution. And the raffle money is coming in all the time. We've got 100 university students out on the street flogging tickets and they're going like hot cakes. I also talked to Tony Pearce. The fundraising race is on at the Ponce [The Ponsonby Yacht Club] – date to be determined – and the auction at the Royal New Zealand Yacht Squadron is all go for the 16th. Tony reckons that it's going to be a biggy. He reckons we should make 15 grand minimum, that's minimum, at that alone, but we got to get cracking on getting that David Barker painting appraised. I'll tell ya something, we'll get your Soviets the 200 grand and it could be a lot more!'

Before he had finished, one of the contribution boxes was brought in and the contents emptied onto the floor before our accountant Vickie Wright tallied it up. 'Look at that, boxes of money,' said Paul. 'Isn't it great?!' We both broke out in fits of uncontrollable laughter.

Independently of the station, and admittedly far less organized, Clive Tremain had set up a *Fazisi* marketing stand on Prince's Wharf. He had missed the first weekend, when most of the boats had arrived, having no stock! By midweek, however, he was in top gear, with several styles of *Fazisi* shirts, and also pants, posters and pins. His biggest money spinner was the T-shirt that said across the front, 'The Russians are Coming!'

Even though, by week's end, the fleet was all in, the wharf was filled to capacity almost every day for a month by an inexhaustible supply of curiosity-seekers and well-wishers. They would scrutinize the yachts on the pontoons, watch for hours the crews at work on the rigging and sails, or just amble through the sponsors' exhibition stands and eat fast food. You could buy a balloon, donate blood or get your blood pressure checked, buy any number of different raffle tickets and, for $2, have the privilege of adding your signature to a huge poster as a contributor to the *Fazisi* Fund.

153

I have never felt an atmosphere like it, at least not for a yacht race. Maybe this is another of New Zealand's secrets: they made a yacht race more than a yacht race by providing a venue for a family day out, with all the trappings of a well organized carnival.

Julia from Queensland had flown over, and we were leaving for a 10-day cruise with friends down to Milford Sound on the South Island. I admit I was glad to be going, and things seemed under control – until we ran into Eugene in the wharf's car park. He was driving the truck and had Juri, Igor, Viktor Kamkin, Elephant and Edgar with him. He didn't look happy.

'Have you heard the news?' he snarled at me. 'Three new crew members have just arrived from the Soviet Union. Did you know about it? Our administration [Vladislav and Chumakov] informed us only this morning.'

'Well, Vladislav and I talked about it a few weeks ago on Leg III,' I said.

'Skip, maybe we are going on strike. Tell the administration and radio station that maybe we will not participate in the "Soviet Union" day on Sunday.'

'Yes, I'll tell them,' I said, as Eugene put the truck in gear and roared out of the carpark in a cloud of smoke.

This was a mutiny of sorts. The implications of the arrival of three new crew members were clear – three of the present crew would be sent home. Nobody knew who would be sent home so they all banded together, in solidarity, as a revolutionary group. Their ammunition was the obvious publicity scandal.

I had indeed discussed this with Vladislav. We had agreed that we needed better crew to improve the performance of the boat. But I had made it clear that I valued the ambience on board more than I did the results. My feeling was that any outsiders who hadn't participated in the gruelling construction would be immediately resented and the whole exercise would be counterproductive. But they were sent for regardless, at the cost of $6,000 in air tickets from Singapore Airlines as there were no direct Aeroflot flights. Not only that, but sending the crew home would be another expense, which the administration obviously intended should be paid out of the *Fazisi* Fund. This was tantamount to having the people of Auckland pay to have people sent back to the salt mines – at least that's how Barry interpreted it.

'No bloody way are we gong to pay to send guys back to the Soviet Union,' said Barry, when I told him what I'd heard. 'If the media gets a hold of this they'll have a field day, and I can tell you right now this fundraising thing will sink like a stone. How could Vlad do something so stupid?'

'I've got Jim rounding up all the crew,' I said, 'and Monica is looking for Vladislav and Chumakov. We need to have a crew meeting pronto and sort this bullshit out.'

'Too bloody right we do.'

Everyone concerned filed into Barry's office later that afternoon for the revolutionary council. Barry, Paul, Vladislav and I had already agreed that the new guys would have to stay and two Soviets – yet to be determined – would go home, not immediately, as Fazis originally intended, but after the boat had left on Leg IV, so they could at least enjoy their stay in Auckland. We hoped this would be enough to assuage the crew.

I explained my feelings to the crew and so did Vladislav, to whom they were not so sympathetic. Almost immediately 12 Soviets began to yell and shout at each other, and the din was so deafening that the 'Politburo' retreated behind the soundproofed glass doors of the inner office and watched them thrash out their grievances. After one hour, with no let up in sight, Barry called a halt and explained the situation.

'Look, guys, let me assure you, nobody is going to be sent home, that's the first thing. We, that means Paul and myself, agree that this was not handled in a correct manner, all right? But we have to come to a solution. We've agreed with Vladislav and Skip that they will decide which two will have to go home after the start, and we're asking you to abide by that decision.'

They all agreed, feeling comfortable with a third party arbitration. The crisis was temporarily over. They would participate, as expected, in the special Soviet Day down at the wharf, and continue working on the boat. Later, Vladislav assured me, after canvassing the crew, that the consensus decision was to send back Juri and Viktor Kamkin. I could accept Viktor being replaced, but I wasn't so sure about Juri, not for his sailing ability, but for the weird *ad hoc* installation of pipes, valves and tanks he had concocted called the 'plumbing', which would not have been out of place on Captain Nemo's submarine and was surely engineered to guarantee his own irreplaceable position. Vladislav assured me that one of the three new crew, Valeri Alekseev, was a marine engineer and could easily figure it all out.

Vladislav was again slipping in the crew's popularity polls with this last *fait accompli*. About the same time he also came under attack from the design group in the Soviet Union which had been involved in *Fazisi*'s original concept. In a critical letter to the editor of the January issue of *Yachting World* magazine, they wrote:

> We write regarding the original underwater profile of *Fazisi* with the keel and rudder that were envisaged by our design. . . . The problems concerning the 'IOR' rating were connected, we believe, with the fact that the owner (Fazis) did not pay much notice to our calculation and recommendation. . . . It is a pity that the owner did not consider it necessary to consult with the designers of the yacht, instead taking into account the opinion of Murnikov, who is not a specialist in this area, although he is introduced abroad as the designer. . . . We believe that the changes made caused an effect similar to tying two or three buckets from the stern, or nailing some pairs of galoshes to the keel.

The letter was signed Oleg Larionov and Alexander Filippov – Mobile Company Leningrad.

Imagine his ego: recalcitrant crew, a project subsisting on financial ruin, the design of the yacht exposed as a muddled failure and his own role as designer in question, and, once again, the financial reins of the project taken out of his hands – this time by the radio station. While he and Chumakov were left to ponder these and other difficulties alone, the crew went out on Saturday night to the fundraising party for 800 in Tim Gurr's mast-building shed and proceeded to get completely legless. To be 'in charge' is to reap the 'rewards' of a Whitbread campaign.

Before I left for the South Island, I met the new crew: Valeri

Alekseev and Victor Pogrebnov, both from Sochi and both Black Sea offshore sailors, and Sergei Borodinov, a dinghy champion from the competitive Flying Dutchman class. The boat had been hauled out of the water at McMullen and Wing's yard and was undergoing bottom and deck painting, and the rudder was under repair at Cooksons. All seemed to be organized, and I left confident, with Jim and Dale once again in charge of the worklist.

When I returned, 10 days later, in time for the Ponsonby fundraising sail, the boat was back in the water and ready to go sailing – the first time we had been ready so long before the start. Only Monica seemed to be suffering, continually plagued by Chumakov for money. He was angry that the radio station wasn't releasing any directly to Fazis, which was intentional because they didn't think it fair for Auckland to have to pay old debts still outstanding in the UK. Monica tried to explain this, but was met with his stony stare and mutterings. In addition, every morning at 7.30, 15 hungover Soviets would invade her bedroom (only because her bedroom doubled as the office) to get their marching orders for the evening, drop off laundry so they could have a clean uniform and get reimbursed for petty cash expenditures.

'Where's Juki?' I asked her. 'I haven't seen him around.'

'When he went off with the blonde, his message was, "If Skip Novak can take holiday, Juki take holiday".'

'Well, fair enough,' I said. I could hardly gainsay Juki; as he told me once, 'Me Juki, very important person, from Georgia'. And indeed he was. He won the beer-drinking competition and he and the Elephant came second in the winch-grinding competition in an events day between the crews. Everyone in the fleet, and possibly in Auckland, knew who Juki was.

Alexander Kedishvili arrived from Moscow 10 days before the start. He was just in time to take part in the ticker-tape parade down Queen Street on 26 January, in honour of the Whitbread crews. I rode in a car holding a big American flag with Vladislav, who held the Soviet flag, and behind in a flatbed truck were the crew and supporters, waving to the crowd of 30,000 on the street, hanging out of office windows and on top of buildings. There were no police barricades, no confusion of any kind, nor a single angry face. There was a utopian atmosphere; it was like a parade in a 1940s family film in a small town in America; the kid hanging from the lamppost, the fat, smiling traffic cop standing next to the smiling sewer repair man who shouts 'Good on ya Russians!', the old pensioner waving a New Zealand and a Soviet flag: each memory frozen in time, having all the impossible goodness of a Norman Rockwell painting. I was moved, almost teary-eyed beneath my sunglasses, not by the adulation, but by the simple sincerity. I couldn't imagine how this could be possible anywhere else, certainly not in America or Europe today, where the very act of putting yourself on public display almost ensures you get egg on your face from some righteous special-interest group, or, worse, from someone just for the malicious fun of it.

By that time, it was clear we would probably reach our target of netting NZ$200,000 for the boat, enough to cover our costs and get us to Uruguay, but not the dream sum to enable us to finish the remainder of the race. We hadn't scored any major sponsors who were willing to support us after New Zealand, which was understandable. To date all the contributions had been small donations of the order of $5 or $10; after all it had been the radio station's intention to make it a 'people's boat,' since the big money corporate campaigns of *Steinlager* and *Fisher & Paykel*, had intentionally left the people out of it.

Vladislav and Alexander were, of course, happy about the result, but still had all the old bills hanging over their heads. They felt pressurized, knowing that a campaign like this was impossible to stage in Uruguay, coupled with fear of the unknown in America. We had all been told the story by the raffle ticket-seller about the American tourist from a cruise ship who had said, 'Why the hell should I support the goddamn communists?' A big Maori overheard this argument, jumped into the fray and bought a book of tickets; the ticket-seller left him telling the American what he could do in no uncertain terms. It was an amusing story, but was it a portent of things to come?

Thursday 1 February was our last event, a fundraising

fashion show at the Ellerslie Race Track. Price of admission was $100 a head and we hoped it would draw the cream of Auckland. A few of our crew, Patrick and Neal from *Rothmans*, Jenni Mundy from *Maiden*, New Zealand All Blacks rugby players, cricketers, and 12 athletes from the Commonwealth Games had already rehearsed that afternoon to escort the models down the catwalk. It would be a gala evening.

Julia and I arrived at 7.30 and mingled with the crowd, then Vladislav and Alexander arrived. They wanted to have a meeting the next morning, but I said I was busy until after 12. 'Why don't we have it right now,' I asked them, 'before the show starts?'

We went outside to the terrace and sat on some lawn furniture. They came right to the point and explained that in Uruguay, once again, the money situation would be desperate. They said that it would be impossible to pay Monica or Jim beyond Auckland. Dale was already paid for the coming leg, but beyond that, he would have to go for no pay. They wanted me to stay and I said I was willing to take the risk, but if we made any money further down the road, say in America, I wanted to be reimbursed. I wasn't sure about the others, but I knew Jim would do the same. I didn't like it, but if there was no money, there was nothing else to do. Then they let the bomb drop.

'And another thing, I am worried about the radio station,' said Vladislav. 'Of course, the accounting is completely clear, unlike Clive, which you know is a big mess, but how do we know what they are doing with the money? Every day boxes of money come in and cash contributions. How can we be sure?'

I was shocked. They were accusing the radio station of pilfering funds. I turned red with rage. 'What the hell are you talking about? Do you think Paul Smitt is going to grab five grand out of the fund? The son-of-a-bitch drives a Ferrari, for Christ's sake, you've seen how he lives, Barry the same. Nobody like that is going to risk a scandal, what you're suggesting is completely stupid!'

I saw Barry and his partner Trish walking towards us and cut off the conversation in mid-stream. 'Hi guys,' said

159

Barry, 'I think it's time to take our seats and get stuck into it!'

I was still fuming when I sat down at the head table. The crew were on display, all in their red outfits, on another table to the side of the centre stage and seemed reasonably happy. I couldn't focus on the conversation as we got our starter. I was totally preoccupied by what Vladislav and Alexander had said, their confused ingratitude towards those who had helped them. And on top of that they were going to strip the project of those of us who had got them halfway round the world. I started to turn resentful, then melancholy, the gin and tonics no doubt exacerbating my mood. I was called up to give a short speech in front of the 400 people, but I made a complete balls-up, and had to ask Eugene to bail me out impromptu. I felt like shit.

Lee Ross, a stand-up American comedian, then got up and did his routine. He didn't raise a reaction from what was predominantly a colonial audience – until he did a pantomime about a guy hanging himself – hanging himself, right in front of our crew! I cringed, went red, then I looked down the row of tables past the laughing faces of those who probably hadn't heard of Alexei Gryshenko, to the ones who had, who were visibly embarrassed that such a *faux pas* could have happened, and to the table with our crew. They sat there with blank expressions while the pantomime went on for five minutes. Then there was another monologue, then Ross proceeded to do another pantomime of a guy hanging himself with his dental floss! It was a coincidence too outrageous to contemplate.

'I'm sorry, mate, try to relax,' said Barry. I couldn't look at the crew. I hated the dinner, loathed the whole enterprise – not only the fashion show but the whole damn Whitbread Race. I had trouble getting my food down, in spite of Julia's efforts to appease.

The fashion show went off brilliantly, and everyone quickly forgot the comedian, as you always do when things are unpleasant. But I hadn't. I was forcing down dessert when the PR lady came up to the table and asked that I go outside and do a TV New Zealand interview. The message was clear, I knew what I had to do – to say what fine people we all were and how the Russians would never forget all of this. In the emotional state I was in, this was the last straw. There comes a time in your life when going along with protocol and with what's expected of you is beyond your personal limit, a time to forget the ramifications of what you are about to do – to simply say 'Fuck it!'

I didn't say that to the PR lady, but politely refused, grabbed Julia by the arm and stormed out.

Two days later we were motoring out to the start, bound for Cape Horn almost 4,000 miles away, once again through the clarity of the Southern Ocean. The crowd on the wharf to see us off knew nothing of our little dramas like the mutiny, nor about the fashion show, which was just as well. To them, to all those who gave us support, whether it was a five-dollar note, a helping hand or just a friendly smile, we owe our gratitude.

Just as we cast off, the crew got together and shouted in unison, 'Thank you, New Zealand!' And we meant it.

12

Leg Four – Cape Horn to Port

The lady at the hot dog joint on the wharf summed up all our feelings about the most frenetically enjoyable stopover we had experienced, which also, in a way, explained why New Zealanders love New Zealand. 'After you've all gone,' she said with a smile, 'it's going to be so quiet around here – won't it be lovely?'

For their last hurrah, the people of Auckland had the harbour and outlying Hauraki Gulf churned up good and proper by the wakes of thousands of spectator craft manoeuvring to see the Whitbread fleet on its way to Cape Horn. A light northeasterly made it a windward start, and although we crossed tacks ahead of *Steinlager* just after the gun went off, we quickly slipped behind the fleet in the man-made sloop, while the big ketch, with New Zealand's favourite son Peter Blake driving her, quickly powered up to the head of the pack. Only *The Card* saved us the ultimate embarrassment of being last out of the gulf when she snagged her mizzen mast rigging on the mast of an anchored cruising boat. The video we saw later of this accident was hilarious; *The Card*'s mizzen mast crumpled to the deck in slow motion while her momentum pulled the hooked cruiser right over on her side and the surprised spectators leapt for their lives into the water. Instead of returning to Auckland to step a spare rig, which would have had to be shipped from Europe, they decided to cut the wreckage loose and continue on as a sloop.

We began Leg IV in tenth position out of 15 maxis, in aggregate time overall, which was still respectable, but our

162

old sails would not give us any material advantage over the others, like *Belmont, NCB, Gatorade* and *UBF*, who had budgets for new equipment and would soon be barking up our rear.

We had 14 crew on board, which was still far too many to sail *Fazisi*, and this number was swelled by two more with the late addition of two sailing journalists, making it 16 altogether. Frenchman Thierry Rannou had sailed with Eric Tabarly's *Côte d'Or* in the last Whitbread and would be filming for French TV and writing for the Paris newspapers and magazines. Roger Vaughan, the well known American sailing writer/editor, was on board from *Life* magazine. At 52 years old, he was understandably worried about the rigours to come. He would later write in his article for *Life*, 'my friend Gary Jobson . . . questioned my sanity when I told him that I was going to be crewing on a Whitbread boat . . Jobson (in Auckland to film the start for ESPN) was so distressed that only hours before I was actually about to stow my gear aboard and cast off, he took me aside, put his arm around me and chillingly warned: "If you have any reservations – any doubts at all – don't go." It felt like his way of saying, "I wouldn't go and you shouldn't go either".'

To carry not one, but two journalists (three if you include myself) is considered an extreme measure because, from a racing standpoint, journalists are normally extra baggage. The fact was, however, that these two had more racing experience than most of the crew put together. I explained to Vladislav that it was obvious we needed the publicity, especially in America, to help get support. The *Life* article was scheduled for the May issue and would coincide with our arrival. It was clear to me that the *Fazisi* project was, even now, evolving less into a sailing story and rather into a general interest saga of how we made it round the world. The racing was only a vehicle whereby a private Soviet project could now try – and succeed – under its own steam, in the west. I had no doubts about the obvious priorities, and no illusions about the obvious pitfalls.

The worst thing that could happen would be a rig or rudder failure, which would put us out of the race and strand the project somewhere in the South Pacific. We had no spares and no back-up facility, so it was paramount that we at least got round Cape Horn in one piece. From there, back in the Atlantic, no matter what happened, the boat could somehow make the finish. Consequently Leg IV had become the watershed between success and failure.

This is why I became visibly panicky when helmsman Sergei Borodinov almost drove a hole through the side of *The Card* later that afternoon. In the fluky winds near the Coromandel Peninsula *The Card* had managed to work its way back up through the fleet and was on starboard tack, giving her the right of way, in a dead heat with us on port. Sergei is a dinghy champion from the Soviet Union, so I was not immediately worried when we were 100 metres away, but when he made no preparation to ease the mainsail, or even to suggest that he was thinking about altering course to dive below their stern in the usual way, with only a second to spare I grabbed the wheel and threw it over. We missed *The Card* by about 10 feet and Sergei looked at me as if to say, 'No problem!' Still, it had been damn close.

The spectator fleet from Auckland had long since dwindled to nothing, but now off the lovely green hills and cliffs of Coromandel, local boats came out to greet us and say their last good-byes. Some ageing 1960s hippies motored in close by in an aluminium fishing boat, the crew of four armed with cans of beer. 'Good on ya! Shit eh! Bloody Russians, you're beauties! Hey, your last chance to defect is Great Barrier (Island), ha ha, nothing to do there but grow dope!'

The Elephant celebrated his 32nd birthday while crossing the Bay of Plenty. East Cape would be our last point of land to round, the following evening, before the slog to the Horn. The crew seemed to be rejuvenated after their stay in Auckland, and they all agreed it had been the best place they had visited yet. The three new crew, Valeri, Vicktor and Sergei, were working out great; they were very enthusiastic and certainly seemed to have more basic sailing knowledge. Quiet, and playing it cool, they were also getting along reasonably well with the others. Again, I could only observe this and get the information secondhand, as all three had very little English and my laziness in learning any Russian didn't help. I justified this lack of interest on my slow ability to grasp French after 13 years in Europe, plus the fact it was unlikely that I would ever return to the USSR for any length of time, but of course, as a matter of courtesy, I should have made more of an effort, and when occasionally I uttered a word like 'divai!' (go for it!) the Soviets just laughed.

If the ambience had greatly improved on board, back on shore it was seething. Via the radio I learned that Vladislav and Alexander were still trying to sort out Clive Tremain's muddled accounting on the marketing side, and there was confusion about stock remaining. Now yet another fundraiser had entered the picture. We had met Rae Glasgow in Fremantle and she had kindly offered to help prepare the boat for departure and had also made some significant connections to the Australian Rotarians. She was in the business of buying and selling thoroughbred horses, but a lack of knowledge of sailboats didn't stop her involvement with Fazisi. She had turned up in Auckland a few days before the start, had heard Vladislav's and Alexander's doubts about the propriety of the fundraising in Auckland and had investigated the situation on their behalf.

Out of hand, she declared that Fazis had been hard done by from New Zealand, and if she (a New Zealander herself) had been in charge she could have raised a lot more money. Because of her Monica had come under fire, being accused of filling the role of 'Skip's personal secretary' and neglecting the crew. Yet when I told them that Monica had been sacked, they were incredulous. Six hundred miles offshore, it all started to become clear. I was told that Rae was now being retained by Fazis to act on their behalf in America. This was fine, because we certainly needed someone working there now, on the ground, making the contacts. But her claim that she already had access to $500,000 in sponsorship for the Florida stopover made her immediately suspect. We had all heard these stories of grandeur before. If it was true, she would have done something that nobody in yachting, not even Dennis Conner, has been able to do.

The light northerly persisted through 6 February, and we crossed the International Dateline that afternoon. Eugene the revolutionary sat down next to me on a sail bag on the weather rail and said, 'Skip, have you heard the news? The administration had decided that I will go home from Punta, and looks like Anatoly too.'

'Yeah, I expected that. I fought for you on the last leg, but I don't think there's much I can do now. You're just too radical and too much of a threat to Vladislav.'

'Any way,' he continued, 'with no money, no new sails, the racing is over.'

'You can say that again,' I said. 'When you get back to Punta you will have done the circumnavigation, so I wouldn't worry about it. I've also heard that some of the wives are coming over, flown in compliments of Aeroflot. That'll be good.'

'Yes, but with project and no money – imagine all the crew with their wives living in a tent in the car park, Rami sitting by a big iron cook pot stirring the borscht while Navigator plays his guitar!' he said with a laugh.

'I know what you mean – like gypsies – and Chumakov guarding the perimeter fence with a shotgun and notepad!'

We all knew that Anatoly was certainly on his way out. From the beginning he had been a thorn in the administration's side, always pushing his ideas and using the loyalty of his boys from Odessa in a tricky power struggle. Anatoly was a skipper reduced to maintaining the running rigging, and he did his job with all the dedication that was required; but it was clear that while doing the repetitive work of splicing and seizing rope and wire his thoughts were elsewhere – four years down the road, holding the wheel of his own Whitbread maxi. The project already had a name – 'Odessa 200' – and its logo, designed by Anatoly, turned up often enough in place of the *Fazisi* logo to create a never-ending feud between him and Vladislav. When he wasn't doing anything else he was filling notebook after notebook with specifications and making sketches for his boat, in what would obviously be an attempt to right the wrongs of the present and at least vindicate himself and his methods.

Clearly, for a lot of the crew on board, although we were still only just halfway round the world, the voyage was close to an end, and they were throttling down. Not so the fresh blood, who were still very enthusiastic, so much so that they got the halyards in a complete muddle on the night of the 8th, and it took Edgar almost two hours aloft in the boatswain's chair to unbraid the cables, some of which had chewed through the plastic headfoil. In an unprecedented performance on *Fazisi*, Edgar, who was becoming one of the strongest players, took charge and gave Valeri, Viktor and Sergei a half-hour lecture on how to keep the halyards organized and untangled. At last there was some civilized communicating going on.

Juki celebrated his 33rd birthday on 10 February, still in calm seas. Champagne was produced, of course; his favourite music, 'Gypsy Kings', played endlessly all evening while Rami cooked another superb meal, not merely because it was Juki's birthday – superb meals were now standard fare on *Fazisi*. That night it was chops and rice, garnished with tomatoes, fresh spring onions, garlic and dried figs. Each meal was different and beautifully presented, each plate individually wiped clean with a cloth before being filled, like in expensive restaurants. We had a lot of fun comparing The Doctor's cooking to Rami's, while Roger and Thierry could hardly believe that it could have been that bad.

I listened to the BBC World Service later that evening. When I told Rami about the anti-semitic pogroms going on in Leningard, he wasn't visibly shaken as I had expected, but only said quietly, 'This is nothing new'.

A Latvian Jew, Abram Leibovich was the oldest member of our crew, born one year after the Second World War ended. His mother came from a family of ten, and she and her husband, both pharmacists with university degrees, had the sense to move to Tashkent in the Soviet Union in 1940. She was one of only three of the family's children to survive Hitler's genocide.

Rami's uncle built a beautiful 30-foot wooden yawl in the late 1940s which Rami sails out of the port of Riga – when he's not working on his antique Amilcar (1924) and going to car shows. He says he became a waiter to pay for his winter skiing in the Caucasus mountains, where he still teaches the sport. Among this crew, he would be considered a Renaissance man.

I told Rami that he should try to do some deck work if he wanted, and how I thought it was a shame that he got stuck with the cooking job. 'I didn't like the idea of cooking at first,' he admitted to me. 'Of course I would rather sail, but with all the confusion in this group, now I prefer my job – it's fine.' A man of few words, I could tell he was not impressed with the crew without his having to say it, at times I think he was embarrassed, not by the lack of technique, but by the behaviour.

We didn't cross the Antarctic Convergence until 11 February, at 53 South. We still hadn't had a good blow yet. We were south of the bulk of the fleet and were slowly moving back up through the competition. The predominantly northwest wind we had been getting was fine in the first half of the stretch to the Cape, and we reckoned a southwesterly front must give us an advantage later on.

Thierry Rannou, however, was getting nervous, not because of the latitude, but because we hadn't had any hard running conditions that he could film. He had promised the media, as well as his personal sponsor, the French men's perfume company Paco Rabanne, that he would come back with all the spectacular footage a Southern Ocean leg is famous for, and on the Soviet maxi, a mainstream news story.

'You had better start using your life harness,' I said to him as the air temperature took a nose dive that afternoon.

'Yes, I know, but on *Côte d'Or* we never used them. I know it sounds stupid – we never used them because Tabarly never used one. Now I find it hard to get used to.'

I pointed at the water, then registering a frosty 3°C and said, '*Mon cher*, you will have a hard time getting used to that too.'

The next day, neither the crew nor the journalists had any complaints when we sailed by ten icebergs in rapid succession. All cameras and video equipment were in use as we altered course 10° for 20 minutes to pass within less than 50 metres of a magnificent ice castle, guarded by a moat of swirling growlers and brash ice that had broken off. Altering course to go touring is, of course, a sacrilege on a race – certainly for skippers like Lawrie Smith or *Merit's* Pierre Fehlmann. But who could ignore the temptation? Imagine a giant natural diamond, 50 metres tall and blindingly blue-white, the first few facets already cut by what can only be the hand of a God, and the crystalline debris scattered randomly on a sea of blue velvet.

It's an axiom that the bigger the iceberg, the safer it is. At night they glow from reflected moon and starlight. It is the growlers and house-size 'bergy bits' that can be the heart-stoppers. Two nights later, in fog, we passed two of these, awash in a heavy swell, unnoticed until they were abeam. I suppose the odds of actually hitting one head-on are pretty slim, but there they were, nonetheless. We didn't see any other growlers, but the big bergs were almost constant features on the horizon for the next week.

We bottomed out at 61° 40' South on 16 February – and still no gale. With roughly five days to go to Cape Horn, We found ourselves the southernmost boat in the fleet with the likelihood of a struggle to get back up north. Perhaps I had made a navigational blunder coming this far south (not the first time). The law of averages, notwithstanding known wind conditions, said it should soon blow from the south and push us back up, but what if it didn't? It could mean either a seventh or fourteenth place at the Horn.

While I pondered our future, Roger and Thierry were busy getting their stories in the easy weather, quietly interviewing the crew, one by one. Eugene says the crew had been warned about the journalists by Vladislav and Alexander, while in New Zealand. They were told to be careful what they said. Eugene and Roger shared a bunk, since they were on opposite watches, and they often joked about how Roger's Western ideology would soak up into Eugene's brain via the common pillow.

On 20 February we heard on the radio sched that *Steinlager* and *Fisher & Paykel*, again not far away from one another, had rounded Cape Horn at 1130 GMT, almost 300 miles ahead of us. We had just been close reaching for the last three days, in miserable conditions, fighting to regain northing. It looked as if seven maxis would converge on Cape Horn within a few hours.

Our first landfall, in the predawn darkness on the 22nd, was the tiny island of Diego Ramirez, which lies about 60 miles southwest of Cape Horn. The Chileans have a weather station here and maintain a navigation light. But, like a lot of things South American, the light wasn't working and the island, which is really only a rock outcrop, was instead backlit by the waning crescent moon low on the eastern horizon. By 5 o'clock in the morning, with daylight coming on, the wind piped up to 25 knots and we shot out of the black hole of a northwesterly rain squall to see the snow-capped mountains of the Cordillera Darwin, which is the high mountain range in Tierra del Fuego. While these high peaks were lit up like fiery beacons in the early morning sun not yet above our horizon, Cape Horn was just visible, low on the water, still cast in shadow and tormented by a succession of what looked like nasty squalls.

Juki was silent, staring ahead, watery-eyed. 'Me looking,' he finally said, 'read books, thinking, now looking – there is – Gorn!' I don't think anybody could have been more profound, or needed to be. Cape Horn, 'Gorn', call it what you will, we had made it!

The northwester died away later that morning and a new breeze filled in from the north northeast. This giving us a close fetch to our penultimate turning mark – Cape Horn to port – under a warm, sunny sky. Although it wasn't the story-book stuff of raging storms and near-shipwreck, everyone was elated to be there, and we toasted the occasion fittingly with a magnum of champagne and, of course, the token bottle of vodka.

We were not alone with our thoughts for long, here at the uttermost ends of the earth. Our competitors, *The Card* and *Belmont*, were a few miles ahead, while *NCB* and *Gatorade* were a few miles astern, reminding us that today's adventure was first and foremost a boat race. And somewhere to the west, out of range, were *Fortuna* and *Satquote British Defender*. Thus far we had not done badly.

By late that afternoon we were heading northeast, towards the Straits of Le Maire that separate mainland Tierra del Fuego from the rugged Staten Island. This would be our geographical gateway back into the Atlantic Ocean which, after the cold, the privation, the isolation and maybe the fear of the Southern Ocean itself, is the metaphorical safe harbour – giving the illusion of a refuge after a long storm.

In spite of this feeling of relief, most of us were disappointed that *Fazisi* didn't get another chance to show her form in some extended surfing conditions. We hadn't even any wounds to lick. As though we had climbed a tough alpine peak without any difficulties, we were now coming back down the relatively easy gradient of the glacier, where we could amble along, let our guard down and relax. . . .

And as they always do, the avalanche came without warning, right out of the west, and bowled us over, only a day later. Just abeam of the Falkland Islands, a vicious westerly buster, born from a cold front over the Andes, gathered steam and spilled out over southern Patagonia and, with a 50-knot vengeance, promptly stripped away our security blanket.

I'm not being metaphorical here – the security blanket was our mainsail, that already had a triple reef. We broached badly, dipping the belly of the sail in the water which smartly tore it to smithereens. West Falkland Island was not far downwind and weathering off with a No. 5 jib and a storm trysail was not the cosiest of thoughts. Luckily the storm abated after 15 hours, and thoughts shifted from safety back once again to the race. Without a full mainsail, with no spare and the prospect of a long repair, the consequences of this setback were obvious. Six other boats were within only 40 miles of us, and the end of the leg was not far away. If we slipped behind, which was now certain, a last place was as sure as if we had planned it.

On the evening of the 24th, with the wind safely down, it was time to start the repair. I reckoned it would take at least ten hours, hand stitching the 15-foot gash back together and then overlaying the whole area with large sheets of heavy dacron material. We set up lights, organized the sewing equipment and teams of two began to pass needles back and forth through the heavy Kevlar sail which was still draped across the boom, now lifeless in the dwindling breeze.

Cleverly hoisting a No. 1 genoa up the mast track, after jury-rigging some sliders, we were able to make reasonable speed, and the work involved in sheeting it correctly also had the beneficial effect of keeping idle minds occupied.

Although this was certainly an unfortunate set of circumstances, I can remember feeling completely content working all night, overseeing the repair, doing my share of sewing, revelling in the joys of manual labour for a change, instead of my self-imposed exile at the chart table, from whence I sallied forth only occasionally to growl the odd order – a style of management the Soviets seem to expect and prefer. I dreamed of doing some single-handed sailing for a change, maybe the BOC race, where one man does – has to do – everything. Here on the Whitbread it is not so demanding, because if you can't or won't 'do it' there are ten others who probably can.

Viktor Pogrebnov, affectionately known as the 'Teddy Bear' by the crew, had his 38th birthday party, on deck, in the middle of all this confusion, but it only added to the good cheer and camaraderie. By the time Venus heralded a spectacular dawn sky of pastel pink and turquoise, the repair was finished. Anatoly, who had stayed up all night with Vladimir, collapsed in an exhausted heap on the afterdeck looking as though he had aged ten years. With his torn clothes and three-week-old beard, he would not have been out of place asleep on the streets of New York City. Soon after, the sail was bent back on the boom by the light of an inspiring sunrise, but the wind had quit entirely, so there was no sense in hoisting the sail only to flog it against the rigging. Not until midday did we make full sail.

We crossed tacks with *Fortuna* during the night of the 24th. We went west, away from the fleet going east, in our last effort to gain the ground lost from the last storm. The next morning, struggling in light headwinds, (because west had not been the way to go) we passed 15 Soviet trawlers steaming south in a single file along the edge of the continental shelf of Argentina. Anatoly contacted them by radio and the crew sent telegrams home to their families. One of the trawler captains was amazed to hear that they had an American skipper – and no Kommissar!

'Look at those bastards,' the well-off American environmentalist said to Eugene, 'they're raping the sea!'

'Yes, but the Soviet people have to eat,' he answered.

Touché. Edgar didn't agree. 'With all those fishing boats, how can there be no fish in our markets at home?'

Thierry, always on the prowl for video material, asked him to repeat that statement for French TV. 'Oh no,' he said, 'for TV is too political.'

With hard times past, and an amble to the finish in prospect, once again the old newspapers came out, and instead of yacht-racers we all turned into idlers. Old animosities also have a way of surfacing when the pressure is turned off.

I woke up the next morning to horrendous yelling on deck and I could clearly make out it came from Juki and Eugene having a go. We had just tacked, and neither Thierry, who was at the chart-table, nor I could understand what it was about. By this stage we were used to these performances, but this one sounded uncharacteristically vehement. Edgar later translated the gist of it, and it went something like this:

Eugene: 'Wind has shifted, we must tack again.'

Juki: *'Tos gesagt?'* (Who said it?) 'Better ask Skip.'

Eugene: 'Why ask him? It's obvious. If you want to ask him, ask him yourself.'

Juki: 'No, my English is not so good, you ask him.'

Eugene: 'It's not difficult, your English is good enough!'

Juki: 'No, you're the English expert, like when you called my girlfriend Jenny up in New Zealand, and said I'm no good, better go out with me, because I can speak English!'

At this point I stuck my head out of the hatch, and saw Juki drop Eugene in between the grinder pedestals with a swipe to the jaw. By the time I jumped on deck it was all over and everybody was feeling bad, not least of all Eugene, who was still stunned and massaging his cheek. Juki apologized to me, but I don't think he did the same to Eugene.

Our own troubles, minor or major as they might have been, were temporarily overshadowed two days later when it was reported that the Finnish maxi *Martela* had issued a mayday, just before their keel had fallen off and the boat capsized through 180°. The old repair from Uruguay after Leg I had just made it – at least far enough to get the crew into warmer waters where they were rescued by the crews of *Charles Jourdan*, *Merit* and *UBF*. When *Martela*'s crew had noticed that the keel was loosening for the second time, near the Falklands, they began sleeping on deck, with only one man below at the radio. If it had happened but one week ago, it could have been an all-time Whitbread disaster.

In a twisted sort of way, I couldn't help but laugh at their misfortune. No lives were lost and in the Whitbread breakdowns, however severe, are all part of the game. At least we would be certain to beat one maxi in the overall results.

On the last day before we arrived in Punta, at the tail-end of the fleet, but on the verge of completing our circumnavigation, the wind veered 20°, freeing us up from a beat to reach. I suggested that someone move the genoa sheet lead from the inboard track to the outboard rail, which was a standard routine. As usual, as one who plays the game right to the end, Dale Tremain without hesitation said, 'I'll do it'.

'Why doesn't someone else do it for a change?' I asked, trying to encourage another 'volunteer'.

No replies. 'Better Dale,' said Navigator Sergei with a barely noticeable sense of humour, 'He is paid for it!!'

Maybe it was time for this Soviet crew to go off on their own.

13

In Search of the Promised Land

We scored four out of four at the finish in Punta, with yet another dead-of-night arrival. There was not a lot to celebrate and the atmosphere was low-key. At the post-race press conference, I let slip that my advisor's role in training this crew was now at an end and I was not sure if I would be continuing to Fort Lauderdale. The press interpreted this as meaning that the Soviets were unable to pay me – which was not entirely incorrect – but the real reason for setting the stage for my departure was simply because I was tired – tired of the racing, which was really more like a yacht delivery, tired of worrying about money and tired of being spokesman for the Soviets. I was running out of steam telling their story, who they were and why they were here, and consequently had the enthusiasm of a bored high-school science teacher explaining the life cycle of angleworms in a jar for the thousandth time.

Franco greeted us with open arms at the Palace Hotel, in spite of the rumour circulating that we were again without funds. In fact, Otegui Wool Exporters would come through with their promised $15,000 and Chumakov arrived with enough to pay the remainder of our necessary expenses. Once again, we were fortunate that we had had no major breakages, save for the mainsail, which had to be repaired in the best fashion we could, using as little new material as possible.

The Russian secretary who was to replace Monica turned out to be Alexander's wife Valentina, who admitted she was on holiday and would not be going on to Fort Lauderdale.

Luckily there was not a lot for anyone to do under the circumstances. It was also fortunate this was a short stopover and in two and a half weeks the fleet would be on its way.

Roger had left almost immediately to return to Maryland and write the story for *Life*; Thierry returned to France, but would be returning for the fifth leg and Dale decided to return to New Zealand, having done a superb job of backing the crew up through the Southern Ocean. 'I don't want to go to Fort Lauderdale – been there, done that,' he said, almost too casually, when making his good-byes to the crew.

The wives of most of the crew arrived after five days and since Chumakov had successfully found free accommodation for half of them in private homes of Russian emigrés, the absence of the familiar red rugby shirts round the office, the boat, the yacht club and its environs was particularly noticeable.

I spent my day checking the office for faxes, answering the odd telephone inquiry, checking the media centre, visiting the boat as little as possible, then ending the day with a run on the beach followed by a nice dinner in a local *asado* joint down the road – no panics, no tension, reduced to the routine that the successful skippers with organized projects had been accustomed to since the start, except in our case it wasn't good organization, nor bad, but total lack of.

Vladislav was still in Fort Lauderdale during the first week of our stay in Punta, and apparently he and Rae had made some headway setting up local fundraising activities. Other reports from America were not so encouraging, especially the feedback I was getting from journalists about how Rae was maligning the New Zealand effort, and especially the radio station, about what she thought were unnecessary expenses incurred in fundraising. 'We [*Fazisi*] didn't need New Zealand' was the message. A Kiwi fundraiser also in Fort Lauderdale, helping the perrennially impoverished *Liverpool Enterprise*, got wind of this and informed the media in New Zealand, so I was soon getting it from both ends. If that woman persists in what I gather are insinuatious that the station has misappropriated funds,' said an angry Barry Everard on the phone, 'she'll soon be talking to my lawyer.'

'The fact is, to raise money, you have to spend money,' I tried to explain to Alexander and Chumakov, this time with greater clarity since Valentina, a professional linguist, was translating. 'The fact that we had to spend $8,000 to run a party that grossed $19,000 is perfectly normal. I see the situation very simply – we made $11,000 that we didn't have before. OK, we didn't get $400,000 out of New Zealand, but we made almost $200,000 net to the boat – $200,000 that we wouldn't have had if we hadn't trusted the station and Clive. You know, sponsorship can never be expected to be a profit-making exercise. If you cover your expenses you should be happy, and in New Zealand we did more than that.'

'We are not ungrateful,' said Valentina, translating Alexander's reply with such accuracy and emotional inflection that I felt it was the first time I had really communicated with the man. 'But our experience in the West has not been good. When we began this project we were told that we would find $5 million, but it was soon obvious that it would not be possible. But even trying to get smaller sums of money, it is very difficult and confusing for us. Most people seem to say one thing and then do another.'

'It's because of Vladislav,' added Chumakov, 'that we are in the mess today. Always we have a big story about how people will help us, but as you can see, we have gone almost all the way around the world with no money and the company in big debt. Now he is in Fort Lauderdale spending money, but I don't think he will make any. That is why it is now decided that Vladislav will be eliminated from making any further financial decisions, so please do not involve him in any. When he arrives this week, he will be only in charge of technical matters.'

They were disillusioned with the West, while I was hardened to it. There was not a lot I could say to console them; the mood was dispairing, like shipwrecked sailors stranded without a hope of rescue. It was clear I couldn't leave the project completely, but I suggested that maybe I shouldn't sail the next leg, and instead go to Fort Lauderdale to try to help the fundraising. I told Alexander that I was not particularly enjoying myself out on the water, and I made the point that the crew could handle the boat themselves (which they could), but he wasn't keen to discuss this question.

It was unthinkable that I shouldn't do the entire race, not only by Fazis, but also by the press, who hinted that it would look bad if I bailed out, for whatever reason, on the crew. This was really a warning that I might get a good roasting in the papers because of it. Peer-group pressure also was brought to bear, even from some of my old crew on *Drum*.

Phil Barrett, a Hampshire man, sailing with the Irish on *NCB*, which was as good a test-bed of moral fibre and stick-to-itness as any project, said to me in the bar, 'You wouldn't bail out now, would ya? After having gone this far?' He thought about it for a while, screwed up his eyes and twitched his outrageous moustache and then made up his own mind, without waiting for my answer, 'Naw, I know you wouldn't, just like you know I wouldn't.' These and other conversations had more effect than I would have thought possible, but again, I was 37 years old, I had done the race four times, and had, or should have had, my thoughts sufficiently gathered by that stage to make my own decision. Also hanging in the balance was the chance to go to northern Argentina to spend time on a friend's *estancia*, a change of pace that was not without its attractions.

But most people would say, 'You've got to go to America! The American skipper of the Soviet boat, Christ, they're all expecting you, and besides, think of the publicity! Think of the next race!' But all I could think of was a sea of long grass, an uncomplaining horse to ride, no publicity and no Russians. It was their project after all, not mine. Why not let them get on with it? There was no mistaking that I faced a dilemma within myself.

When I broached the subject for the third time, the matter was finally put to rest. 'We started this project with you, and we want to finish it with you,' said Alexander. 'You are morally obliged to help us.' I caved in. The new plan was to have a new Soviet co-skipper, not Anatoly, who was still in disfavour, but Valeri Alekseev, a Black Sea skipper, but one who hadn't done the graft back in Poti. Everyone assured me that the crew was in favour of the decision.

The idea was to get back to the original arrangement which had ended tragically six months before in Uruguay with Alexei's suicide. 'And now,' said the press release I wrote later that day, 'It is fitting that we resume our original concept of a joint venture, having a Soviet and an American skipper.' In practice, Valeri and I agreed that he would run the entire show; I would play a lesser role in the tactics and leave Sergei Akatyev to do more. In reality, I was going along for the ride and to be on board when we hit the States. It is easily understandable that Fazis did not want to have to explain why I was not on board and instead somewhere out of touch on the Pampas.

Gary Jobson arrived two days before the start to interview the skippers for ESPN TV in America, and film the re-start. He pulled me aside in the media centre on the Friday and said, 'Listen, I got to tell you something. What kind of an agreement did the Soviets have with Dennis Conner?'

'As far as I know, none at all,' I answered.

'Well, I talked to Dennis before I left, and told him about how big the Whitbread Race is, about you and the Russians. And he said he was furious with the Russians, how they owed him a fortune in commissions for the Pepsi deal, and when the boat got to Fort Lauderdale he was going to have it chained to the dock.'

I started to laugh. We hadn't even got $200,000 out of Pepsi! You tell Dennis that we're bucks up, rolling in sponsorship money, let him chain us to the dock – then I'll blow him right out of the water!'

'You know something,' said Gary, 'when this is over, you should go on a lecture circuit in America – make some money, then go and do the next one.'

'I'll be in the Antarctic next year, right out of it. But yeah, I'd like to do the next one, without rock stars, without Russians, for once my own project. But someone else is going to have to do the leg work and raise the money. I don't want to go through anything like this again.'

On Saturday 17 March, we left the dock for the start. Anatoly and Eugene waved us goodbye. Valeri Safiullin was back on board for the last two legs, and we hoped Thierry Rannou would be able to catch a motorboat to the starting line because, at one and a half hours to the gun, he was still sitting in the office at the Palace Hotel trying to negotiate a contract with Fazis about the video film he would be shooting – part of the new Fazis 'get tough, mean and nasty like in the West' campaign. He jumped on board, sweating, 15 minutes before the start. 'Those bastards, *faire un contrat maintenant, c'est con!'*

Sergei Borodinov drove the boat at the start while I shot video for the TV pool. We were last across the line and managed to maintain that position for most of the way to Fort Lauderdale, with an average wind of only 10 to 12 knots for almost 6,000 miles. *Fazisi*, with her tattered sails, lumbered in the wake of the fleet right from the start. The enthusiasm for racing never took off but levelled out somewhere just above mild interest. I think Valeri the skipper, Sergei and Viktor would have liked to push harder, but the weariness of this routine for the old crew had the effect of dragging them down as well.

It was predominantly a tropical leg and soon after leaving Punta I settled into my own routine of sleeping 8 or 9 hours a night, waking up with a bucket of sea water tossed over my head, followed by 50 deep knee bends. After breakfast came the morning radio sched, leaving the remainder of the day clear to devote to my extensive and varied library, between cups of tea.

Like the paranoid American that I am, I avoided the midday sun which is especially ferocious in these latitudes, while the Soviets were content roasting away on deck, even on their off-watch, soaking up the ultra violet all day – which in a way is really an environmental impact statement that has far greater implications than a bit of skin cancer.

Sergei was now in charge of the tactics and only occasionally would I interfere with the deck work, but it was still distressing to find that after all these miles they were still sailing in light winds at the wrong angle, had the spinnaker pole set at the wrong height, with the boat generally out of trim.

'Come on, Edgar,' I said one morning. 'You know when the wind changes you have to re-trim the sails.'

'Skip, I know, but I don't want to make war in crew.'

I sighed and went back down below to continue reading the biography of Pablo Picasso. He once said, 'It is not necessary to paint a man with a gun, an apple can be just as revolutionary'. Maybe I had been using the wrong psychology all along.

After one week, Thierry realized that it had been a mistake for him to return for another leg. The filming material was non-existent ('uncommercial' it's called in the trade) – naked Soviets sunning themselves in the tropics and not interested in doing any interviews – hardly an adventure story for television. When he was not annoying the watch by suggesting they trim the sails and steer in the right direction ('Not your problem, you are journalist,' they told him) he was on the radio to *Charles Jourdan*, *Gatorade* and *Merit* gossiping in French as only the French can do, or speaking to his sponsor in France, dictating articles, with a highly cynical flair, about how the American skipper was in the depths of depression.

As evidence that his opinions were not necessarily appreciated, Navigator Sergei left a small drawing on the back of a chart for him to see – a live frog on a dinner plate garnished with lemon and parsley, *à la* Rami, with knife and fork at the ready.

Rothmans had finally broken the stranglehold *Steinlager* had been maintaining on the fleet and by 29 March, twelve days out of Uruguay, she was miles ahead, having sailed a spectacular course far to the east of the fleet.

That same night we could see the outline of the Brazilian city of Recife, and occasionally silent explosions of lightning, coloured orange by the city lights, would illuminate big thunderland clouds along the coast – nocturnal tropical showers were giving the citizens there some relief from another stifling day.

Not so on board *Fazisi*. Offshore, the sun beat down on us continually during the day, with no prospect of rain. Down below, the deck head was too hot to touch and the interior became an oven by midday. In these conditions the cornflakes served with tepid milk for breakfast and the warm fruit juice had to be forced down to prevent dehydration, and were not consumed for pleasure. My biggest fear wasn't a

181

tropical storm, nor pirates in the Caribbean, but the likely breakdown from overuse by my bunk fan, which ran about 20 hours a day.

Even the little inconveniences began to rankle, like when the crate of fresh grapefruits we had all been looking forward to were finally broached, only to discover they were desiccated, high in fibre and little else. And when Pierre Fehlmann, skipper of *Merit*, informed us that his crew had just finished another two litres of icecream – straight from the deep-freeze – our situation began to grate on the nerves.

A day later, we turned the northeast corner of Brazil and made a course for the Virgin Islands, our next likely landfall, some 2000 miles away to the northwest. That afternoon, with the low-lying mosquito coast quickly slipping below our horizon, we sailed through a fleet of native fishing craft – rough and ready open wooden boats, brightly painted with lateen sailes, some sporting an outboard motor, crewed by a handful of black Brazilians.

I tried to get our crew to drop the spinnaker for ten minutes and come alongside one of them so the Brazilians could trade some fresh fish for the spare $10 bill I had. It is strictly against the race rules to take on provisions at sea, but I thought, under the circumstances, the crew would welcome a bit of excitement in an otherwise uneventful passage.

Not all, but a few shouted at me, '*Nyet*! we are racing!' Viktor and Sergei Borodinov actually got quite aggressive about it. In spite of evidence to the contrary, I had to concede we were, at least, supposed to be racing, but there were far greater implications in this little incident. I had been effectively emasculated – stripped of all authority. The crew knew it and I knew it. My involvement in the sailing was really over. Thierry, almost beside himself with joy grabbed his notepad and wrote the story down, and I admit to doing the same, the victim of my own journalism.

This was in reality a good sign, an indication that the crew wanted to go it alone. But after a day of obligatory enthusiasm, they slipped back into their old apathy, fickle as a spinnaker that momentarily fills then again loses the breeze and collapses.

Gorbachev sent the troops in to Lithuania during this leg,

but the crew, even Edgar and Rami from Latvia, didn't seem too interested. 'What did your wife say,' I asked Rami, 'you know, about the conditions in the Soviet Union with all the reform?'

'Not a lot. We didn't talk about it much – didn't want to. Those problems will all be there when we go back.'

As if to explain this crew, Juki told me that the problem with the Soviet Union was surely a problem of culture, and of course he used his beloved Georgia as an example, 'Everywhere *Fazisi* go, England, South America, Australia, New Zealand, there are Russian peoples, Ukrainian peoples, Moldavian, Lithuanian, Latvian, but no Georgian. Why? Because Georgian peoples love Georgia!' He gave me an interesting lecture on Georgian history and concluded it by saying, 'Georgian peoples, Russian peoples no same, no same, Georgian people friendly people, smile, speak to everyone!' He then makes a long face and says, 'Russian people, hoooh!'

With one week to go, we were again becalmed and *Steinlager*, who had regained the lead from *Rothmans'* with not much difficulty, was a staggering 500 miles ahead and would easily make five wins in a row. I played a game with the crew, who, if the truth be known, were dying to get off the boat and into the hot dog and hamburger world of America. 'Juki,' I asked, 'how much money would you give to be in Fort Lauderdale today?' He thought about it for a while and finally said, with no shame, 'Fifty dollars!'

Both Thierry and I, equally frustrated and having a similar sense of value, would offer $400. But most of the other crew refused to play, instead making vague idealistic propositions: 'All my money if we could do better'. 'Money is not important', 'I'm happy to be here', and so on. I didn't know whether to be impressed, feel sorry for them or laugh. I wasn't even sure why I played the game.

We missed the blow that funneled the leaders into Fort Lauderdale for a spectacular surfing finish, three days ahead of us. Instead we had to gybe back and forth in almost no wind, trying to get through the gap in the Bahama Bank appropriately known as the 'Hole in the Wall', before reaching across the Gulf stream to Florida. Almost twenty years ago I was going the other way, on one of my first big yacht deliveries, on a plastic 40-footer bound for the fledgling charter trade in the British Virgin Islands. I can remember quite clearly the big storm we had, how the engine had filled with water and when I got lost how we almost accidentally beached the boat on a deserted islet south of San Salvador. That's how my career started, at the bottom, culminating in this voyage with yet another crew, naive, but possibly clever enough to have started at the top.

At midday on 11 April *Fazisi* crossed the finishing line, reached through the narrow channel of Port Everglades and turned right towards the dock in Fort Lauderdale. We had landed in America – the Promised Land – the heart of the ideological West: all that is good, or all that is bad, in the world. Not just a country, but a concept that our crew had heard about ever since they could remember. And now they were embarking on the ultimate voyage. I was as curious as they were to see what we would discover.

Epilogue

Unlike the other Whitbread ports of call, Fort Lauderdale, Florida, is an anomaly, off the track of any logical circumnavigation of the world. It's also probably about the least traditional venue that you could possibly think of if you had to take a round the world race into America. Unlike Newport, Rhode Island, or Annapolis, Maryland, or for that matter New York City itself, there is very little sense of marine history there. A satellite of the better known city of Miami which lies only 20 miles to the south, Lauderdale is an enigmatic community: a strange amalgam of elderly retirees with leathery sun tans, a meeting place for rowdy college kids during spring and Christmas holiday breaks, and host to a permanent population of itinerant boat builders, boat mechanics, boat painters, delivery skippers and yacht brokers who sometimes appear to be the only working class.

With one of the highest proportions of water craft to residents in the country, Fort Lauderdale, like a lot of places in America, makes up for any deficiency of character with volume and pizzas. After all, 70 years ago it was nothing more than a mosquito-infested swamp, part of the Everglades, inhabited by an assortment of crocodiles, alligators, snakes and waders. This was before land speculators dredged and filled the area just behind the natural waterway known as the 'Intercoastal' which separated the swampy area from the barrier beach. When the water filled the new canals it created what is possibly the world's largest marina village, and now is filled to capacity with medium to outsize homes sporting their family yachts tied up on pilings out front.

185

Apart from the residential areas tucked away on their private canals, the commercial districts are concrete arteries of streets and wide boulevards festooned with signs that scream at the clientele advertising fast food joints, bars and restaurants, hotels, shops, gas stations, motels, even more bars and restaurants and of course the banks that proliferate on every corner to fuel this powerful holiday economy which throbs with energy 24 hours a day.

I have spent a fair share of my time in Fort Lauderdale over the years and I have to admit the atmosphere there is no longer my cup of tea. It typifies all the stereotypes of liberal America – the choice, the vibrance, the vanity, the congestion, the consumption, the eternal optimism, and the excess. If this was a spiritual purgatory for me, for the Soviets it represented a materialistic paradise. From the time we threw our lines ashore on the jetty of the Pier 66 Hotel which served as the Race centre, the crew loved every minute of their stay until they left for England three and a half weeks later.

Rae Glasgow had secured cheap accommodation for the crew in the exclusive Bahia Mar Resort Hotel, which saved the project a small fortune. From the complimentary office there she had also organized the marketing of the *Fazisi* T-shirts and other paraphernalia. She negotiated a new suit of sails via local sponsors and drafted another gruelling schedule for the crew for fundraising evenings, some of which, like the judging the 'Hot Body' competition, were understandably more enjoyable than others. The crew even got a sponsored haircut and manicure at an upmarket hair stylist who put on a champagne and caviar reception.

Fazis had arranged for 58 works of art to be donated to the project from Soviet artists which were sent over in a last-minute air cargo consignment and the Palm Beach magazine publisher Frank Lennon organized an art auction and other events in what is probably the wealthiest community in America.

There was a feeling of good will from everyone we came in contact with and almost from the moment they arrived the *Fazisi* crew were local celebrities. Even the Lithuanian protesters marching up and down in front of a Palm Beach restaurant that was hosting a cocktail party for us were almost benevolent, well mannered as the crew, and turned out to be the only negative vibe.

Although a lot happened in Fort Lauderdale, there was a lot that didn't happen, or go exactly to plan. We never found the dream sponsor to pull Fazis out of debt back in England, but instead raised only subsistence money from a grass roots campaign, similar to, but not as successful as New Zealand. It was clear even to an unintelligent observer that the boat would in any case finish the Race, with or without a big sponsor – and the Race was to all intents and purposes over. Dennis Conner never showed up to collect his money, which was unfortunate because we could have used the publicity. We managed to get only two new sails out of the budget, due to infighting between the sailmaker and the fundraising organization. Sadly, the art auction realized only a small part of its intrinsic worth. And many other fundraising ideas just never happened.

What *Fazisi* did bring about was some understanding between the Soviet Union and America that was not reported in *Time* magazine or *Newsweek*, but possibly was more significant, albeit on a small scale. It gave many Americans their first experience of knowing, or at least meeting, people from the Soviet Union, and I think many were pleasantly surprised. It was really public relations at its best, which was even more appreciated when the Soviet Ambassador to America, Yuri Dubinin, and his wife Tatiana, spent three days with the project. He was probably the most eloquent spokesman *Fazisi* had enjoyed. He spoke at the press conference for the art auction, made an appearance at another press conference at the Bahia Mar Hotel and spent an afternoon at the helm of *Fazisi*. 'The good will and general good feeling I have found in this project,' he told a TV film crew, 'would be a good lesson for world diplomacy.' If that wasn't a platitude, and I think it was not, the *Fazisi* project would have to be considered a milestone, and not just in a yacht race.

Again, there was no time for the crew really to relax, to take stock of where they were and what they were doing. Late in the stop-over when I asked them out of all the countries they had seen, which one they liked the most, almost all said America. But most of them added, 'Maybe New Zealand, nice country too,' which was said as if they weren't quite sure why. Possibly they realized the relative rural sanity of Auckland was more representative of New Zealand than what can only be described as the pleasantly hedonistic world of Fort Lauderdale could ever be representative of America. A few of the crew commented that when they saw the stately homes in Palm Beach they were amazed to find that people really lived like that, simply because they had always been told in the Soviet Union that no one could possibly have that much wealth. They were making an observation, not a value judgement.

It is hard to get a well-rounded view of America in a place like South Florida in three and a half weeks, but I'm sure that's not what the *Fazisi* crew got out of their visits to glitzy night clubs, their one-day trip to Disney World, their expensive receptions and dinners with the mega rich, a few of whom were there not because they were necessarily interested in the Soviets, but because the Soviets were now fashionable, and the event was on their social charity schedule – Tuesday night the Soviets, Thursday afternoon the Heart Foundation. . . .

It is a great pity that the crew was too busy to explore the different sides of America: to have a drink at the South Port Raw Bar where the locals hang out, have a meal at 'Dirty' Ernies down on US 1, the last original eatery in an otherwise modern watered-down cuisine, have breakfast at the topless doughnut joint, or maybe even take a closed-window cruise through the racial war zone west of Biscayne Boulevard in Miami where the blacks and Hispanics carve each other up on a regular basis. When Rami took the bus up to Washington DC to visit a Latvian relative now working for Voice of America Radio, I told him, 'Make sure you see more than the Washington Monument – walk through the negro ghetto as well!'

On 5 May *Fazisi* began the last leg to England. She finished an outstanding 8th place after 18 days at sea, and retained her 11th place overall for the Whitbread, beating four maxis out of the fleet of fifteen led by the stunning performance of

Peter Blake's *Steinlager 2*. During the summer *Fazisi* toured in America in hopes of finding support for another joint venture project, this time with a proper Western sponsor for the next Whitbread Race in 1993/4. With good contacts now established, this will be their future.

I was not on board for that last voyage, but instead waved the crew goodbye and godspeed from a rubber dinghy. At the start, I wouldn't have felt comfortable riding across the Atlantic like a publicity potentate as I did on the fifth leg to America. But by now I was more than content about this decision, besides, I had this book to write; a story that needed to be told which would surely be newsworthy while *Fazisi* and her tumultuous history was still fresh in the minds of the interested public.

Granted, it has been a story mainly about problems: battles with not only the sea, but against each other and battles within ourselves. It is set in a period of social conflict for the Soviet Union, its people struggling to be released from the repression which the long overdue events of the last twelve months have helped to break down.

It is only because of this conflict that the *Fazisi* project ever existed. The *Fazisi* story took place simply because in these changing times it was meant to happen. To go against the established system, to try something new like the Soviet team did, and then to succeed, turns the story of whatever conflict they suffered into one of great achievement. *Fazisi* and her crew should not be judged by the conflict, but by the result. They are true revolutionaries.

In his epilogue to *War and Peace*, Tolstoy said that great events in history like the Napoleonic Wars could not have happened simply because of the actions or willpower of individuals like Napoleon or Czar Alexander, but took place because of an almost unexplainable mass movement that was simply destined to be.

Maybe so. On the last day before *Fazisi* left for England I ran into Viktor Tichov, Alexander Kedisvlili and Vladislav in the hotel elevator. 'Big trouble,' they said. 'Problems with getting fundraising money, we are off to see lawyer.'

We looked at each other for a moment. We had been down this road before. Then it all was put in perspective when the four of us burst out laughing. The boat had come 11th but this Soviet management team had won their race in the end. They had come to grips with the wild West, and after all the strife they still had a sense of humour. I thought back to a conversation I had during the 5th leg when some of the crew were complaining about the Fazis administration.

Juki, the great communicator, could have told Tolstoy a thing or two about destiny and those who make it. He said to me, 'Everyone complain about Fazis company. If no Fazis company, me no see world!'

AUTHOR'S NOTE

I would like to thank Tony and Gill Crossley for providing the peace and solitude at their farm *Milima* in Queensland, Australia, where I traded a rolling ocean for seas of grass in May 1990 to write this book.

Appendix I

Fazisi's *design and deck plan*

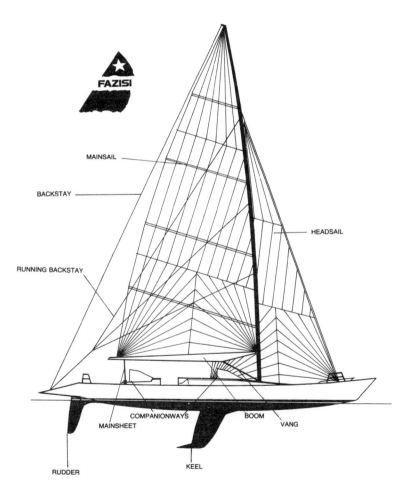

MAINSAIL

BACKSTAY

HEADSAIL

RUNNING BACKSTAY

COMPANIONWAYS

MAINSHEET

BOOM

VANG

RUDDER

KEEL

<u>Deck plan</u>

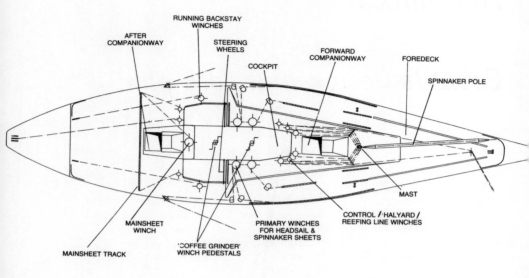

RUNNING BACKSTAY
WINCHES

AFTER
COMPANIONWAY

STEERING
WHEELS

COCKPIT

FORWARD
COMPANIONWAY

FOREDECK

SPINNAKER POLE

MAST

CONTROL / HALYARD /
REEFING LINE WINCHES

MAINSHEET
WINCH

PRIMARY WINCHES
FOR HEADSAIL &
SPINNAKER SHEETS

MAINSHEET TRACK

'COFFEE GRINDER'
WINCH PEDESTALS

<u>Accomodation</u>

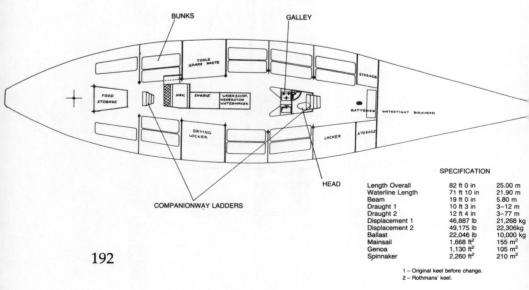

BUNKS

GALLEY

HEAD

COMPANIONWAY LADDERS

192

SPECIFICATION		
Length Overall	82 ft 0 in	25.00 m
Waterline Length	71 ft 10 in	21.90 m
Beam	19 ft 0 in	5.80 m
Draught 1	10 ft 3 in	3–12 m
Draught 2	12 ft 4 in	3–77 m
Displacement 1	46,887 lb	21,268 kg
Displacement 2	49,175 lb	22,306kg
Ballast	22,046 lb	10,000 kg
Mainsail	1,668 ft²	155 m²
Genoa	1,130 ft²	105 m²
Spinnaker	2,260 ft²	210 m²

1 – Original keel before change.
2 – Rothmans' keel.

Appendix II

Crew list

Name	Age	Profession	Home town	Legs raced
Sergei Akatyev	33	ship's navigator	Kiev	3,4,5,6
Valeri Alekseev	38	sailing coach	Sochi	4,5,6
Sergei Borodinov	32	professional sailor	Moscow	4,5
Juri Doroshenko	31	ship's navigator	Sevastopol	1,2,3
Alexei Drosdovski	38	doctor	Odessa	1,2
Alexei Gryshenko	42	electronic engineer	Kiev	1
Brian 'Mugsy' Hancock	32	property developer	Boston, USA	1
Mark 'Herbe' Hauser	26	professional sailor	Auckland, NZ	3
Roland Jourdain	25	professional sailor	La Rochelle, France	2
Viktor Kamkin	37	architect	Dnepropetrovs	1,2,3
Guennadi Korolkov	28	ship's navigator	Odessa	1,2
Vladimir Kulinichenko	27	mechanical engineer	Odessa	3,4,5,6
Rami Leibovich	47	waiter	Riga	3,4,5,6
Igor Mironenko	32	mechanical engineer	Kiev	1,2,3,4,5
Vladislav Murnikov	37	civil engineer	Moscow	3,6
Eugene Platon	31	applied mathematician	Kiev	1,2,3,4
Viktor Pogrebnov	38	sailing coach	Sochi	4,5,6
Thierry Rannou	32	journalist	Paris	4,5
Jim Saunders	42	marine engineer	Hamble, UK	2
Valeri Safiullin	33	engineer	Alma Ata	1,2,5,6
Sergei Stanetsky	32	electrical engineer	Odessa	1,2,3,4,5,6
Nodari Teneishvili	31	ships navigator	Tshaltubo, Georgia	1,6
Edgar Terechin	34	sailing coach	Riga	1,2,3,4,5,6
Dale Tremain	32	boat builder	Auckland, NZ	2,3,4

Fazisi: The Joint Venture

Name	Age	Profession	Home town	Legs raced
Jumberi 'Juki' Tsomaya	32	sailing coach	Poti, Georgia	1,2,3,4,5,6
Roger Vaughan	52	editor/journalist	Oxford, Maryland, USA	4
Anatoly Verba	44	marine engineer	Odessa	1,2,3,4
Viktor Yasykov	41	professional sailor	Sochi	1,2

Appendix III

Competitors

Boat Name	Nationality	Skipper	Length (ft)	IOR rating foot	Dis-placement pounds (approx)
Division A – IOR 70 foot to 62.5 foot					
Merit	Switz.	Pierre Fohlmann	80	70.00	65,200
Steinlager 2	New Zeal.	Peter Blake	84	70.00	78,400
Fisher & Paykel NZ	New Zeal.	Grant Dalton	82	70.00	72,000
Satquote British Defender	GB	Colin Watkins	80	70.00	67,200
The Card	Sweden	Roger Nilson	80	70.00	66,841
Union Bank of Finland	Finland	Ludde Ingvall	79	70.00	63,000
NCB Ireland	Ireland	Joe English	79	69.12	69,440
Martela of	Finland	Markku Wiikori	78	70.00	65,400
Belmont Finland II	Finland	Harry Harkimo	80	70.00	61,730
Fortuna Extra Lights	Spain	Jan Santana Jose-Luis Doresto Javier de la Gondara	76	68.00	51,520
Fazisi	Sov. Union	Alexei Gryshenko Valeri Alexeev Skip Novak	82	69.99	47,400
Gatorade	Italy	Giorgio Falck Herve Jan	80	70.00	60,000
Charles Jourdan	France	Alain Gabbay Max Phillippe Couteau	76	70.00	35,000
Liverpool Enterprise	GB	Bob Salmon	80	70.00	66,140
Rothmans	GB	Lawrie Smith	78	70.00	58,973
Division C – IOR 55 foot to 47.5 foot					
Equity & Law II	Holland	Dirk Nauta	63	54.61	42,900

195

Fazisi: The Joint Venture

Boat Name	Nationality	Skipper	Length (ft)	IOR rating foot	Displacement pounds (approx)
Division D – IOR 47.5 foot to 40 foot					
Maiden	GB	Tracy Edwards	58	45.92	48,000
La Poste	France	Daniel Mallo	51	40.46	28,600
Rucanor Sport	Belgium	Bruno Dubois	56	46.15	36,512
Esprit de Liberte	France	Patrick Tabarly	56	51.50	32,928
Schlussel von Bremen	West Germany	Harm Muller-Rohlck Rolf Renken Dr Jochen Orgelman	63	47.49	52,535
Cruiser Class – IOR 70 foot to 40 foot					
Creightons Naturally	GB	John Chittenden	79	71.89	76,174
With Integrity	GB	Andy Coghill	68	67.80	73,020

Appendix IV

Results

LEG I – The Solent to Punta del Este

Name	Elapsed Time				Place
	D	H	M	S	
Steinlager 2	25	20	46	27	1
Merit	26	08	11	20	2
Fisher & Paykel	27	03	50	26	3
Rothmans	27	07	29	00	4
The Card	28	06	43	25	5
Fazisi	28	13	20	18	6
Gatorade	28	13	22	58	7
Martela O. F.	28	13	54	58	8
Satquote British Defender	28	14	23	52	9
Fortuna Extra Lights	28	19	49	45	10
Charles Jourdan	28	20	10	18	11
Belmont Finland II	28	20	21	15	12
NCB Ireland	29	05	27	46	13
Union Bank of Finland	29	13	49	05	14
Equity & Law II	31	09	57	53	15
Liverpool Enterprise	32	03	15	55	16
Creightons Naturally	34	07	59	15	17
L'Esprit de Liberté	34	09	02	59	18
Rucanor Sport	34	10	20	03	19
Maiden	35	00	46	44	20
With Integrity	35	07	11	47	21
Schlussel von Bremen	35	11	46	37	22
La Poste	37	20	04	18	23

Fazisi: The Joint Venture

LEG II – Punta del Este to Fremantle

Name	D	H	M	S	Place
Steinlager 2	27	05	34	44	1
Rothmans	27	07	07	28	2
Merit	27	07	07	56	3
Fisher & Paykel	27	08	30	20	4
Charles Jourdan	27	22	16	41	5
The Card	27	22	57	57	6
Martela O. F.	28	01	27	57	7
Union Bank of Finland	28	05	13	52	8
Fortuna Extra Lights	28	05	52	22	9
Fazisi	29	01	40	15	10
Gatorade	29	05	39	14	11
Satquote British Defender	29	10	01	43	12
NCB Ireland	29	10	39	02	13
Belmont Finland II	29	15	57	55	14
Equity & Law II	31	22	28	36	15
Liverpool Enterprise	33	03	00	26	16
Maiden	35	11	11	41	17
Rucanor Sport	36	17	57	43	18
Schlussel von Bremen	36	18	06	42	19
L'Esprit de Liberte	36	18	09	59	20
With Integrity	37	18	19	55	21
Creightons Naturally	40	09	45	43	22
La Poste	40	15	33	31	23

LEG II – Combined Times

Name	D	H	M	S	Place
Steinlager 2	53	02	21	11	1
Merit	53	15	19	16	2
Fisher & Paykel	54	12	20	46	2
Rothmans	54	14	36	28	4
The Card	56	05	41	22	5
Martela O. F.	56	15	22	55	6
Charles Jourdan	56	18	26	59	7
Fortuna Extra Lights	57	01	42	07	8
Fazisi	57	15	00	33	9
Gatorade	57	19	02	12	10
Union Bank of Finland	57	19	02	57	11
Satquote British Defender	58	00	25	35	12
Belmont Finland II	58	12	19	10	13
NCB Ireland	58	16	06	48	14
Equity & Law II	63	08	26	29	15
Liverpool Enterprise	65	06	16	21	16
Maiden	70	11	58	25	17
L'Esprit de Liberte	71	03	12	58	18
Rucanor Sport	71	04	17	46	19
Schlussel von Bremen	72	05	53	19	20
With Integrity	73	01	31	42	21
Creightons Naturally	74	17	44	58	22
La Poste	78	11	37	49	23

LEG III – Fremantle to Auckland

Name	Elapsed Time				Place
	D	H	M	S	
Steinlager 2	12	17	33	00	1
Fisher & Paykel	12	17	39	04	2
Merit	12	18	44	17	3
Rothmans	12	18	54	37	4
The Card	12	20	49	50	5
Fortuna Extra Lights	12	21	22	22	6
Martela O. F.	12	22	42	57	7
Satquote British Defender	12	23	29	25	8
Charles Jourdan	13	02	53	49	9
Fazisi	13	04	40	30	10
Gatorade	13	05	11	08	11
NCB Ireland	13	10	50	24	12
Belmont Finland II	13	14	27	42	13
Liverpool Enterprise	14	14	17	58	14
Equity & Law II	14	16	55	13	15
Union Bank of Finland	14	20	40	06	16
With Integrity	14	22	50	02	17
Creightons Naturally	15	04	12	04	18
Maiden	15	05	27	14	19
L'Esprit de Liberte	15	06	17	16	20
Schlussel von Bremen	15	08	21	58	21
Rucanor Sport	15	23	31	41	22
La Poste	18	23	18	23	23

LEG III – Combined Times

Name	Elapsed Time				Place
	D	H	M	S	
Steinlager 2	65	19	54	11	1
Merit	66	10	03	33	2
Fisher & Paykel	67	05	59	50	3
Rothmans	67	09	31	05	4
The Card	69	02	31	12	5
Martela O. F.	69	14	05	52	6
Charles Jourdan	69	21	20	48	7
Fortuna Extra Lights	69	23	04	29	8
Fazisi	70	19	41	03	9
Satquote British Defender	70	23	55	00	10
Gatorade	71	00	13	20	11
Belmont Finland II	72	02	46	52	12
NCB Ireland	72	02	57	12	13
Union Bank of Finland	72	15	43	03	14
Equity & Law II	78	01	21	42	15
Liverpool Enterprise	79	20	34	19	16
Maiden	85	17	25	39	17
L'Esprit de Liberte	86	09	30	14	18
Rucanor Sport	87	03	49	27	19
Schlussel von Bremen	87	14	15	17	20
With Integrity	88	00	21	44	21
Creightons Naturally	89	21	57	02	22
La Poste	97	10	56	12	23

Fazisi: The Joint Venture

LEG IV – Auckland to Funta del Este

Name	Elapsed Time				Place
	D	H	M	S	
Steinlager 2	22	20	41	53	1
Fisher & Paykel	22	21	03	11	2
Rothmans	23	09	00	11	3
Merit	23	10	30	32	4
Charles Jourdan	23	14	18	05	5
Union Bank of Finland	23	18	12	29	6
Gatorade	24	17	28	29	7
The Card	24	18	12	47	8
NCB Ireland	24	23	31	22	9
Belmont Finland II	25	00	45	54	10
Fortuna Extra Lights	25	01	17	31	11
Satquote British Defender	25	01	31	12	12
Fazisi	25	07	01	15	13
Liverpool Enterprise	26	02	56	09	14
Equity & Law II	26	15	34	24	15
Creightons Naturally	26	16	10	48	16
L'Esprit de Liberte	29	03	25	51	17
Schlussel von Bremen	29	20	33	28	18
With Integrity	29	21	14	03	19
Maiden	30	12	06	48	20
La Poste	30	15	21	39	21

LEG IV – Combined Times

Name	Elapsed Time				Place
	D	H	M	S	
Steinlager 2	88	16	36	04	1
Merit	89	20	34	05	2
Fisher & Paykel	90	03	03	01	3
Rothmans	90	18	31	16	4
Charles Jourdan	93	11	38	53	5
The Card	93	20	43	59	6
Fortuna Extra Lights	95	00	22	00	7
Gatorade	95	17	41	49	8
Satquote British Defender	96	01	26	12	9
Fazisi	96	02	42	18	10
Union Bank of Finland	96	09	55	32	11
NCB Ireland	97	02	28	34	12
Belmond Finland II	97	03	32	46	13
Equity & Law II	104	16	56	06	14
Liverpool Enterprise	105	23	30	28	15
L'Esprit de Liberte	115	12	56	05	16
Maiden	116	05	32	27	17
Creightons Naturally	116	14	07	50	18
Schlussel von Bremen	117	10	48	45	19
With Integrity	117	21	35	47	20
La Poste	128	02	17	51	21

LEG V – Punta del Este to Fort Lauderdale

Name	Elapsed Time				Place
	D	H	M	S	
Steinlager 2	22	16	41	11	1
Fisher & Paykel	22	17	15	41	2
Rothmans	22	21	33	04	3
Merit	23	10	52	24	4
The Card	23	15	24	19	5
Satquote British Defender	23	18	49	47	6
Union Bank of Finland	24	00	33	43	7
NCB Ireland	24	00	24	54	8
Belmont Finland II	24	04	23	00	9
Gatorade	24	05	03	34	10
Fortuna Extra Lights	24	10	07	15	11
Charles Jourdan	24	11	34	24	12
Fazisi	25	01	57	37	13
Equity & Law II	25	20	45	39	14
Creightons Naturally	25	21	22	18	15
Liverpool Enterprise	26	01	36	30	16
L'Esprit de Liberte	27	02	41	10	17
Rucanor Sport	27	06	14	10	18
With Integrity	28	01	17	10	19
Schlussel von Bremen	28	02	43	03	20
Maiden	28	03	35	18	21
La Poste	30	20	57	38	22

LEG V – Combined Times

Name	Elapsed Time				Place
	D	H	M	S	
Steinlager 2	111	09	17	15	1
Fisher & Paykel	112	20	18	42	2
Merit	113	07	26	29	3
Rothmans	113	16	04	20	4
The Card	117	12	08	18	5
Charles Jourdan	117	23	13	17	6
Fortuna Extra Lights	119	10	29	15	7
Satquote British Defender	119	20	15	59	8
Gatorade	119	22	45	23	9
Union Bank of Finland	120	10	29	15	10
Fazisi	121	04	39	55	11
NCB Ireland	121	05	53	28	12
Belmont Finland II	121	07	55	46	13
Equity & Law II	130	13	41	45	14
Liverpool Enterprise	132	01	06	58	15
Creightons Naturally	142	11	30	08	16
L'Esprit de Liberte	142	15	37	15	17
Maiden	144	09	07	45	18
Schlussel von Bremen	145	13	31	48	19
With Integrity	145	22	52	57	20
La Poste	158	23	15	29	21

Fazisi: The Joint Venture

LEG VI – Fort Lauderdale to Southampton

Name	Elapsed Time				Place
	D	H	M	S	
Steinlager 2	17	00	23	15	1
Fisher & Paykel	17	00	59	40	2
Merit	17	02	43	45	3
Rothmans	17	12	50	03	4
The Card	17	19	07	25	5
Belmont Finland II	17	20	35	27	6
Fortuna Extra Lights	17	21	44	56	7
Fazisi	18	04	21	09	8
Union Bank of Finland	18	06	08	57	9
Equity & Law II	18	10	08	48	10
NCB Ireland	18	13	29	10	11
Gatorade	18	15	44	49	12
Charles Jourdan	18	16	01	34	13
Liverpool Enterprise	19	03	45	24	14
Creightons Naturally	19	19	04	50	15
Schlussel von Bremen	22	05	35	46	16
L'Esprit de Liberte	22	05	59	01	17
Rucanor Sport	22	17	45	56	18
Maiden	22	17	59	08	19
La Poste	22	23	40	48	20
Satquote British Defender	23	16	26	24	21
With Integrity	24	17	26	10	22

Whitbread Final Results

Name	Elapsed Time				Place
	D	H	M	S	
Steinlager 2	128	09	40	30	1
Fisher & Paykel	129	21	18	22	2
Merit	130	10	10	14	3
Rothmans	131	04	54	23	4
The Card	135	07	15	43	5
Charles Jourdan	136	15	14	51	6
Fortuna Extra Lights	137	08	22	11	7
Gatorade	138	14	30	12	8
Union Bank of Finland	138	16	38	12	9
Belmont Finland II	139	04	31	13	10
Fazisi	139	09	01	04	11
NCB Ireland	139	19	22	38	12
Satquote British Defender	143	12	42	23	13
Equity & Law II	148	23	50	33	14
Liverpool Enterprise	151	04	52	22	15
Creightons Naturally	162	06	34	58	16
L'Esprit de Liberte	164	21	36	16	17
Maiden	167	03	06	53	18
Schlussel von Bremen	167	19	07	34	19
With Integrity	170	16	19	07	20
La Poste	181	22	56	17	21

202

Index

Index

204

Index

Index